*Ancient Society and History*

# The Roman

# SUZANNE DIXON

# *Family*

The Johns Hopkins University Press
Baltimore and London

This book has been brought to publication with the generous assistance of the David M. Robinson Publication Fund.

The Johns Hopkins University Press
701 West 40th Street
Baltimore, Maryland 21211-2190
The Johns Hopkins Press Ltd., London

The paper in this book meets the minimum requirements of the American National Standard for Information Sciences—Permanence of Paper for Printed Library Materials, ANSI Z39.48–1984.

Library of Congress Cataloging-in-Publication Data

Dixon, Suzanne.
  The Roman family / Suzanne Dixon.
     p.     cm.—(Ancient society and history)
  Includes bibliographical references and index.
  ISBN 0-8018-4199-2.—ISBN 0-8018-4200-X (pbk.)
  1. Family—Rome—History.  I. Title.  II. Series.
HQ511.D59   1991
306.85′0945′632—dc20                        91-25876

*To my children, Clem and Christabel*

# Contents

Contents

# Preface and Acknowledgments

The family continues to be a topic of public debate. From time to time, editorials or politicians tell us it is "breaking down," a recurrent theme of moralists through the ages. I monitor such statements with interest—as I do information about changes in contemporary family patterns—and never fail to be impressed by the strength of popular fantasies about the role and nature of the family in the past which emerge from such generalizations. It seems to me that we need a good, rigorous base of knowledge about families past and present if we are to make sensible comments about current developments and future plans. We need to understand the roles which families can perform and the variety of ways in which they can be organized. History, sociology, psychology, and anthropology all furnish us with important material for an informed understanding of what goes on within families. This book is intended to contribute to that understanding.

The opening chapter reviews the controversies which have occupied historians of the family in general and historians of the Roman family in particular, considers the problems of evidence, and looks at Roman conceptions of the family and at the functions commonly performed by families. It is a pity in a way that convention and logic require the author to set the scene at the beginning of the book. It is important to have all these elements in mind while looking at more specific aspects of Roman family relations, but such generalities usually have less appeal than discussion of concrete examples. It is, however, important to acknowledge the influences, political as well as academic, which affect approaches to the history of the family and to note the changes in direction. Even in the few years since I began this book, the focus has changed greatly, and I have not only updated my bibliographies constantly but completely recast drafts as new perspectives and information presented themselves.

Chapter 2 considers the legal setting, contrasting the formal legal position with the reality. This is important because the Roman family has often been represented as a summary of such formal statements. In practice, many relations not recognized at law—such as the slave family or the marriage of imperial soldiers—were tolerated socially and even given some legal acknowledgment. Chapter 3 is a study of Roman marriage, and chapter 4, of children in the family. There is inevitably a certain overlap between the two. The legal and social aspects of relations between spouses and between parents and children are offset against emotional links. In chapter 5 we see the way in which the family adjusts to the changes which occur throughout its life course—how it adapts to the introduction of new members by birth and marriage and to the aging or death of others.

Whether we make it explicit or not, our interest in families in other cultures is often tied to curiosity about similarities and differences between their practices and our own, as we perceive them. There is at the same time a certain scholarly posture of "objectivity" which pretends to present material neutrally. I have attempted a compromise. Certainly feelings, which are so difficult to reconstruct from ancient sources, are too important to omit from any account of family relations. The dangers are legion—it is so easy to assume that certain verbal formulae or gestures have the same meaning which we expect in a particular context. Perhaps some epitaphs which we invest with strong sentiment were merely formal acknowledgments of duty to the dead, and certainly the gesture of husband and wife holding hands was merely a symbol of the married state rather than any intimacy. The death of young children probably had a different impact in a society where it was such a common occurrence, but there is evidence that it affected some parents very strongly. I have chosen to explain the problems of assessing these and other questions, to provide the available evidence, and to state my view in such a way as to allow the reader to come to an independent conclusion.

I gratefully acknowledge the support of the Australian Research Council, which made this book possible. It enabled me to have computing, research, and typing assistance which were essential to its completion. The support was particularly welcome because it came at a time when the humanities, particularly history, were under attack from many quarters, and the council had even been criticized publicly for supporting my earlier project on Roman motherhood, which was stigmatized as being of "no relevance or benefit to the community." Many projects were included in the criticism, but the Roman mother somehow struck the media as newsworthy and either headed the list or stood for outlandish academic endeavors. And yet family relations, as I have said, continue to be a topic of great public debate. People do talk about universals in family relations, particularly between the generations and the sexes, and they need to have an informed basis for making these statements. History has a lot to offer, particularly in demonstrating the flexibility of the family as an institution, a major theme of this book. Looking rigorously at our own practices and at those of other societies is not only fascinating in itself but of obvious relevance to everyone with a stake in "the family" as an institution. Augustus's legislation is a good example of the folly of attempting to manipulate the family through state intervention without a sound basis of information and a successful public relations program (although his promotion was very wide-ranging), a lesson which could save money for many governments engaged in attempts to encourage or limit population growth.

I wish to acknowledge the assistance of the following sources for photographs: the Vatican Library collection (Biblioteca apostolica vaticana) for plate 1; Carlsberg Ny Glyptotek for plate 2; the

Trustees of the British Museum for plate 3; the photographic archive of the Palazzo dei Conservatori, Rome, for plates 4 and 8; the J. P. Getty Museum for plates 5, 6, 7, 20, 21, and 22; the Soprintendenza archeologica di Pompeii for permission to reproduce plate 9; the Australian National University Antiquities Collection for plate 10; the German Archaeological Institute in Rome for plates 11, 16, 17, and 24; the Assessore of the Department for Antique Monuments and Excavations, Rome, for permission to reproduce plate 12; the photographic archive of the Vatican Museum for plate 13; Art Resource, New York, and Photo Alinari for plate 14; Mr. P. Hall, of the Yorkshire Museum, York, for plate 15; the Rheinisches Bildarchiv, Cologne, for plate 18; Dott.ssa Anna Gallina Zevi, of the Soprintendenza archeologica di Ostia, for plate 19; and the Marburg Archiv for plate 23.

I wish to thank Mrs. Penny Peel for her work as research assistant and Ms. Erica Maddock for her typing. In an emergency close to the end, Mrs. Dorothy Owen came to my aid, and for this she deserves special appreciation. I was physically handicapped throughout this project and therefore literally needed the help which normally is a pleasant extra. Because of this I owe particular thanks to all involved. Karen Ascani and Bente Rasmussen, of the Danish Academy in Rome, were very helpful in securing photographs from Italian sources.

My family were a wonderful support throughout. My husband's contribution cannot be itemized, because it was so extensive, and my mother encouraged me and helped proof the typescript at a crucial stage. I wish to single out my children for special thanks. At a time of life when they could be forgiven for self-absorption and even for embarrassment at my unmotherly incapacity and odd interests, they were always ready to help me in practical ways and to tolerate my preoccupation with my work and my physical difficulties. They provided me with an example of another theme of this work—the mutual support provided by different members of the family across the generations at times of need.

The Roman Family

gained currency in so many European languages that it can come as a surprise to learn that the Romans rarely used it to mean family in the sense of kin. The imperial jurist Ulpian, who flourished in the early third century A.D., devoted part of his forty-sixth book, *On the Edict,* to the various legal meanings of the word.[1] In most contexts, *familia* was more likely to signify the collection of slaves and freed slaves attached to a married couple;[2] indeed, in strict legal parlance husband and wife each had a *familia* of slaves, although the jurists recognized that in practice their slaves could be treated as one community.[3] The term was commonly employed to mean also those freed slaves who bore the family name of the former owner and owed him or her certain obligations for life.[4] Nor was this a legal formality only: the evidence of sepulchral inscriptions suggests that slaves and freed slaves tended to marry (or, where status prevented this, to form *de facto* unions) within the *familia* and even to group in kinlike clusters for such purposes as funeral commemoration, in addition to performing such services for the former owner. Indeed, reciprocal obligations between *familia* and owners could extend over several generations and even involve sentimental links across the status boundaries.[5] By an extension of this meaning, *familia* could also signify a business. This was because most Roman "industry" was based on a number of specialist slaves within or beyond the household.[6]

The Roman did sometimes use *familia* to mean family or kin, but in technical discussions rather than common parlance. Ulpian stated that a woman was the beginning and end of her own *familia,* apparently meaning that she could not pass on to her children her family name or her sacral and inheritance rights as a man could his.[7] Not unnaturally, the law concentrates on those aspects which affect status and access to property and inheritance. Legal language reflects this emphasis, with words containing the old genitive *familias* (of the *familia*). A Roman male, once released from the power of his own father, *paterfamilias*, usually by the father's death, was technically a *paterfamilias* (father of the *familia*), even if he was a celibate and immature ten-year-old.[8] If he married, his children were in his power and were *filiifamilias* (sons of the "family") or *filiaefamilias* (daughters of the "family").[9] His wife, however, was technically a *materfamilias* (mother of the "family") only if she had entered the husband's *manus* (hand) on marriage and thereby submerged her property in his and transferred her entitlement on intestate succession from the family of her birth to that of her marriage.[10] The association of the family estate with the term *familia* is apparent in these expressions, and *familia* can be used, as Ulpian points out, to mean the estate, as in the Twelve Tables rulings on inheritance.[11] So *familia(s)* in the expressions just listed signifies the estate as much as the kinship unit. In fact, as Saller has demonstrated (1984a), Romans commonly spoke of the "house" (*domus*) rather than the *familia* when they wished to refer to the lineage or kinship unit.

But whatever variations there might be in the constitution and description of the family, it is a universal human institution, and the Romans were human. They unquestionably had families and saw the family as central to their personal lives and to society. We have already seen that some family terms had specific legal implications. Indeed, for the first half of the twentieth century, most studies of the Roman family were based on legal sources and were concerned with legal relationships within the family, particularly with rights of inheritance and power relations between *paterfamilias* and *filiusfamilias*. There was, moreover, greater communion between classicists and anthropologists at the turn of the century, and many classical scholars looked to comparative ethnographic data to find the key to an understanding of Roman marriage rules and ceremonies and the nature of the Roman household. The influence of LePlay (1871), Morgan (1871, 1877), Engels (1884), and Frazer (1890) is evident in the imaginative reconstructions of Roman family life and the fascination with ritualized bride capture and bride price, with comparisons from colorful cultures.[12]

The stress on the wide-ranging powers of the Roman *paterfamilias* (see chapter 2) and the rules of inheritance on intestacy together formed the basis of a dominant view of the typical Roman family as a three-generation household, containing married sons and their wives and families, a model of patriarchy in which the oldest ascendant male had supreme powers over his wife and children. This was termed a "joint agnatic household," and kinship

3

relations through the male line (agnatic connections) were seen as central. This line of argument was decisively attacked by Crook (1967b) in a leading article about the extent of the powers of the Roman father (*patria potestas*). Crook argued that the literary evidence did not offer any support for the view that the Roman household commonly contained coresident married brothers and that such households as were known were mentioned as atypical. By 1986, when Rawson reviewed trends in the scholarship, the prevailing view was that the Roman family was nuclear. This view had been elaborated and substantiated by Saller and Shaw.[13]

Much of the earlier scholarship now seems somewhat misguided. Arguments from the system of inheritance on intestacy or kinship terms were given undue weight as indicators of actual relations and residence patterns. The "evidence" consisted primarily of overgeneralization from formal legal principles of inheritance on intestacy through the male line and the fact that a Roman woman could not transfer her name or family rites to her children as a man could. This was bolstered by comparative material and somewhat strained arguments from kinship terms, supported by the conviction that the *linguistic* term *Indo-European* reflected common racial and social origins, including a common prototypical family form.[14] Perhaps the fundamental problem was a failure to define the terms of the discussion and therefore to distinguish clearly between (1) the composition of the *household,* or domestic unit; (2) the working concept of *kin,* with its elaborate system of obligations as attested by practice and explicit ideology; and (3) the hierarchy of kin definitions revealed in the formal rules governing *inheritance* on intestacy.[15]

We began this chapter with a reminder of the different meanings we assign to one's "family." It does not follow from the fact that a Roman *paterfamilias*'s estate could be divided on his death among his wife, his children, and his sons' children that all of these people necessarily inhabited the same house, but authors often spoke as if this was the case. Moreover, definitions of *kin* are not the same as those of *household structure:* in Roman society, as in so many others, children (of both sexes) might leave the parental home on marriage but did not thereby weaken their bonds with their parents and other family members whom they regarded as close kin. And the law tells only part of the story. Women who passed formally into their husband's family and men who were adopted into another family ceded their claim to inheritance within their "blood" family but still acknowledged firm ties to their own parents, brothers, and sisters, just as women who now change their family name on marriage maintain affection and loyalty for their "blood" kin.[16] Indeed, prosopography, the detailed investigation of individual careers and family backgrounds of Roman political figures, has emphasized the close bonds between brothers, sisters, in-laws, half-siblings, and cousins.[17]

Up to a point, earlier scholarship on the family was based on the belief that certain institutions were fundamental to the social evolution of the European "races," a view that is unlikely to find much credence post-1940s. Murdock (1949) represented the dominant postwar sociological view, that the nuclear or conjugal family of mother, father, and dependent children was universally the most popular family form and the best basis for socializing children. This approach was reinforced for historians of the family by the findings of Laslett and the Cambridge Group for the Study of Population and Society, especially the edited collection *Household and Family in Past Time* (1972). The book opposed the common view that the English family (i.e., household) had been more "extended" and the primary unit of production as well as reproduction until industrialization forced a separation of home and the workplace and laid the ground for the modern, nuclear family as a focus of reproduction, socialization, and consumption. The argument for the English material was based on the analysis of census data, but the collection included studies of different regions in different periods and led to the tentative notion that the nuclear household might in fact have been the norm for most places throughout history. Advocates of this view pointed to preindustrial mortality patterns for the improbability of finding three generations simultaneously living. Since this work appeared, Saller and Shaw have collaborated with the Cambridge group to produce computer-generated simulations of Roman populations which confirm that many Romans would not have had a living father by the time they entered their twenties.[18] This virtually dissolves the image of the three-generation agnatic household with a tyrannical patriarch at its head.

Household size was a great issue in the 1970s among historians of the family, partly because the Laslett study undermined a picture of the past that had been firmly entrenched in the public consciousness and was central to Marxist analysis of the modern family as the product of industrialization. Many reacted against the idea that the nuclear household had always been the norm. Berkner (1975) attacked the use of census material on the grounds that it captures one moment of a household's state and that household composition necessarily alters through the life course of family members and should be viewed as cyclic.[19] This qualification has now become standard; in fact, Laslett maintains that the 1972 study did acknowledge this essentially dynamic character of the household.[20] Hareven (1987) insists that *life course* is more appropriate than *life cycle,* which presupposes that each generation eventually repeats the pattern of the earlier generations,[21] but there is a sense in which household composition does go through a fairly predictable cycle. Typically, it is nuclear (married couple and children), sometimes including an aged (grand) parent, then changes as children leave for work or marriage. It might include day laborers and single relations staying for a time, or married children who stay only until they have children of their own or are economically capable of forming a new nuclear household. Grandchildren might be sent back while the parents seek work elsewhere. Stone (1981:63) likens the family to a concertina, contracting and expanding. A census can clearly represent only part of such a mobile scenario and is insufficient for forming a refined view of the relations between coresidents or between nonresident kin; all things being equal, one would expect ties of sentiment and obligation between parents and an apprenticed son in another village to be stronger than those between the parents and their boarders or resident day laborers.

The wish to explain the emergence of the "modern" European family lies behind this continuing debate. Scholars of the Roman family seem to have lost interest in it. Just as they once assumed the family to be multigenerational, now they assume it to be nuclear, and they generally use the word *family* to mean coresident kin. But we need to be sensitive to the implications: even if life expectancy imposes a nuclear structure on most households in practice, this does not obliterate firmly entrenched ideas about obligation and the way things should be. Stone points out that in one nineteenth-century English community, where grandparents were found in only 9 percent of households, 80 percent of the people over the age of sixty-five who had surviving children did live with them.[22] The Romans whose family arrangements we know best are the political elite of the city of Rome, where the older generation could afford separate accommodation with ample slaves and attendants to care for their physical welfare and their children could attend them for regular visits.[23] So the idea clearly persisted that aged parents had a right to live with their married children; or perhaps their married children lived with them. It could be that many Roman households did conform to this code, which is obscured for us by concentration on the literary evidence from the late republican urban elite. Even within the elite, we know of households that included aged parents and married children. In the second century B.C., Cato the elder's married son lived with him, and the household then expanded to contain Cato's much younger second wife, then their child. In the first century B.C., Julius Caesar's mother lived with him and his young bride. The aged Appius Claudius was admired by later generations for maintaining an active tyranny over his children and grandchildren in spite of his blindness. So, even if most families were essentially nuclear and relatively few people survived after their children reached the adult years, those who did might well have lived with their married children. Most people could not have afforded separate residences.[24]

There are even examples of coresident married brothers, such as the Aelii Tuberones of the second century B.C. and the Licinii Crassi of the first century B.C..[25] General opinion appears now to follow Crook's view that this particular arrangement was unusual, at least by the late Republic. I have no serious quarrel with this opinion, but we do need to keep an open mind about the diversity of relationships, even if we all agree that the residential family usually consisted of husband, wife, and young unmarried children.[26]

There have been some attempts to introduce complexities and nuances to the prevailing opinion that the nuclear unit was the dominant household form and the primary focus of obligation in Roman society. Barker (1985) has pointed out that Roman Egyptian censuses reveal a significant proportion of "extended" households that included three generations or elderly parents living with a newly married son or daughter or married brothers or sisters. He has, moreover, contrasted the pattern of kin obligation reflected in the commemorative inscriptions used by Saller and Shaw (and, I should add, Rawson and myself) with that displayed in dedicatory inscriptions.[27] Both findings merit serious attention. There were probably regional variations, but it is possible that we are unduly influenced by the limited evidence for Italy and the Western Empire.

In my study of Roman motherhood I stressed that economic, social, and demographic factors necessarily widened the circle of people with whom the young Roman Italian child was likely to be associated. Some women died or were very ill following childbirth, servile or mercenary wet nurses and attendants cared for the babies of the elite, the free poor apparently made use of babysitters, and slave children were sometimes—perhaps routinely—separated from their mother at birth.[28] All such arrangements have implications for the composition of the household—its inclusion of slaves and childcare personnel or of non-kin children—and for relationships within the household. Even relatively modest homes generally contained slaves or dependent workers, and children and youths were exchanged as apprentices. We hear of nuclear families at the top of the social scale with few children in which the daughters left to marry, and the sons to establish a bachelor household or to pursue their education in Greece. Such households would have contained hundreds of slaves and dependents, as well as relatively honored boarders/guests, such as philosophers. Those slaves or freed slaves who provided such personal services as nursing, secretarial work, or personal attendance might have strong bonds of affection and patronage with the individual or couple at the

center of a huge unit of production and consumption that constituted the city base or at one of the country estates that were home
for the elite family. The terms *nuclear family* and *household composition* take on new significance in these circumstances.

There seems, moreover, to have been a certain pragmatism in
Roman family relations which allowed for flexible childcare or
child custody arrangements and a general readiness to extend the
kinship definitions to accommodate in-laws and step-relations.
The process is referred to very casually and incidentally in the
sources and contrasts markedly with modern trauma over child
custody. The death, divorce, or travel of parents occasioned permanent and temporary accommodations of children which made
free of kin and patronage links.[29] Plutarch begins his biography of
Cato the younger with an account of the household in which he
was reared with half-relations during the civil war; and we know
that Cato continued to have strong links with his half sister Servilia, just as her son Brutus had strong links with *his* half sisters,
the Iuniae.[30] Brutus cooperated with his brother-in-law Cassius in
the conspiracy to assassinate Caesar, and the family meeting (*consilium*) held in June 44 B.C. to take stock of the political situation
created by the assassination included Brutus, his half sisters and
their husbands as well as their mother Servilia (who seemed to
take the chair), Brutus's wife and cousin Porcia (Cato's daughter),
and sundry friends of the family.[31] As we shall see, in-laws were
expected to provide support for many purposes, and all kin could
be called on in a time of crisis.

Many marriages in the ancient world were dissolved by death
which by modern standards was premature. Others were dissolved by divorce. Remarriage was common in both cases and
caused a proliferation of step- and half-relations which were encompassed in the network of kin. Bradley (1987) argues that this
necessarily caused such dislocation in the life of a Roman child of
the political elite that we cannot possibly equate its situation with
that of a child in a modern nuclear family. He examines closely the
marital ramifications of Sulla and Pompey, who perhaps show
more conjugal mobility than most, but within the political elite
this pattern was not so unusual, and remarriage operated at all

social levels.[32] Bradley sees such fluidity as a disruptive and inse-
cure background for child rearing. This is probably true, but it
might have had a positive side which we can appreciate once we
rid ourselves of the culturebound notion that the intense, one-to-
one maternal-child relationship idealized in modern consumer societies is the only acceptable model for childhood. The Roman setting reveals an elastic concept of kin that continues to apply in
adult life, as shown in the examples above for the family of Cato
and Servilia. In the speech *pro Cluentio,* Cicero cites the example
of his client's deceased stepfather Oppianicus sending a message to
a former wife to bring their young son to him, a proceeding they
followed on holidays, we are told. This is interesting because fathers always had the right to take children with them after divorce,
and indeed at the time Oppianicus did have a child of a subsequent marriage living with him, while he contemplated yet another marriage with Sassia, the villain of Cicero's speech, who had
children of her own.[33] It may still be true in these circumstances
that *family* means nuclear family, in the sense that the core of kin
at the center of the household was husband and wife (or husband
and wife and wife and wife), but the actual configuration and even
the kin relations within and outside the household were subject to
great change, and this needs to be acknowledged in any study of
Roman family forms. The term *nuclear* can cover different arrangements even within the same family over a period of time.[34]

Slave families raise other questions. At law, slaves had no capacity to marry, and there was very little acknowledgment of family ties.[35] Some literary and other references suggest that slave children were reared together, perhaps in a separate household from
their mothers. We know that many children were sold at an early
age without their mothers and that brothers and sisters were separated.[36] Yet slaves did form *de facto* unions, and epitaphs testify to
the fact that some maintained these after gaining freedom. Men
and women commonly referred to each other as *contubernales*
(slave spouses) even when they had both been freed and were entitled to use the standard terms for husband, wife, or marriage.[37]
Wallace-Hadrill (1991) points to the artificiality of separating out

"the slave family" or "the lower-class family" when these so often encompassed people who spent much of their life within the homes of the propertied classes. If slave and free children grew up together during their early years and acknowledged for life the bond forged by having once drunk at the same breast,[38] we should be clear that "family life" bore little resemblance to that of the small suburban unit in the modern West, and we should be wary of language that might conjure up this cut-and-dried imagery.

For those who did not enjoy the active patronage of the upper classes, economic exigencies would have imposed certain alterations on the family structure at different stages. Within the families of the free poor, children could be apprenticed or start other work from early ages, sometimes leaving the parental home to do so. Enlistment in the Roman army (or, for noncitizens, the auxiliary forces or the navy) would take very young people out of the residential group, but like guest workers in modern Europe, they would still maintain strong bonds with their families and send money back to them.[39]

It is still acceptable to assert that most Romans lived for most of their lives in nuclear households, but only if we appreciate that this covers a multitude of changes and accommodations over the individual life course and that "the household" was likely to differ significantly from its modern urban equivalent. It would often have included slaves, boarders, and apprentices, as well as other relatives. Regional and class customs and economic constraints would often have imposed specific conditions, such as the separation of young children from the parental home so that they could work or the separation of babies from mothers to free the mothers for work. Remarriage would have disrupted households and formed new residential groupings while often extending kinship relations. Most cultures have a certain notional family form that is regarded as the norm, but even when this is the most common form, there will inevitably be many variants. Residential arrangements, like inheritance practices, are essentially strategies adopted in response to particular circumstances, and the Roman family was above all a flexible and pragmatic institution.

*Other Trends in Scholarship on History of the Family*

The particular interest of the 1970s and early 1980s in defining the domestic group and household has somewhat petered out in recent years.[40] As we have seen, the history of the Roman family is influenced by external intellectual movements, including the work of historians of the family in other periods. There is therefore a case for reviewing some of the major trends in this work over the last twenty years and relating it to developments in studies of the Roman family, but there are important differences. Studies of the family in the Early Modern period tend to be dominated by the need to explain the "modernization" of the family, particularly the impact of industrialization on family relations.[41] This consideration does not, of course, bear directly on the history of the Roman family. It is raised indirectly by the question whether the nuclear family and the modern sentimental stress on the family as a "haven in a heartless world" is a purely modern ideological construct.[42] It is my belief that we can parallel this sentimental picture of family life as a refuge in the literature of late republican Rome.[43] The question is linked with the continuing controversy about whether childhood is a modern invention and people in other historical periods failed to appreciate the specific characteristics of childhood as a stage of life.[44]

The other major difference between Early Modern history and that of the Roman family is the source material. The recent interest in history of the family was characterized at first by a strongly quantitative approach, particularly among the French historians, who were able to produce detailed regional studies of wet-nursing practices, age at marriage, frequency of remarriage, and so on.[45] Historians of the Roman family have also produced statistically based studies, but they have had to rely on the documentary evidence from Roman Egypt, which includes some census material, and the evidence from tombstone inscriptions, which lends itself to numerical analysis but does not provide a representative "population" and frequently cannot be classified accurately by dating techniques. The material used by Roman historians has sometimes been used to determine questions of status but is increasingly applied to discussions of feeling and patterns of obligation within the family.[46] This trend has been influenced by the necessary concentration on the sepulchral inscriptions, which represent the fulfillment of a duty and, by definition, a display of proper sentiments. Even the computer simulations of population patterns prepared by Saller and Shaw in conjunction with the Cambridge Group for the History of Population and Social Structure were used to throw light on Roman family relations, as in Saller's (1986) study of *patria potestas*. The distinction that is drawn (sometimes explicitly and frequently implicitly) between quantitative and qualitative history in reviews of Early Modern family scholarship is not really applicable to Roman family studies.[47]

Other trends are relevant, but indirectly. Thus the interaction between the family and wider social structures, a growing concern of Early Modern historians, has always been a feature of Roman family studies because of the traditional concentration on the political role of the elite families and the role of marriage alliance in this. This feature parallels, to an extent, the earlier concern of historians such as Stone with the elite family in other periods of history.[48]

The modern interest in "history from below" has had an impact on studies of the Roman family, and there has been a serious attempt to study the lower class. In practice, this has tended to be the slave family. Peasants probably formed the great bulk of the ancient free population, but unfortunately they left few archaeological, literary, or inscriptional traces for the historical record.[49] It is therefore almost impossible to reconstruct histories of the peasant family as such and certainly impossible to reconstruct regionally based studies of the peasant family. Surviving Roman inscriptions have a skewing towards urban examples, and this inevitably affects their style. The overrepresentation of the military in inscriptions may give us (indirectly) our nearest guide to peasants, since the army provided an obvious avenue of social mobility for dispossessed peasants and agricultural laborers with few prospects.[50] Otherwise, the studies of the lower-class Roman family tend to be studies of people who are clearly slaves or freed slaves and can be designated as such by status indicators in inscriptions,

13

particularly epitaphs. This has been the basis of studies in lower-class kinship by Rawson, Treggiari, Flory, and Bradley.[51] We need, however, to remind ourselves that the distinction between upper and lower class has to be tempered by the fact of patronage and slave ownership, which meant that slave families were sometimes closely associated and coresident with upper-class families.[52]

It is very important to know the general demographic pattern of a population—age at first marriage, median life expectancy, frequency of child mortality and of remarriage, and so on. Roman statistical studies have been progressively refined, and the use of computer simulations has enhanced the discipline.[53] But although the techniques have become more sophisticated, the usual basis of the information remains the epitaphs, which are not consistently informative. Romans sometimes recorded the age at death of the person commemorated, and sometimes the length of that person's marriage, but this is by no means standard. It is also clear that children were not routinely commemorated, particularly if they died very young, and there are likely to be variations according to the region in which the inscriptions are found.[54] Nonetheless, these inscriptions do provide some sort of basis for calculations, and they have been skillfully used by some to form a picture of life chances and the ways in which they might have affected the Roman family. We have to remind ourselves that marriages in earlier periods were much shorter than they tend to be now because of different mortality patterns and the common age differential between husband and wife. Children were frequently orphaned because their mothers had died in childbirth (or as a result of ailments based in reproduction), and some fathers died of natural causes or military activity before their children attained adulthood. Such factors created a particular sort of demographic background in which remarriage was frequent and many children grew up in blended families or with a variety of caregivers, not necessarily kin.[55] Whether the incidence of early child mortality actually affected the attitude of people in preindustrial societies to young children is an issue that continues to be debated by historians of the family and of childhood in all periods. The controversy is discussed in chapter 4, below.

The human body, particularly the body as a cultural construct, has been the subject of many recent works. Oddly enough, they have not had a great impact on family studies in general in spite of their obvious relevance for attitudes to sexuality, reproduction, and child health. The works of Daly, Lacan, Cixous, and Clément have influenced feminist studies,[56] but they have not generally been related to work on the family, in spite of the continued connection between feminist studies, women's history, and history of the family.[57] Some French scholars have shown an awareness of the connection: Étienne on the medical treatment of young children, Néraudau on the child's physical development, and above all Rousselle on sexuality and the body in the ancient world. All display a strong interest in aspects of the life cycle and reproduction and their impact on human relationships, particularly within the family.[58] Classical scholars have also looked at aspects of the female life cycle.[59] It is nonetheless a pity that the great mass of material currently being published on ancient medical writings, particularly as it relates to women, is not often connected directly with history of the family in spite of the importance of such issues as the spacing of the ancient family. Étienne's contention that the ancients had little interest in childhood illness because it was not an area of proper concern for (male) doctors is an interesting one that could be tested in part by further reference to the medical literature. There is also scope for greater cooperation between archaeologists and historians of the family. Thus, Frier compared the evidence of skeletal remains with life expectancy figures that he had gleaned from the jurist Ulpian.[60]

Ancient historians are less inclined than their "modern" colleagues to confine themselves to one type of source. Historians of the ancient family tend to use literary sources and inscriptions as well as legal texts to reconstruct different aspects of family life. The literary texts necessarily provide an anecdotal and somewhat impressionistic basis for knowledge, but they are vital to any reconstruction of feelings. At the end of the 1981 conference that resulted in the collection of papers edited by Rawson (1986a), Professor Keith Hopkins commented that few of the participants had openly discussed feelings, which were such an important part

15

of family life. At the second conference, in 1988, participants with acknowledged expertise in law and epigraphy (areas usually associated with "hard data") showed a consistent regard for feelings and relationships. Moreover, these participants had published in the area of sentiments and relationships in the intervening period. This put their work firmly in the category of *mentalité,* the study of "the values, beliefs, emotions, and passions of individuals and groups,"[61] a study closely associated with the French *annalistes* of the Centre Nationale de Recherches Scientifiques (CNRS) and pioneered by Febvre, Bloch, Braudel, and Leroy Ladurie. Romanists commonly combine the methods that Wheaton characterizes as typical of the approach: scrutiny of a particular document and "thick description," that is, the use of disparate evidence to support a particular view of family relations.[62]

In his introduction to the forthcoming collection on the history of the family in Italy, Saller comments that the contributing historians and anthropologists continue to consider issues of household size and complexity, but in a different way from the 1970s approach to static household composition, and take a neutral stand on issues of emotional relationships within the family. He perceives a general tendency in the scholarship to move away from generalization and concentrate instead on specific strategies and regions. Ancient historians, particularly those of the British empiricist school, have been criticized in the past for taking too narrow a view of social institutions and failing to look at the wider picture. Ironically, this process is now reversed, and it would seem that historians of the Roman family are more prepared than anthropologists or historians of the medieval and Early Modern family to consider general issues such as marriage preference and inheritance strategies or the function of dowry.[63] Perhaps this will become one of the differences between the studies of the Roman family and those of other families.

Another difference, one that is vital to the "modernization" debate, lies in the role of the family vis à vis social institutions. The question that concerns Early Modern historians is whether the family is best seen as an active agent of social and economic change or, in the traditional fashion, the passive object of larger transformations.[64] The issue is an important one, with implications for the study of the Roman family, in which we attempt to make sense of apparent changes in family obligation over long periods of time.

At the same time, it is worth noting that most historians of the family were trained first in traditional political history. They therefore sometimes retain the habit of seeing history primarily in terms of political periodization and the need to explain political change; indeed, in the past this has almost been a definition of history. This perception carries with it the danger of assuming that periodization—the distinction between the Roman republican and imperial eras, for example, or the notion of the Renaissance—has general application. Questions have arisen whether there ever really was a "Renaissance" for most of the European population and specifically for women, even those of the elite. By the same token, it could well be that areas such as literature, the law, and the family, though influenced by changes involved in the centralization of Roman government associated with the establishment of the Principate, retained the major features of earlier society. Laslett rightly questions the urge to relate the family to political and economic change in the "wider" social context. It could be that the family generally belongs to *l'histoire immobile,* an expression of the CNRS school that stresses the continuity of social institutions as determined by factors such as geography.[65]

Historians of the family and anthropologists now acknowledge that it is a mistake to assign a single family form to any period of history. There are always going to be great divergences in family structures, particularly between regions and classes and in response to various factors, geographic and economic. This diversity cannot be properly addressed in studying the ancient world. Yet ancient historians must either give up entirely or deal with the evidence which is available to them. As long as there is a critical understanding of its limitations, this seems reasonable enough. The literature is predominantly a record of the norms of the upper class, particularly the men of the political elite based in the city of Rome itself. The inscriptions have a wider social base but a strong urban bias and a tendency to record only the bare bones of family

17

ideology. The law tends to record the ideology of the ruling group as applied to the problem cases of the population at large. The training of ancient historians in close linguistic and textual analysis is important in assessing this type of evidence and in attempting to piece it together. It is to be hoped that the written material can be combined with the material evidence of archaeologists and art historians as people within these groups become increasingly interested in areas to do with kinship studies and social history generally.[66] This might even enable us to draw some conclusions about regional differences in household structure and other factors which affect the family but it is unlikely that we shall ever be able to draw firm conclusions about the diversity of family forms and ideals throughout the Roman Empire. To date, the best material on regional differences has been based on tombstones and other inscriptions.[67]

In sum, work on the ancient Mediterranean family by ancient historians will necessarily differ from that of family historians based in other periods. The modernization of the family does not bear directly on their work, and their material does not lend itself to the same demographic analysis or close reasoning about individual and regional variation. At the same time, ancient historians are part of the intellectual movements of their own times and are necessarily influenced by trends within their own societies as well. More than this, ancient historians have specific contributions to make to the study of the family in general and to the family within European history in particular, not only because Roman law formed the basis of several later systems and Roman culture permeated so many parts of Europe but also because debates within the modern family and related issues often concern the timing of certain developments. Thus it can be true that while childhood is in a sense a modern invention and the nineteenth-century family marks the development of a sentimentally defined unit, these developments were also present in Roman society. If this can, as I believe, be demonstrated, it changes our view of the history of childhood and marriage in a general way and is a salutary reminder that history is not a matter of social evolution; that is, there is not a linear development within which children gradually and progressively improve their position or the family moves towards a more "civilized" or isolated mode. Such developments can take place and then change again.

## The Myth of the Archaic Roman Family

Historians agree, then, that the family has changed in the last few centuries: it has shrunk in size, and more emphasis has been placed on the emotional bonds between husband and wife and parents and children than in the past, when the stress was on material obligation and the economic role of the family. There is little agreement apart from this. The popular consciousness also acknowledges a change in the family and interprets it primarily in moral terms as a decline from the sense of stronger obligation in the past, particularly the obligation towards older members of the family and a willingness to look after them. These changes have also been interpreted morally by historians and by governments, and they are invoked in the modern world in the public sphere, sometimes with very specific political consequences. Thus the *Code civil*, also called the *Code Napoléon*, of 1804, which spread with French power to many other parts of Europe, was based ultimately on Roman law and specifically admired the power that Roman law had given to the *paterfamilias*.[68]

The influential nineteenth-century historian LePlay argued (1871) that the stem family had dominated French history until the modern period and had shown a less selfish and more stable approach to family life. LePlay's reasoning had an enormous influence not only on historical thinking almost until the present day but also on popular and government approaches to proper family behavior.[69] In the twentieth century such views have been taken up by Ariès, whose work on the history of childhood has had such an impact on family studies. Ariès was originally a right-wing apologist who used historical reasoning to argue for particular attitudes in the modern world towards the family.[70] In general, conservative sentiment has emphasized this earlier family form, characterized by the authority of the father or grandfather, by strict gender divisions within the family, and by the deference of young people and women to the leading males of the older generation. This was also the model idealized by the fascist regime in Italy under Mussolini, which consciously elevated the early Roman family as it was perceived by public figures of the time and found its way into scholarly literature.[71] In the Italian context, there was often an explicit comparison with early Roman history and the position of the *paterfamilias* within the family.[72] More recently, the traditional family and its values have been invoked by the Tory government in Great Britain as a rationale for taking responsibility away from the state and putting it back with the family, for example, in the care of helpless invalids and the aged.[73]

The romantic and moralizing view of the past also plays its role in the politics and history of the left. Like other nineteenth-century historians, Engels saw the family as a development from early, primitive communism, which existed in a period of matriarchal power. The family then developed, according to this view, as an extended patriarchal unit which was ultimately transformed by industrialization into the modern nuclear family, characterized by the separation of the home and the workplace and the eventual exclusion of women and children from the public employment sphere.[74] In more recent times, this view has been analyzed more closely and modified by Marxist feminist historians, who have revised many of its aspects and developed new ones.[75]

Politicians as a breed are fond of making pronouncements about the family. So are newspaper editors and ministers of religion. The presumptions sometimes vary, and the purpose of particular pronouncements can involve a reduction of public funding or a simple condemnation of existing morals, but the underlying assumption is usually that people in the past were finer, that they had a better sense of family obligation and a more spiritual set of values than those in the present. The assumption is usually underpinned by a particular picture of the family as a large unit in which the mother was dedicated to the regular production of a great number of offspring and the children were obedient to their parents. The implicit contrast is with the modern family, characterized as selfish, materialistic, and overly individualist. This image has not been greatly affected by demographic information from historians, and the enormous body of scholarship on the subject has had little impact on the popular perception of the family in earlier times as being large, generous, and content. This particular consciousness, as we have seen, can have specific, material results for contemporary cultures.

The ancient Romans also had a particular picture of their past that included a perception of the earlier family as morally superior to the family of their own day. As in the modern case, there is a sense in which this consciousness and ideal had a life of its own. It is therefore important to form a picture of what the Romans *thought* about the family of the past, because that reflects something of their own values and because the myth of what the family ought to be can actually affect legislation and practice in later ages.

In the modern world, there is dissonance between the image of the past as a more moral and more spiritual place than the materialistic, restless present and the equally firm and widespread view that we have improved over the ages and that the present age represents a peak of civilization and material progress. In the ancient world there was no such conflict, for the view was general that the current age represented a decline from the standards of the past. In fact, the past was usually mentioned in order to underline this contrast and to set an example to readers of the behavior to which they ought to aspire. Romans associated the decline with growing luxury and security. The stereotype was that early Romans were always physically brave and prepared to go to war, that they were poor, that they lived essentially in peasant families.[76] The precise timing of the decline tended to be vague, but there was general agreement that the particular age in which the authors wrote was a considerable step below this earlier, golden age. As in the modern world, women and children were often used to symbolize the moral decline, and their faults were sometimes related to their role within the family. Thus Lucretia, the subject of an early political legend, was seen as the perfect wife of early Rome, chaste and industrious. Juvenal contrasted the hard-working women of archaic Rome with their modern equivalents, who were frivolous and adulterous, and Tacitus contrasted the virtuous women of the German tribes with their decadent counterparts in urban Rome of his day.[77]

21

The youth of an earlier day, so ran the myth, had always been better trained and more respectful to its elders. Stories circulated of sons in earlier times who had been killed by fathers for disobedience and of aged patriarchs who dominated not only their children but their grandchildren, all housed under the same roof.[78] When the emperor Augustus attempted to foster a moral regeneration in Roman society, he revived the temples and religious practices of a past age and traditional family values as he saw them. He deliberately used speeches from the past to justify his own legislative program, which encouraged marriage and (legitimate) procreation. He made a point of claiming that this was a historical revival and emphasized the links with early Roman virtue, both in his own specific propaganda and in the works of poets who were associated with him, such as Horace and Vergil. In his *Res gestae* Augustus claimed that he had set a good example himself and that he had shown by examples from the past that he was bringing Romans back to their earlier virtuous traditions. The poet Horace contrasted modern behavior, which had led to the civil war, with the virtue of early Rome, including the family.[79]

It might be improbable statistically that there ever had been a great number of three-generation households dominated by aged patriarchs, but the position of this sort of household in the Roman consciousness was quite strong. In chapter 2 we shall look at the pattern of transmission of property, particularly by inheritance, and see that this ideal form of household and family relations seems to underlie the Roman system of succession on intestate death. That authors of the late republican and imperial periods retained stories of earlier virtue from different eras shows the persistence of Roman admiration for these earlier prototypes. Valerius Maximus devotes a chapter to the subject of austere living (*de paupertate*), which seems to be equated with a peasant-based economy in an earlier period, and another chapter to the severity of parents, that is fathers, towards sons.[80] Later authors, such as the Greek biographer Plutarch, had a stock of such stories on which to draw. He continued the tradition, for example, in his praise of the family of the Aelii Tuberones, when he wrote in the second century A.D. of their lifestyle in the second century B.C., contrasting the harmonious communal life of the impoverished married brothers with the morals of his own day, when brothers squabbled about the finer points of their inheritance division.[81]

This persistent literary tradition probably reflects general thinking. It has occasional echoes in tombstone inscriptions, when people commemorating a dead spouse comment on the length of their marriage and add that it is unusual "these days" to have a marriage that ends with death rather than divorce.[82] Augustus's legislation and some of the works connected with it are clearly part of a conscious propaganda program, but they might well have originated in his sincere belief that Rome needed to get back to its traditional devotion to personal and religious values (as perceived by him).

Certainly Augustus's laws continued to be resisted, and the consensus of the ancient sources is that they were unsuccessful in their aim of forcing the nobility in particular to have more children. But in spite of cynicism about their efficacy, there seems to have been general agreement that family life had declined. Authors sometimes contrasted Romans with "noble savages," that is, foreign groups who were perceived as less civilized but more moral, such as the Scythians of Horace's day or the Germans of Tacitus's time.[83] Even these comparisons, however, contained the implicit notion that Romans had once been simple and poorer and therefore more virtuous and had declined from this earlier model. Thus Tacitus, in discussing the Germans, adds the comment, "Their good morals have greater force than good laws do elsewhere," where *elsewhere* obviously refers to Rome. This echoes the sentiment of the Augustan poet Horace, "What good are our laws without morals?" while his contemporary Livy comments in his Preface that people of his own day have reached a stage at which they are unable to endure either their own vices or the remedies to these vices, presumably the Augustan legislation or simply improved morals.[84] This gloomy view about the decline of morals dominates the attitude towards the family and has specific implications, for example, in the reluctance of the law to put formal checks on the power of the *paterfamilias* and in the very slow accommodation of the reality of family obligations in the area of inheritance, two aspects of legal family relations which we shall examine in the following chapter.

The picture of the family also reflects a system of ideal morals and ideal relations between the generations which underpins actual relations, just as it does in our own day. This intangible and probably inaccurate view of the past maintained by Romans is therefore an essential part of the *mentalité* that had specific and sometimes concrete implications for their approach to family matters in the sphere of public rhetoric and public policy.

## The Function of the Roman Family

The family performs a number of roles for its members and for society. Some scholars argue that it is not useful to define the family in terms of its functions because so many of these functions can be and are performed by non-kin groups and because kin do not themselves necessarily fulfill the same roles in the economy or in people's lives.[85] Such scholars argue that the family ought to be defined and analyzed "structurally,"[86] although the particular meaning of this term varies with different schools of thought. Others would argue that the family is itself a social construct and that in treating it as an organic unit scholars simply obscure the manifold interests represented within families.[87] Descriptions of the family in terms of its function do tend, it is true, to stress the solidarity of the family unit and imply a rather harmonious model that is unrealistically static and does not properly show the many changes that can occur within families. Within this book I attempt to show different transformations within the family and the role of conflict in the usual family life course. It has also been pointed out that historians tend to treat the family as a passive object and that this in turn obscures the dynamic role the family can play in history, sometimes as a force for subversion and resistance to ruling groups.[88]

In spite of these points, it remains useful to elucidate the diverse functions that the family performs both for society and for family members. As far as the state is concerned, the family is usually perceived as a nursery, a breeding ground of soldiers and future taxpayers in particular. Governments inevitably begin census and even benevolent operations with a view to providing the nation or city-state with future defenders and contributors to state revenue. From any point of view, the family is the basis of reproduction, both physical reproduction and the reproduction of culture, that is, morality and national character. The family traditionally produces and trains a new generation in the specific economic tasks of the particular group, such as farming, crafts, clothes production. Historically the family has been an economic unit, although it is true that kin can cooperate with other groups or coopt other groups into economic production with it, so this is not an exclusive function of kin. At a subsistence level, however, the family does tend to work together to produce the basics of existence, namely, food, shelter, and clothing. In most societies the family is an important means of transmitting and redistributing property and intangibles such as honor, a family name, and the family cult. Families usually have the understanding, whether explicit or not, that some members will require material support at certain stages of their life—early childhood, old age, a period of specialist education, or pregnancy—and that they in turn will support other members at the times when they are able. That support clearly consists again of the provision of food, shelter, and clothing. In most systems, this is elaborated into other expectations, such as respect and affection for the elderly, in addition to the provision of material needs. This ideal and the reality are studied in more detail in chapters 4 and 5. It is clear that children in the ancient world were expected to repay the care spent on them in their early dependence by looking after parents and other family members when the children reached their prime.

It was not only the old who hoped for respect and affection from other members. The persistence of the family as a human institution suggests that it is reasonably successful in performing the basic functions of economic and emotional support. Societies can be organized in many ways, and families, as we have seen, can take many forms, but kinship is everywhere an important principle of social organization and identification. Most people seem to find it important to be able to associate themselves with kin notionally as well as in the other ways noted here. People who have never met relatives in another country cherish the idea of the relationship, and adults who were given up as babies to institutions often suffer from a lack of identity (because they do not know who their parents and other kin are) even when they have built up families of their own. This is not to deny the role of non-kin in Roman society. In a culture in which patronage and slavery were so important it is to be expected that households include non-kin members, and it should not be surprising that slaves not only formed biological kin units but also tended to create non-kin groupings, usually based on the *familia* (even after manumission), for purposes such as funeral commemoration. In other cases, slaves and former slaves were sometimes included by favor in large tombs established by their owners.[89]

Even in a society such as the Roman, where it was possible to leave property to people outside the family, inheritance within the family was overwhelmingly the most common way of transmitting large-scale property. This was usually from parents to children, although other channels were used, especially by the childless.

The family also fulfilled economic roles by means of training, which was part of the socializing process. Senators' sons would be trained by their fathers or by family friends and patrons, and children at all social levels would learn their gender roles through their parents and other close relations of the same sex. It is clear from Roman legal sources that teaching relations (and relationships such as fostering and patronage) were acknowledged at law as resembling kinship bonds.[90] This could mean, too, that apprentices would normally form a special relationship with the family of the master who had taught the trade. Groups are clearly linked in an important way through marriage and reproduction, and sometimes the other links would continue through several generations, so that the children of freed slaves would be deemed to owe certain duties to the children of their former patron.[91] In this way, the economic side of family life was extended through patronage and other institutions, including fostering.

We have seen that emotional support was part of the idea of

proper family relations. Both material and emotional support can be necessary at times of crisis, and it was expected that the Roman family, including relations by marriage, would rally round when needed. Since the accounts of the historians of antiquity are dominated by political events, the most dramatic examples of support in adversity tend to cluster around times of general crisis, such as the civil wars or individual political situations, notably Cicero's exile, 58–57 B.C., which is very well documented and provides detail about his expectations of family members and their performance. Cicero in exile relied heavily on the support of his wife Terentia, his brother Quintus Cicero, his brother-in-law and old friend Atticus, and his son-in-law Piso Frugi.[92] I have already referred to the composition of family *consilia,* which could include in-laws, married children of both sexes, and even friends of the family.

We are told that the civil wars yielded spectacular instances of both loyalty and betrayal by family members. The historical tradition preserves both, but loyalty is much more in evidence between husbands and wives and especially children and parents, in spite of the odd comment by Velleius Paterculus that sons (or perhaps children) showed no loyalty at all, that wives were most loyal, freedmen reasonably loyal, and slaves sometimes loyal.[93] One famous example is the woman Turia, whose protection of her husband is recounted by both Valerius Maximus and Appian.[94]

The heading of the long but defective inscription conventionally termed *Laudatio Turiae* has been lost, so we do not have the name of the commemorator or the wife whom he describes and addresses. The identification with Turia and her husband is not generally accepted, but the label persists. The inscription apparently records a funeral speech *(laudatio)* in which a man eulogizes his wife's outstanding loyalty during the civil war, and the heroic acts he recounts do bear some resemblance to the stories about Turia. He also mentions her general family feeling—*pietas*—and cites everyday instances of it. These include her loyalty and respect to her mother-in-law and her economic generosity to her relations, including a tendency to contribute to the dowries of female relatives and to bring some of them up herself, a generosity which was eventually curbed by her brother and husband lest she run down the family estate.[95]

This is a reminder that family solidarity could be shown in more routine "crises," the sorts of things that happen normally in the life course of any family. There are always young women to be dowered for marriage, as well as family members in need of some other economic assistance. There are also times when families need to rally in specific ways, for example, within the political elite, at election time, when it is necessary for all family members to call in their economic and patronage assistance for the candidate.[96] Even a successful childbirth normally requires some help from family. Aulus Gellius shows a mother tending her daughter's lying-in and making subsequent arrangements.[97] If the woman died in childbirth, the family would have to supply some sort of substitute for her, as in the case of Quintilian's children, where the grandmother (probably his mother) filled this role or an aunt, as in the case of Pliny's wife.[98] The law allowed certain exceptions to its rulings on the ground of the duty family members owed each other; for example, the customary ban on gifts between husband and wife could be waived if the gift were to enable the husband to advance politically or to help him in exile (or to avoid exile). Women were prevented by an imperial ruling from being guarantors for third parties, but, again, an exception was allowed to a woman who had pledged herself to protect a father from exile or to support a close relation in court.[99] So the law reflected the general view of society that it was only proper for relatives to help each other out, even in contravention of certain rules governing the distribution of property. In chapter 2 we shall look in greater detail at the accommodation of such family practices by the law.

The family continued throughout the imperial period to be the main basis of economic production and the most important locus of the preservation and redistribution of property through marriage and between the generations upon death. The emphasis on the material aspect in these ancient accounts sometimes seems very prominent to the modern reader used to the modern concentration on the sentimental role of the family. It seems clear, however, from the inscriptions and the literary sources that the family was also a focus of emotional satisfaction for Romans. They did arrange marriages on what seem to have been fairly hard-headed grounds, and they did perceive their children at some level as an economic investment, but this does not preclude the importance of the family as an emotional unit, and there is evidence that at least from the late Republic (for which we have richer sources) the family was perceived as a refuge from the other problems of life.[100] The perception of the family as haven is often described by historians of the eighteenth and nineteenth centuries as a modern development; therefore, it is important to note that the same attitudes seem to have existed in Roman times, sometimes expressed in terms strikingly similar to the modern ones. Lucretius pours philosophical scorn on the stock behavior of mourners at a funeral, who lament that a young man who has died in his prime will no longer return to his happy home, his excellent wife, and his sweet children running to be picked up and to kiss him.[101] In other words, the delights of life are represented as the emotional pleasures of domesticity. This is precisely the picture Cicero paints at a low moment when he writes to Atticus that he has no real friends while Atticus and Quintus are out of Rome, in spite of being surrounded in the forum by supporters. He claims that his only real pleasure is gained in the time spent with his wife, his little daughter, and his young son, Marcus Cicero.[102]

In trying to deal with the opposition to his marriage laws, Augustus referred to the joys of marriage while acknowledging that marriage and parenthood had their problems, and in the debate in the senate about whether governors' wives should accompany them to their posts, the prince Drusus pointed out that the empress Livia (Drusus's grandmother) and Augustus had traveled together to the provinces and that he himself, though prepared to do his public duty, would not do it so happily if he were unable to take with him his wife, the mother of their many children.[103] This debate shows that the sentimental representation of family life had permeated the language of the public sphere and could openly be invoked in it as an attractive social ideal. As in any culture, the ideal was not necessarily realized, and it was doubtless the case

29

that some marriages were loveless and that many parents abused their children. This is also true of modern cultures, but the ideal is strong, and most families achieve moments, at least, that would reinforce this picture. The many epitaphs praising spouses and children in stock terms at least indicate the strength of ideals of marital harmony, affection for young children, and regret for "children" of all ages who die before the parents. Parents do also mourn their offspring because the death of a child signifies the loss of many hopes, but it is clear that there is some feeling behind the ideal.[104]

The functions of the family can best be summarized as social and physical reproduction, the transmission of property, honor, and the family cult, economic subsistence, and material and emotional support between family members, particularly at peak periods of the life course or at times of specific crisis or need. The family itself was a dynamic unit which responded to particular economic and demographic factors and to the changing stages of the life course. It could adapt to circumstances—a lack of children in one branch could be remedied by specific strategies such as adoption or fostering—and it could expand to take in people who were not biological kin but who had some claim to kinlike support, such as slaves, dependents, and people who were linked by fostering and other relationships. A strong sentimental ideal of family feeling developed in Roman society. It overlapped with and supplemented the traditional stress on obligation. Both concepts were absorbed into the term *pietas,* which characterized Roman family and, to an extent, patronage relationships.

## Conclusion

The family has always been a political football, and perhaps the Roman family has been kicked around more than any other through the ages. The Romans themselves reflected idealized views of its function in their legal rulings, their literature, and their political pronouncements. The emperor Augustus saw it as the basis of his program of moral renewal, the Christian fathers attacked its treatment of children, the Napoleonic Code looked to it as a model of proper power relations and stability, the Italian fascist regime revered it as an enduring symbol of the Italian virtues, many scholars viewed it as an interesting example of Indo-Germanic virtues (apart from some Anglophones who took for granted its moral decay).[105]

Theoretical constructs based on the analysis of kinship terminology and archaic inheritance schemata have largely yielded place to empirical investigation—the study of actual behavior, popular norms, statistical likelihood, and recorded feelings. Such "hard data" have changed the received opinion of who comprised the Roman household and how Roman fathers actually exercised their notorious powers over their children. The new picture is in some ways uneven but far more believable: a picture of households which responded to the changing needs of the family economy and the individual life course, of fathers who cajoled and nagged recalcitrant children, of mothers who engineered their children's marriages, of single-parent families, of working mothers, of elite children growing up with slave children and a number of intimate nurses and babysitters, of blended families abounding in step- and half-relations which extended kin ties almost indefinitely. On the other hand, we need to remind ourselves that myths and ideals play an important role in cultural consciousness: that Romans regarded with admiration the large household run on frugal lines by an inflexible *paterfamilias* is itself a significant piece of historical information about the Romans and their *mentalité*.

Within any society and, indeed, any particular section of a society, families will differ from each other and will respond to circumstances—death, marriage, changes in local markets or land use. Individual variation will play its part—the paternal style of the orator Cicero differed from that of his brother Quintus.[106] The Roman Empire was huge. It embraced many different ethnic and religious groups, and it had a wide range of status differentials and a relatively high degree of social and geographic mobility. What we conveniently but inaccurately term *the* Roman family manifested itself in a multiplicity of forms and institutions, even more, perhaps, than "the French peasant family of the eighteenth century" or "the modern Australian family." Roman historians have attempted to include the lower orders in their family studies but acknowledge the class and regional bias imposed by most of the available sources. Some have begun tentatively to examine regional differences.[107] The material from Roman Egypt, which does contain concrete information from household-based censuses and individual wills and contracts of sale, adoption, and apprenticeship, is enriching our knowledge of Roman families.[108] The changes introduced into family ideology and practices by Christianity continue to be examined intensively.[109] Historians of the later European family still look to the Roman family as the basis of many later developments, not least because Roman law was consciously adopted and adapted by so many societies.[110]

We are all creatures of our own culture, and we all have a vested interest in the family. We tend inevitably to focus on current interests—in the role of women, especially mothers, within the family, in the attitudes to young children and the care of the aged—to see the ways in which Roman attitudes, values, and practice resembled or differed from "ours," whatever they may be. The current stress on the nuclear character of the Roman family is itself a reflection of modern practice and ideology, just as the earlier emphasis on patriarchal authority and historical continuity arose from the concerns of an earlier generation of scholars.

Roman family studies reveal that companionate marriage and the perception of childhood as a distinct stage of the human life course are not wholly modern inventions. Even our limited evidence makes it clear that the ideology and practice of Roman families changed slowly within ancient times, perhaps in response to external factors such as imperial legislation and Christianity but sometimes for reasons which are not clear, as in the shift in marriage preference which placed the married woman legally in her natal rather than her conjugal family. The problems of explaining such changes and the inconsistent rate of change both highlight the continuity of family structures and the pragmatic nature of families, which must always balance ideology against demographic and economic contingencies. Thus Roman republican society, in which widows and divorcées normally remarried, continued to idealize the woman who married only once (just as many modern societies view marriage in ideal terms as a lifelong partnership, founded in exclusive romantic love, against a reality of divorce and a predictable level of widowhood). It is surely untenable to retain any vestigial tendency to discern linear social evolution, whether on the nineteenth-century model of moving towards "civilization" or its modern equivalent, the (often implicit) view that people have only recently begun to place a "proper" value on human relationships. This is as pointless as the recurrent moralizing of the modern media (or their ancient Roman equivalents) about a "decline in the family."[111]

And yet it is true that the state of the family at any period is quite rightly a matter of general concern. Study of its history can readily be justified in terms of the light it throws not only on other historical institutions and events but also on our own societies.[112] It is too easy for the uninformed to make generalizations about motherhood, the role of women, the "normal" behavior of children in the family, and the care of the aged which are based on erroneous conceptions of what "the family" has been in the past.[113] It is right and proper that scholars should rigorously research these areas and, if possible, communicate their conclusions to the community at large, especially when such issues are the subject of debate and affect public policy. This topicality, however, has its own drawbacks: "Social scientists, like everyone else, are participants as well as observers in families; and they tend rather easily to universalize experiences which reflect their own gender and class relations."[114] And, one could add, their own generational bias, their own experience as daughters, mothers, cousins, grandfathers.

It is easy enough to see the bias that others bring to the subject, but one's own omissions are not always clear. Engagement lends the study great appeal but makes any notion of scholarly objectivity even more elusive than in political history, to which one also brings inevitable bias. It is difficult to study alien practices such as the routine abandonment of newborn babies or arranged marriages without wondering about the difference in feelings of the participants. It is difficult to think of familiar relationships such as those between young children and their grandparents without assuming that they carried the same sentimental implications attributed to them by contemporary ideology.[115] Yet feelings and norms are such important elements of family studies that they cannot simply be passed over.

The general problems of writing about kinship are increased in the case of the Roman family by the well-known source problems of a literature dominated by the viewpoint of the middle-aged male of the ruling class (even if the writer is a young man, such as Catullus, or the son of a freed slave, such as Horace), who sees women, children, slaves, and agricultural workers as existing (if noticed) on the periphery of life. Roman historiography was concerned with wars and public political life, not with the everyday business of family and marriage and parenthood, which impinge on the accounts of Tacitus, Livy, and Sallust only when they inform the political and military account. Even when ancient authors speak theoretically of the family, in their philosophical and juristic works, they sometimes invoke an ideal which might not be close to the reality of their own lives. Seneca the philosopher gave theoretical reasons why the wise man should not marry but was known for his passion for his own young wife.[116]

It is nonetheless possible to form some notion of norms and even of population history. Romans do speak of their feelings (however formulaically and economically at times) in epitaphs, law court speeches, and letters. They do tell us something of their marriage and dotal arrangements, their inheritance practices, their material obligations to family members, and the occasional dissension between the generations. The material available has not changed greatly in the last hundred years, but the approaches to it have altered enormously. Roman historical studies continue to use the traditional classical techniques of intensive linguistic and literary source analysis, legal theory, and epigraphy but these are now commonly supplemented by statistical material and concepts drawn from comparative studies of the family in other historical periods or sometimes from sociology and anthropology. The source material and sometimes the concerns of French regional history or the postindustrial family can be very different from those of the Roman historian of the family, who then has to make choices about how to apply the findings from these kindred disciplines.

The questions being asked now are not those of the 1970s, and the scholarship of the 1990s will probably bring new perspectives, sometimes as a direct reflection of modern social and intellectual trends. Historians of the Roman family will probably maintain their dual function, for they are ancient historians, trained first in philological analysis and political history and secondarily as students of the family, but show themselves (intermittently) to be alert to the issues that concern other historians and social scientists. This book is designed to explain basic ideas and major developments in the study of the Roman family and, to a limited extent, of the European family, but it necessarily reflects the views of the author. The very arrangement and selection of topics represents a certain approach to the subject. The chapter headings, not to mention their content, would have been quite different fifty or even twenty years ago, and even contemporary colleagues in the discipline adopt different modes of organizing the material. The discipline shows the same dynamic quality as the institution of the family and will doubtless continue to grow and to develop. The questions will change, and so will the answers, and that is as it should be.

# Two

# Roman Family Relations
# and the Law

We saw in chapter 1 that Roman family studies have traditionally paid great attention to the law, especially to the wide-ranging powers of the Roman father (*paterfamilias*) and the rules laid down for inheritance in cases where persons died without a will, the laws of intestate succession. This concentration is understandable, given the importance of power relations and the transmission of property within families, but it is necessary to look beyond the letter of the law to discover not only the practice but the socially determined norms that actually governed behavior between family members. For example, Roman fathers did not habitually kill their adult children, although they had the right at law to do so; mothers seem commonly to have arranged their children's marriages, although they did *not* have a legal power to do so; and even humble Romans commonly made wills in accordance with popular notions of rightful inheritance rather than the strictly agnatic system of intestate succession enshrined in the legal system.

In any society there is likely to be some discrepancy between the law and general practice, not only in such consciously illegal acts as brigandage, murder, or fraud, which are unlikely to win general approval, but in the ideology of competing systems of obligation and priority. In the modern world there is often a conflict between laws such as death duties, designed to increase state revenue, and the general feeling that children are entitled to inherit unencumbered parental estates. Where statutes penalizing "victimless crimes" (e.g., vagrancy, homosexual acts, and smoking marijuana) are seen to be needlessly oppressive, the activities are effectively tolerated on the assumption that the law will eventually change to keep pace with altered community standards.

Roman culture and the Roman *mentalité* revered the lawmakers of the past. The term *mos maiorum* (custom of the forbears) could be applied to law or custom and was usually invoked to attest the morality or legality of some contemporary proposal. The Law of the Twelve Tables was traditionally supposed to have arisen from the struggle of the patrician and plebeian orders in the early republican period, when the lower orders objected to the whimsical exercise of power by the officeholding upper classes, who had the monopoly of a knowledge of law and religion. As a result, the laws (so goes the traditional story) were recorded and available for public consultation from the fifth century B.C.[1] They were routinely learned by Roman schoolchildren. They survive now only in scattered quotations which scholars have assembled from law court speeches and the works of jurists.[2] Modern opinion is divided on whether they represent a codification of existing principles or a development of the law.[3] In either case, later generations revered the Twelve Tables even more than other types of recorded law, and there was great reluctance to tamper with the tradition.

This is not to say that Romans made no new law. A glance at Rotondi's (1922) guide to Roman statutes shows how much legislation built up over the years. We need not concern ourselves here with the technical distinctions between the different types of law, but a brief outline is necessary. It was possible for the consuls to introduce bills to the elite senate or for plebeian tribunes (*tribuni plebis*) to take them to the popular assembly. In either case, they could eventually be treated as statute law (*ius civile*), each statute taking its name from the family (gentile) name of the proposer(s).[4] Thus a law proposed by the consuls Pl. Licinius Crassus and

C. Cassius Longinus and authorized by the senate would be the *Lex Licinia Cassia,* its function often specified by a subsequent title; [5] a law proposed by the tribune P. Clodius Pulcher and passed by the popular assembly would become the *Lex Clodia de iniuriis publicis.* It was, however, rare for Romans to *revoke* existing legislation. Confusion sometimes resulted from the fact that the relation of new laws to existing statutes was not always made clear. [6]

The praetorian judicial system allowed a little leeway in interpreting and executing the laws. Like consuls, praetors were annually elected officials who were expected to relinquish office at the end of the calendar year. Both consuls and praetors enjoyed certain other privileges and responsibilities, and both acted in a judicial capacity, but the praetors tended to be the regular presidents of courts. Their chief function was to determine whether a particular case fitted an existing definition of a legal suit (*actio*), to appoint a judge (*iudex*), and to supply him with the appropriate formula for determining the outcome of the case once he had made a decision about the facts. [7] Towards the end of the Republic, standing courts for criminal offenses increased, and such charges were judged by a large jury. Most family suits, however, were more likely to be determined by formulary procedure. The praetors would hear disputes about return of dowry, for instance, or the registration or contesting of wills, applications for a guardian (*tutor*) for a minor or woman, and so on.

Praetors were ambitious senatorial politicians with no particular expertise in the law. Each year the chief praetor read out an "edict" stating his approach to various aspects of the law. In practice, this tended to be a cumulative document, with some changes from year to year, and there was no means of appeal against a praetor who failed to follow his own avowed principles. Roman law was essentially casuistic, so praetors sometimes made judgments on specific issues which could be incorporated by subsequent praetors in the edict and used as a guide. (This had none of the authority of precedent in modern common law countries, but it did have a certain influence.) In some cases, praetors were able to soften slightly the effect of laws that were out of step with current thinking. They were, for example, inclined to favor the claims of "blood" kin to a deceased estate over those of legally defined relations, but they were not supposed to overstep the law. Thus a woman's claim to the estate of her deceased children who had died intestate had to be determined in accordance with the rules *unde cognati,* but sometimes the praetor could award possession to the person perceived as the "rightful heir."[8] In this way, a separate system of praetorian law, *ius honorarium,* grew up beside the system of statute law, *ius civile.* The opinions of praetors in real cases and of legal experts in real and hypothetical cases came to be collected by students of the law, and praetors would often seek advice from a committee (*consilium*) of friends who made a particular study of the law and were able to cite such cases.

Again, we have to rely on reconstructions of the edict from scattered quotations from later sources,[9] while for praetorian practice we are often reliant on Cicero's account of Verres's governorship (as *pro praetore,* or propraetor, that is, in the years following his praetorship at Rome) of Sicily and his use of the provincial edict, which probably paralleled the edict of the urban praetor (*praetor urbanus*) at Rome.[10] Statutes occasionally survive on inscriptions, sometimes provincial copies or parallel legislation, such as the *Lex Salpensana.*[11] Otherwise statutes are known primarily from references in literary sources such as law court speeches, letters, or histories, which do not necessarily quote the laws directly. In the sixth century A.D., the Christian emperor Justinian commissioned the jurist Tribonian to organize a compilation of Roman law under subject headings.[12] This compilation was completed under great pressure of time. It includes judgments by jurists and praetors from the republican and imperial periods, as well as references to the emperors' own rulings, which had come to have the force of law. The opinions of certain jurists—a class which virtually became professional academics by the second century A.D.—were regarded as authoritative, but since the juristic schools frequently took opposing views on legal questions, the law was not always certain.[13]

Those scholars of the Roman family who made law their chief interest in the earlier part of the twentieth century tended to use the material from the *Digest* and the other imperial compilations,[14] which included imperial rescripts, replies by the emperors to individuals who had written to them about specific cases.[15] These studies paid little attention to historical change or to the social significance of legal developments. The approach of historians such as Crook has been to use the law as a historical source, together with other sources such as republican speeches and letters, imperial biographies and letters, and so on, in an attempt to reconstruct developments in social and economic history. The works of Humbert, Garnsey, Treggiari, Y. Thomas, Dixon, Saller, and Corbier fall into this category. All are legal historians in this mode.[16]

It is, in any case, important for the reader to understand the basic legal principles traditionally governing Roman family relations before we embark on an account of ways in which these were modified by practice, judicial interpretation, and statute. Perhaps the most famous—or most notorious—is the extreme power of the Roman father, the *paterfamilias*. His legitimate children were in his paternal power (*patria potestas*) from birth.[17] They had no power to own or manipulate property in their own right, nor could they make valid wills. The father retained the power of life and death (*ius vitae necisque*) over them until he died unless he chose to release them from his power, for example, by adopting them into another family, by "emancipating" them, or by transferring daughters to the family of their husband on marriage; the procedure in each case entailed a formulaic ceremony of great antiquity.[18] The marriage of a person in paternal power, a *filiusfamilias* (son of the *familia*) or *filiafamilias* (daughter of the *familia*), was not valid unless it was performed with paternal consent.[19] A few paternal rights were limited in early Roman society; for example, fathers were not able to sell daughters. They could sell sons or bind them over to a creditor, and the early practice was that a bonded son would revert to the father's power after emancipation, but this was eventually changed so that the son achieved full legal freedom if he went through this process three times! According to later tradition, regal laws limited the father's power to expose newborn infants—a standard method of family limitation in the ancient world.[20] He was bound to rear one daughter and any healthy sons. This law had certainly lapsed by the late Republic, when fathers had full powers to expose any newborn child at will and appear to have exercised these powers.

Unless the father initiated the steps outlined above to free his children from his power, they became legally independent (*sui iuris*) only on his death. If he had not made a will, the children shared equally in his estate. They were all termed *sui heredes* (their own heirs, or heirs to their own property), an odd expression which the jurists explained by the notion that the *paterfamilias,* for all his extensive powers, was in effect a trustee for life of the family estate but that it belonged in a sense to the family forever.[21] The *paterfamilias* could make a will (another solemn ceremony, bearing certain resemblances to the ritual of emancipation, *coemptio,* adoption, and so on) in which, in theory, he could leave the estate to whomever he wished as long as he conformed to the many rules governing Roman testaments and explicitly excluded *sui heredes,* naming the sons and including daughters and the children of deceased sons in the expression "Let all others be disinherited";[22] but in practice there was a strong presumption that children would be the heirs.

Children of a legitimate marriage always belonged to the family of the father, but if the father's father were alive, they were in his power, passing into that of their own father on the grandfather's death. If a son predeceased his father, the son's children received their father's share and had then to divide it equally among themselves. A woman could pass on marriage from the *potestas* of her father into the *manus* of her husband (or of her father-in-law, for if he were alive, her husband would be in his *potestas*). This signified at law that she became a member of her husband's family. Any property she owned or acquired, in addition to her dowry, became her husband's, and on the husband's death she inherited equally with her children. If she did not make the legal transfer on marriage, she remained at law a member of her own natal family and retained her right of equal inheritance with her brothers. Both types of marriage existed in Rome from earliest times, but there was a change in fashion. In the early Republic, most women seem to have transferred to the husband's *manus* on marriage, but by the first century B.C. it seems to have been usual for women to

41

remain in the family of their birth, although the children of the marriage still took the father's name, were in his power, and were his *sui heredes*.[23]

It is quite possible that this system of inheritance was closely linked with the conditions of Roman society in the early Republic. As we saw in chapter 1, the Romans had a particular image of their own past, characterized by self-sufficiency and simplicity. Historians now dispute the dramatic contrasts implicit in this folk history, but it remains true in very general terms that early Roman society was a more basic agrarian culture. It conquered most of Italy, but the upper class seems to have been characterized by honors—religious, political, and military—and inherited status rather than by much greater wealth and the conspicuous spending that became so typical of the senatorial elite from the second century B.C., when the Roman Empire extended beyond the Italian peninsula and the massive importation of slaves transformed the economy.[24] Roman stories about famous consuls and generals who were called from the plow to take command of the Roman army and about their virtuous wives, who worked into the night spinning and weaving, naturally have a mythic and symbolic element but could well reflect an earlier reality.[25]

Within such a setting, the Roman system of inheritance and marriage makes a certain sense. The family, headed by the oldest male ascendant, would work the land as an economic unit. Women who entered the family by marriage would bring with them as dowry their intestate portion of land, which would then be merged with the family holding. If her husband died and the widow stayed on with her children, this would postpone the splitting of the estate. As in many systems, the movement of women by marriage from one family to another was a biological and economic necessity, for only in this way could the family extend into another generation and gain land to offset the possible divisions in each generation. Where the preservation of the family and the land is prized, there is sometimes a resentment of this necessity and a suspicion of women, who change family membership and potentially threaten estates—those of their natal family because the dowry entails a loss of land or goods and those of their conjugal family because a widow is able to leave and take with her her share of their estate. The father's death and the consequent removal of her portion of the estate as dowry could therefore be seen by her brothers as an unfair loss. It is typical of dowry systems that men accept the provision of dowry for sisters or daughters as a charge on their masculine honor, but they perceive it and speak of it as a burden and a loss, failing to offset it against the dowry that they themselves virtually acquire on their own marriage. Such talk can often be an excuse for boasting about the extent of dowry, but the resentment is reflected at times in a suspicion of women, who are perceived as robbing their brothers or children by reducing the family estate.[26] If continuity of family is prized, the very mobility of women between families becomes suspect.

It becomes understandable that the Roman system had safeguards to minimize the disruptive effects of such transfers. Thus the married woman became at law a member of her husband's family. If he died, she became *sui iuris,* just as her children did. If they were young, they required a *tutor,* who could be appointed in the father's will or determined by the same rules as those governing succession on intestate death; that is, the *tutores* were likely to be the father's brothers. The function of the *tutor* was to administer and maintain the child's estate until he reached puberty. A girl, however, retained a *tutor* for life or until she passed into the *manus* of a husband. In the case of women over the age of puberty, the function of the *tutor* was somewhat different. His authorization was necessary if the woman wished to perform certain legal acts, such as selling *res mancipi* (slaves, land, certain cattle), pledging dowry, making a will, or manumitting slaves. The *tutor* did not, however, administer the woman's property, and she was able to conduct certain types of business, including cash transactions. Both women and children *in tutela* were capable of owning property and accepting inheritances, but children were not able to make valid wills. At least by the mid-Republic, women could make wills as long as they underwent a ceremonial *coemptio* for the purpose and had the authority of the *tutor.* The word *tutor* is often translated as "guardian," and in the case of children this is reasonable, as long as people understand that the *tutor* did not live with the children or have any particular say in their lives (e.g., their marriages or education). It is not apposite in the case of women. In both cases, the institution of *tutela* was originally tied to the inheritance system and designed to protect the family property, not the person *in tutela*.[27]

By the late Republic, the women of the elite seem to have made wills as a matter of course and to have engaged freely in property sales. By the first century B.C., most wives remained after marriage in the family of their birth. The reason for this change in marriage preference is not clear, but it is probably connected with the economic changes mentioned above. From at least the second century B.C., Italy became a slave-based economy, and elite attitudes towards land changed. It was no longer something to be kept within the family at all costs but something to be exploited for profit, whether by cash cropping, sale, or leasing out for specialist uses. The senatorial class was still a landed aristocracy, but it no longer worked its own land personally. Senatorials tended to live in urban centers—that is, to view their Roman or municipal homes as their base—and to acquire estates from all over Italy. According to Plutarch, the second-century B.C. censor Cato the elder led the new style of profit agriculture, and the self-sufficient peasant family, once the backbone of the Italian countryside, was squeezed out by the vast estates, *latifundia,* worked by foreign slaves and producing specialist crops for sale and export.[28]

Certain changes in family legislation and practice are probably to be dated to this transition, although the source tradition makes it difficult to plot developments precisely. The problem is that we have much more information about *everything* from the late Republic, while our knowledge of earlier institutions is largely culled from later sources with an interest in propagating myths about the past. This leaves us with a stark picture of the simple but virtuous life of early Rome, where the tyrannical *paterfamilias* reigned supreme over children and wife alike, where women worked too hard to have energy for adultery or were beaten to death for drinking wine and there was no divorce.[29] Later authors typically invoked this past (favorably!) to contrast it with the decadence of their own day. Thus Cicero (through the *persona* of Cato the elder) admires the tyranny exercised by the aged Appius Claudius over his household, Plutarch compares the harmony and simplicity of the Aelii Tuberones brothers with the inheritance squabbles of his own day, and Juvenal admires the women of old who were too tired to think of adultery.[30]

Some elements of the traditional stories are certainly garbled or exaggerated and sometimes contradictory. We are told that there was no divorce before 230 B.C. but hear of early laws allowing a husband to divorce a wife for adultery, poisoning the children (perhaps secret abortion?), or stealing the household keys, as well as the censure of a husband for divorcing a blameless wife.[31] Yet the anecdotes can be interpreted plausibly: divorce was probably rare in early Rome and initiated only by the husband for serious marital offenses. The significance of the "first divorce" of 230 B.C. was the establishment of a set legal procedure (*actio*) for the recovery of dowry on the dissolution of marriage if the usual methods of negotiation between families had failed.[32] By the first century B.C., divorce was quite straightforward, could be initiated by either party, and involved no recourse to the law unless there was some dispute about property. There were, then, some changes in legal procedure, but they did not keep pace with the changes in practice and ideology concerning the proper obligations between family members. In the following subsection we see ways in which the strict, legal view of family relations was modified by legal and customary means to accord with contemporary morality.

### The Accommodation of Social Rules within the Legal System

Most legal systems display a certain conservatism. In the Roman case this conservatism was accentuated by the reverence for *mos maiorum,* the custom of the ancestors. By the first century B.C. Roman law was the subject of study and analysis by sophisticated scholars, but it was still based to an extent on the simple "If man hit man, let man pay" principles of the Twelve Tables and earlier.[33] We have seen that legal relations within the family probably reflected the norms and customs of a much earlier society. By the late Republic, the rules of succession on intestacy no longer reflected community ideas of how property ought to be transmitted, for the stress on agnatic relationships often excluded the obligation of a mother to her children. The lifelong *tutela* of women seemed odd in a culture in which elite women, like their menfolk, apparently took full advantage of opportunities for capital investment.[34] These anomalies continued in the imperial period, in spite of the fact that there was now more scope for centralized, forward-looking legislation. Career soldiers from the time of Augustus (at least) had no capacity to form valid Roman marriages during service but naturally wished their *de facto* wives and illegitimate children to succeed to them, even if they were foreigners without the capacity to benefit from a Roman will.[35]

For all their theoretical reverence for the past, Romans were essentially pragmatic, and a number of solutions to these problems developed piecemeal, consisting sometimes of clever dodges to get around the law, sometimes in virtually ignoring inconvenient laws until they fell into desuetude; sometimes praetorian or imperial decisions in individual cases would be cited and eventually find their way into statutes. The process was not systematic and progressive, nor was it internally consistent. Thus, there was a general tendency over the centuries to modify *patria potestas* but a feeling that the state should not interfere too much in this area, and sometimes the powers of the *paterfamilias* were even strengthened.[36]

In this chapter, we look at legal developments in specific aspects of family relations: *patria potestas,* the acknowledgment of maternal rights and obligations, the conception of dowry, the slave and soldier family, and various legal acknowledgments of the obligations of *pietas*. An examination of the strategies adopted reveals that many community notions of proper behavior were absorbed very slowly and erratically into the law in a number of ways and that we must be very careful in studying Roman law to take account of the extent to which formal principles were actually implemented rather than jump to the conclusion that Romans, unlike everybody else, can be described by their laws taken in isolation. This would mean treating them as a historical constant throughout the ten centuries from the publication of the Twelve Tables within a simple, rustic society to the codification of the *Digest* in a Christian era, when the sprawling, long-established, cosmopolitan empire had split into two huge administrative units embracing hundreds of different societies and traditions.

The Roman *paterfamilias* is the most discussed family member. Before the modern interest in social history and the family, works allegedly on "the Roman family" usually turned out to be about the Roman father and son. The Romans themselves knew that such extensive lifelong powers over property and the person were unique to Roman fathers.[37] Because of its association with Roman citizenship, *patria potestas* became a coveted privilege,[38] and in a sense the *paterfamilias* made the law within the family circle, though always on the assumption that he was advised by a family committee (*consilium*).[39] The Twelve Tables imposed a limit on the *paterfamilias*'s power to reclaim a son whom he had sold: after the third time, the son was released from his *potestas*.[40] Anecdotes from the late Republic make it clear that fathers normally consulted other family members, especially wives, about their children's marriages,[41] and the emperor Marcus ruled in the second century A.D. that a father did not have the power to end a daughter's happy marriage against her will.[42]

By the early third century A.D. a father who killed his child could be held to account unless he had acted in accordance with a trial by family *consilium*. This presumably refers to an adult child. In the second century A.D. the emperor Hadrian exiled a father who had killed his son. The son allegedly had been having an affair with his stepmother, but even so, Hadrian reportedly argued that the father's impulsive punishment was not a proper exercise of *patria potestas*, which ought to be characterized by *pietas*, not *atrocitas*.[43] This goes against the theory that the law should not intervene against the father at all and against the tradition of revering examples of paternal severity. We have some knowledge of father-son conflict by the late Republic, and it is clear that such conflict was normally settled, not by recourse to violence and killing or even by exheredation, but by nagging and persuasion.[44] The father's right to reject a new baby was still taken for granted, and the practice of infant exposure seems to have persisted for some time in spite of attempts by Christian emperors to legislate it out of existence.[45] So the famous paternal right over life and death, like the right to determine children's marriages, was tempered primarily by convention, but in general the law supported the conventional distinctions.[46]

It should not be thought that the law consistently eroded *patria potestas*. At times it strengthened the position of the *paterfamilias*. It was deemed unreasonable that a manumitting slaveowner should have greater rights over the dispositions of a former female slave than a father had over his emancipated daughter, so the category of *parens manumissor* was elevated to the status of *tutela legitima* to ensure that a father who had surrendered his *potestas* by emancipating should still have a right of veto over her testamentary and some other dispositions.[47] It is surely not irrelevant that those who made the law were themselves *patresfamilias* and the legal writings are full of the imaginary examples "If I have a son in my *potestas*." They checked what they perceived as excessive imposition of the notional rights of the *paterfamilias* and in individual cases applied personal and community morality about the proper behavior of the father, who was expected to be affectionate and merciful and could be punished if he was not, as in the case of the father who was exiled by *relegatio* for exercising his rights at law in circumstances of severe provocation.[48] The law could be merciful—to father or child—and could operate as a check on itself through the casuistic system, whereby individual cases could be determined on common-sense grounds as well as by strict adherence to the letter of the law.

Just as our picture of the father's powers needs to be modified by reference to the praetorian tradition and convention, so the mother's position is enhanced by a look at socially accepted practice and the evolving law on inheritance. The traditional legal system tied the mother's status to her entry into the agnatic family of her husband. With the changing marriage preference, most women of the late Republic and early Empire did not change status on marriage (that is, they did not enter the *manus* of the husband) and were not therefore members of the same family as their own children. The brothers of a married woman had first claim on her inheritance if she died intestate and had the power to prevent her from making a will if they were her *tutores,* for the *tutor* was determined by the same process as intestate succession if the father of a woman had not specifically appointed her *tutor* in his will. This procedure had been laid down by the Twelve Tables to protect family estates in the hands of women (and young children) who had no *sui heredes* at a time when women could not make wills.[49] By the mid-Republic, women could make wills and clearly did so.[50] The social expectation was that women would pass their property on to their children or grandchildren; indeed, literary and juristic examples make this expectation clear even before the full development of the action against an undutiful will. Cicero, offended at his ex-wife's criticism of his new will, implied that she had not been as dutiful as he. Valerius Maximus castigated a woman who excluded one of two daughters for no defensible, moral reason and records the decision of Augustus to break the will of a mother who had passed over her sons in favor of her second husband.[51]

Given that the *tutor* was originally established to monitor the disposition of a woman's estate, it is interesting to note that women were able in effect to divert their property from their agnates to their children and that this historical development could only have taken place with the complicity of their own families, who appointed or served as *tutores.* But in the case of the woman who died intestate, the rules gave her brother priority over her children. This soon came to be seen as an anomaly and an injustice, and it was modified by successive legislation in the second century A.D. strengthening the reciprocal inheritance rights between mother and child. But even then the legislation applied only to women with the right of children (*ius liberorum*), which could mean three or four, according to the woman's status, and the rights of a paternal uncle to the estate of his sister-in-law's dead children were still somewhat uncertain. These details were remedied finally in the sixth century A.D.[52] We are told that the emperor Claudius had first noted the situation and shown pity towards bereaved mothers. Then a senatorial commendation under Hadrian confirmed the right of mothers to their dead (minor) children's estates, and in A.D. 178 children were able to succeed directly to a mother who died intestate, but there was still some ambiguity about the rights of a maternal uncle.[53] The whole process shows a fairly consistent presumption of maternal rights and duties and even a sentimental feeling for grieving mothers, but the solutions were somewhat *ad hoc* and imperfect, suggesting a lingering reluctance to do away entirely with the Twelve Tables agnatic principle even in an age which had dispensed with so many of the rituals concerning the links of a married woman with her agnates.[54]

The right of a woman to determine the marriages of her children had no basis whatever in law, but it is referred to in the literary sources as part of the process of making marriages and even, in one case, of ending a marriage.[55] Most of the anecdotes show the mother acting in combination with her husband or as a widow in consultation with friends and relations. The *Codex Theodosianus* refers incidentally to the need for parental rather than just paternal consent to marriage,[56] but there is little legal backing for what seems to be an accepted social procedure and apparently little need for the involvement of the law. It might be interesting to compare this with the more recent model of Peloponnesian marriage, in which the father of the bride takes responsibility for negotiations but knows that insufficient attention to his daughter's interests will condemn him to a lifetime of reproaches and reminders from his wife. This is reminiscent of Livy's and Plutarch's stories of the consular second century B.C. husband who returns home to announce to his wife the successful conclusion of a betrothal for their daughter, to be upbraided for excluding the mother from the discussion. The mother is mollified only on learning of the unparalleled distinction of the groom. The story, like all good *topoi*, can be attached to different actors but illustrates the social background: it was clearly a foolhardy father who took his rights at law literally.[57]

Dowry is another area in which there is some discrepancy between the theory of the law and its practice as influenced by social expectation. It is generally assumed that dowry was a feature of Roman society from earliest times, but it was not mentioned in the Twelve Tables, as far as we know. Its first appearance in formal legal history is 230 B.C., with the establishment of the *actio rei uxo-*

*riae,* a legal action for the recovery of dowry on the dissolution of marriage.[58] The action lay to the wife and her father. Roman dowry actually belonged to the husband for the duration of the marriage, but he was expected to return it or its value to the wife on divorce, subject to possible deductions for marital fault or the maintenance of children. If the wife died, he retained the dowry unless it had been given by the wife's father, who had the right to reclaim his contribution.[59]

The immediate function of the dowry was to provide income or produce for the conjugal family, and the husband, as owner, was expected to maintain the substance or capital of the dowry while enjoying the benefit of the income or fruits. There is some evidence that it was a point of masculine honor to do this. When the general Aemilius Paulus died ca. 160 B.C., his sons went to some trouble to ensure that their stepmother's dowry was repaid, although this involved cutting into a meager estate.[60] In the following generation, the death of Q. Aelius Tubero involved the sale of land in a family where the integrity and continuity of the holding was prized, in order to repay the value of his widow's dowry.[61] Both Milo and Cicero went to great lengths (even employing legal dodges) to safeguard their wives' dowries against the possible threat of confiscation as part of the husbands' holdings.[62] That dowry was legally part of the husband's own property did not detract from the popular perception of it as really belonging to the wife. This principle was eventually acknowledged at law. The case of Licinnia, wife of the plebeian tribune Gaius Gracchus, had raised the question in court. She was presumably seeking the return of her dowry after her husband's assassination in 122 B.C. because her dotal property had been damaged in riots connected with his political activity.[63]

It became common for families to negotiate agreements before marriage (*pacta dotalia*) establishing the rules for the return of dowry on its dissolution, and it was customary to review the terms in the case of divorce.[64] Rules also developed for those instances where negotiations broke down, and the *Digest* predictably contains whole chapters about the problems which could arise. For our purposes the notable feature is the central paradox that while

51

the husband was legally the owner of the dowry, his ownership was hedged about by social expectation and, slowly, by legal limitations. In all accounts, dowry is spoken of as if it belonged to the wife. "The money was paid to the women," says Polybius of dowry installments' being handed over to the women's husbands; authors write of "Terentia's dowry" and "Licinnia's dowry."[65] Gaius points to the anomaly of Augustan legislation which still accorded the husband this status as owner but prevented him from alienating or mortgaging his wife's dotal land (in Italy) without her permission, legislation which was later strengthened.[66]

The other great limitation was the wife's ability to divorce her husband with ease and dispatch and require the immediate return of real estate and part of any cash settlement. Indeed, the wife could demand an accounting and even sue during the marriage if she had reason to suspect that her husband was putting "her" dowry at risk.[67] If the husband died, the return of the dowry was a privileged claim on the estate, directly reflecting the practice of the second century B.C. examples given above, where the widows had apparently been in the husband's *manus* and the dowry had theoretically been sunk into a common family fund but had in practice been distinguished from the patrimonial holdings and treated as a preferred debt.[68] By Cicero's day, it was apparently law that any property of a wife *in manu* should be treated as dowry (on the analogy of the separate regime form of marriage), and being treated as dowry seems to have meant essentially that her property was returnable.[69]

Tryphoninus (late 2d to early 3d century A.D.) eventually refers to the notion that dowry is really the wife's and the husband cannot appeal to a fine legal point to escape his obligation.[70] Other jurists make comparable comments from time to time, but these would probably be classed in common law systems as *obiter dicta;* they do not affect the fundamental principle that the husband remains owner of the dowry for the duration of the marriage. They reflect rather the general *social* view, which had a long history, that the good husband maintained the dowry and used it to enhance the conjugal economy but treated it more as if he were an administrator. The laws limiting his behavior were directed at husbands who did not live up to this general ethos. The case law and juristic comments suggest a tendency to sympathize with the wife's claim and the working assumption that the husband should not treat the dowry as his personal property. Even the right of the state to treat the dowry as part of his holdings (its status at law) in the event of confiscation was open to question.

Behind this approach lay the assumptions that marriage was central to society and that marriage required dowry.[71] The importance placed on this is evident in the ruling that even a woman *in tutela legitima* was entitled to have a temporary *tutor* appointed for the purpose of promising dowry in the absence of her *tutor* father or *patronus*.[72] Usually the law was disinclined to treat *tutores legitimi* so cavalierly in a period when other *tutores* were readily replaced or overruled. Dowry is also an exception to the limitations on the power of a *filiusfamilias* to pledge a large amount. The *SC Macedonianum*, of the first century A.D., was designed to prevent *filiifamilias* from borrowing against a father's estate, but if the *paterfamilias* were absent for a long period, the son could legally pledge dowry for his daughter.[73] Again, the guiding principle is the overriding importance for women of having a dowry in order to marry, then remarry. Where this conflicts with other principles— the husband's rights as owner, the patron's right as *tutor*, or the right of a *paterfamilias* to be immune from independent commitments by his son in power—there is a tendency to favor the woman's right to her dowry.

## Slave Families

Slaves had no legal right to marry. Their children belonged to the owner of the slave mother. Yet slaves did form *de facto* marriages (*contubernia*) and attempted to maintain family ties in spite of the great pressures which could be applied, such as the right of the owner to control sexual access to slaves and the real possibility of separation.[74]

Slaves were not even deemed to have *cognati/ae* (the most informal definition of relatives) because of the difficulty of determining these in servile conditions.[75] Even manumission did not alter the former slave's legal relation to existing kin. Freed slaves had no *agnati,* and the only way of acquiring them was for a freed male slave who had gained citizenship to form a proper, legitimate marriage and produce children who came into his *potestas.* These children would be his *agnati* (but not his wife's, unless she had entered his *manus*).

In practice, people knew that slaves did form marital and family relationships and that important social bonds existed between slave and free—for example, between a slave nurse and her nurseling and between her own child and the nurseling.[76] The law had always been ready to enforce the manifold duties of freed slaves to their former owners,[77] but in time the existence of ties of kinship among slaves was occasionally acknowledged at law. On the negative side, kinship was recognized in that it stigmatized incestuous unions; that is, a freed slave could not marry his biological sister or daughter, even if she was a slave or freed slave and therefore had no claim on his estate if he died intestate.[78] More positively, it was possible to get around the restrictions of the *Lex Aelia Sentia* (which set a minimum age of thirty for a slave being manumitted and even a minimum age of twenty for the person manumitting) if the owner was freeing a slave who was a parent or child, brother or sister, or even a foster brother or sister.[79] A man was also granted exemption from the restrictions if he wished to free a female slave in order to marry her.[80] In fact, the law admitted the principle that slave children owed a duty of *pietas* to their parents, and slave parents to their children.[81]

To be sure, the law continued to take the side of the owner or *patronus/a,*[82] but there was some mitigation where the rights of children intervened. The Julian law on marriage forced certain accommodations by posing a conflict between the rights of *patroni* and the rights of children to the estate of a freed slave. A *libertina* (freedwoman) was liberated from *tutela* if she had four freeborn children, and the former owner could not then prevent her from making a will, but a former owner would still be entitled to one-fifth of her estate if she died intestate.[83]

The law is not consistent in its viewpoint. At times it clearly takes the part of the ruling class, and at other times it is amenable to common-sense and humane considerations. The confusion that results from the conflict of assumed patronal rights and Augustan legislation promoting marriage and parenthood shows up the anomalies.[84] It is all the more impressive that there was some flexibility in the approach to the slave family that allowed individual owners to display compassion and acknowledge family ties among people who, *stricto iure,* had none.

## Soldiers' Families

From the time at least of Marius, at the end of the second century B.C., the Roman army became more of a standing professional body than an *ad hoc* citizen militia.[85] In the imperial period, the army continued to be a refuge for the landless or those with poor prospects and offered an increasingly privileged status to serving soldiers and to veterans. It was important for emperors to maintain the loyal support of the military, since power could rest ultimately with them. Given his commitment to encouraging marriage in part with the aim of replenishing the available stock for the army, it is ironic that Augustus was probably responsible for a ruling that soldiers beneath a certain rank were not permitted to marry during service.[86]

The reason for this ban is not clear. It has been suggested that it was to avoid distraction and encumbrance for an army on the move,[87] but the archaeological and epigraphic evidence suggests that soldiers did form liaisons and that their families accompanied them. Epitaphs to and by "wives" and children exist at military sites, as do remains indicative of a feminine and childish presence.[88] The general opinion is that Septimius Severus lifted the ban in A.D. 197.[89] This view is based partly on a statement by Herodian but supported by a number of legal texts.[90]

For the purpose of this chapter, the interesting point is the effective tolerance of soldier unions and the official response to the many problems this caused, particularly in relation to the status of the children, who were deemed illegitimate.[91] In many cases the *de facto* wives were foreigners (*peregrinae*), and even children born after the soldier's term of service would normally have been illegitimate because marriage between Roman citizens and foreigners was not recognized at law. Some military *diplomata* show that emperors granted special privileges to soldiers from time to time, including the right on discharge to form proper unions (*iustae nuptiae*) with *peregrinae* and produce Roman citizen children, and the jurist Gaius seems to imply that this became a general privilege.[92] The *diplomata,* however, sometimes concern naval or auxiliary troops, who themselves only became citizens on discharge. The argument is therefore based partly on the implication that these "lesser elements" would not have gained greater privileges than citizen legionaries or praetorians and partly on specific grants to soldiers of these citizen ranks.[93] Children born during service were probably not included in these special grants.[94]

This caused some distress and confusion among soldiers, a group whom the emperors tended to woo by various means. Even those grants of *conubium* mentioned above were specific to particular groups of veterans; it was not until A.D. 197 that there was a general indulgence of this kind to the military, although it had probably become an expected privilege. Other measures show the *ad hoc* nature of the laws concerning soldier families, which Campbell sees as reflecting the diverse attitudes of individual emperors, with Claudius, Trajan, and Hadrian apparently taking a particular interest in them. Even Augustus introduced the ruling that soldiers who were still *in patria potestate* had a right to maintain the military income as *peculium castrense* although they were still subject to paternal power in other respects, such as the need for the father's permission to marry.[95] Under the Flavians, soldiers were allowed greater latitude in making wills, allegedly because of their simplicity and ignorance, which was surely no greater than that of the mass of the free population.[96] Soldiers were even permitted to leave their goods to people who were not qualified to be heirs or legatees of a normal Roman will, such as foreigners and the unmarried. This would have enabled them to name non-Roman "wives" and children and fellow soldiers as beneficiaries.[97] Under Claudius, soldiers had in any case gained the rights of married men for such purposes.[98]

In A.D. 119 Hadrian wrote to the prefect of Egypt, Rammius

Martialis, granting the right of succession on intestacy to the children of serving soldiers. He tempered this grant, which presumably extended to soldiers elsewhere, with a pious note that it had been only proper to exclude these illegitimates in the past because the practice of forming families was opposed to military discipline but that he was taking it upon himself to mitigate the harshness of past judgments.[99] Yet the ban on soldier marriage remained and continued to cause difficulties. If a soldier died in service, his "wife" had no claim to the return of her dowry.[100] And the retired auxiliary Octavius Valens shows his frustration at the exclusion of his children from Alexandrian citizenship because of their illegitimacy, for they had been born during his service.[101]

It is probable that noncitizen sons of serving soldiers could actually gain Roman citizenship by enlistment in the army, and inscriptions suggest that such men were concentrated in certain legions. It has even been suggested that this might have been a reason for maintaining the ban on soldier marriage—to obtain such recruits.[102] In any case, the legal evidence supports the view that Septimius Severus lifted the ban on marriage during military service. This would have been welcome to many soldiers. Others, who had formed or hoped to form unions with foreign women, probably still had to wait for discharge to gain the privilege of full *conubium*. Until the Edict of Caracalla, in A.D. 212, virtually conferred Roman citizenship on all free subjects of the empire, this constituted a special privilege of the military, perhaps as an inducement for soldiers to settle in the province where they had been stationed, for civilian Roman citizens could not readily gain the right to marry non-Romans.

Campbell rightly emphasizes the haphazard development of the recognition of the soldier family, but his association of this process with emperors' varying attitudes to the military—admittedly an important variable—obscures the fact that it is really typical of Roman law in general. We have seen the same process at work in the expansion of the property rights of the soldier *filius-familias* offset against the reluctance to undermine paternal power in any fundamental way. In other respects, too, military discipline could be balanced with acknowledgment of family ties. Even the punishment of a deserter might be modified if his desertion had been impelled by concern for his relations.[103]

### Conclusion

*Pietas,* proper acknowledgment of family ties, was a factor which could be invoked in legal judgments in this way for the benefit of the person being judged, or it could be imposed on an unwilling subject by the court. Ulpian's guidelines for consular judges on liability for maintenance list a number of obligations to parents, children, and *patroni/ae* or *liberti/ae* but give more general guidance in the principle that need should be the determining factor. Destitute parents were entitled to maintenance by their children by virtue of their condition *and* by virtue of the relationship, for the heirs of a son were not obliged to maintain the testator's father to the same extent as the son himself, had he lived, who would have been moved by his filial duty (*ex officio pietatis suae*).[104] Even if a father had emancipated his child, this did not absolve either of them of the duty of maintenance when the circumstances required it.[105] A range of relations could in fact be judged responsible, but given that competing claims might be complex, the adjudicator had to weigh the propriety and kin feelings involved and use his discretionary power where appropriate to relieve hardship.[106] Obligation, a sense of kinship (*cognatio,* not *agnatio*), and feelings— moral and affective notions such as *pietas, obsequium,* and *affectio*— were thus integral to legal administration.[107] The human face of Roman law.

These examples do not paint a complete picture of the effective law of the family as shown in statutes and judicial policy, but they do demonstrate the process by which the law could accommodate change, however slowly and erratically. In many cases, they show that the apparent severity or starkness of Roman law could be tempered, however imperfectly, by humane and common-sense considerations. The law did treat slaves as chattels who had no legal right to marry and whose parent-child relations were nonexistent in formal law, and yet in various ways the law acknowledged their ties of kinship and affection with free citizens. The law asserted the right of a woman to dowry and marriage even against the usually sacrosanct privileges of her former owner (in the case of a freed slave) and increasingly treated the husband's formal power of ownership of his wife's dowry as a legal fiction, to be hedged about by conditions to enforce the community view of his obligation.

If there is a consistent thread in these disparate examples and the *ad hoc* legal developments, it is in the affirmation of "real" kinship against the formality of kinship as defined by status and agnatic connection. This principle is evident in rulings concerning the slave family, soldier marriage, maternal-child inheritance, and the rights and obligations of children who had passed formally out of the family of their birth by adoption, emancipation, or *manus*-marriage (i.e., *coemptio*). The awesome powers of the *paterfamilias* were (generally) eroded very slowly over time, and the rights and duties of the mother were strengthened slightly. Some practices went by default; for example, the *Lex Voconia,* which forbade testators of the top property class to institute women as heirs, and the practice of lifelong *tutela* of women gradually disappeared.[108] Other practices persisted but were modified in accordance with general principles of obligation. Thus, the allocation of dowry on divorce was based less on the attribution of fault and increasingly on the assumption that a mother should contribute to the maintenance of children of a former marriage. In other words, Roman legal practice largely upheld and propagated the common-sense standards of blood, affection, and patronage, which governed relationships within the community, over the artificial system of agnatic kinship, which had been passed down from archaic Rome and retained in the legal rules determining hereditary succession and *tutela.*

It should be clear from this chapter that the picture of Roman family relations that might be formed by a summary of legal rights is not a sound basis for understanding ancient kinship and its underlying principles. This is an important point not only for Roman historians but for scholars of other periods, who quite properly look to Roman social structures for the explanation of later developments in the Mediterranean. We saw in chapter 1 that myths and models can acquire a force of their own. In this sense Roman law had an independent impact on later legal studies and even legal developments.[109] But in studying Roman attitudes towards the family or the effective law of the family it is essential to look carefully at the law as represented not only by selective quotations of statutes and the alleged rights of fathers and husbands [110] but by praetorian and imperial decisions as well. The tempering of the law by practice and community reaction is well illustrated in Valerius Maximus's motley collection of memorably unfair wills.[111]

To be sure, it is always possible for opinionated or unprincipled individuals to ignore these standards and stick by the letter of the law, and there were doubtless tyrannical fathers who exerted their powers and feckless husbands who wasted the substance of their wives' dowries, but odd cases would make their way into the legal process, and the law would eventually deal with such anomalies by *ad hoc* judgments and even belated and half-hearted legislation. The whole process throws light on Roman thinking not only about the family but about law, tradition, and the proper role of the state. It is certainly more straightforward to stick with a coherent picture of the Roman family defined purely in terms of agnatic relations and dominated by an all-powerful *paterfamilias,* but it is entirely artificial and reflects neither the Roman *mentalité* of the late Republic and early Empire nor the reality of everyday relationships and the acknowledgment of obligations of affection, service, and material support that actually underpinned the living law of the family.

# Three

# Marriage

> Marriage was a matter of intention; if you lived
> together "as" man and wife, man and wife
> you were.
> —Crook 1967a, 101

> Marriage is the union of male and female, a
> partnership in all of life, the conjunction
> of human and divine law
> —Dig. 23.2.1 (Modestinus)[a]

### The Definition and Purpose of Roman Marriage

I f two Roman citizens with the legal capacity to marry one another each had the consent of the *paterfamilias* and lived together with the intention of being married, that was recognized
as a valid marriage (*iustum conubium* or *iustae nuptiae*), and
children born of the union were Roman citizens in the power
of their father.[1] This gives us a basic definition of marriage and a
notion of its purpose in Roman society. We shall trace the different
types of marriage, their legal significance, and their historical development. But first we need to determine what Romans saw as
the essential characteristics and function of marriage. Many past
discussions of marriage have focused on legal oddities, such as the
fact that a valid marriage could be contracted in the absence of the

---

[a] The reference in the second quote to the "conjunction of human and divine
law" is thought to be a post-classical interpolation (see Berger 1953, 578, under
*Matrimonium* for references).

groom but not of the bride.[2] Such points are of legal interest, but they can distract attention from the social reality of marriage.[3]

As we shall see below, the state and the community at large tended to agree that marriage was above all an institution for the production of legitimate children, and Roman legal discussions of marriage commonly focus on this question of the status of children. Illegitimate children could still be Roman citizens and suffered few legal disadvantages,[4] but marriage remained the chief means of determining status from one generation to the next.[5]

Marriage performed a number of roles, many of them common to marriage in most societies.[6] It linked different families both immediately on the marriage and in subsequent generations if children resulted from the union. Dowry and inheritance, the two major forms of property transmission in the ancient world, were both tied to marriage. It should be pointed out, however, that inheritance between husband and wife, though common, was not seen as an obvious or obligatory form of inheritance (as it was between parents and children). Within the political elite, marriage was an important means of forging alliances, and thus mentions of Roman marriages crept into the works of historians, who normally disdained domestic or economic detail. Senatorial men married earlier than men lower down the social scale precisely because they needed the support of two family networks to assist them in gaining political office.[7] Pliny commends a candidate for marriage to his friend's niece by pointing out that the potential groom has already achieved office, so that his in-laws would not be put to the usual expense and trouble expected of the bride's family as part of an electoral campaign.[8] In his difficult exile, Cicero had the active support of his son-in-law Calpurnius Piso Frugi and of his brother-in-law Atticus at Rome.[9] "Turia's" husband exclaims: "And what of your affection and filial piety, when you showed equal respect for my mother and your own family and provided them with the same comfort?"[10] Marriage extended the network of support available for routine family needs and for emergencies.

Roman marriage was clearly perceived as a family affair, not an individual decision based on personal attraction. The marriage of Cicero's brother Quintus to Pomponia, sister of Cicero's great friend Atticus, was intended to cement the ties between the two friends.[11] Delighted to be asked to suggest a husband for his friend's young niece, Pliny enthuses: "You could not entrust me with anything which I value or welcome so much, nor could there be any more befitting duty for me than to select a young man worthy to be the father of Arulenus Rusticus's grandchildren"; and later: "for if I picture you and your brother for whom we are seeking a son-in-law, . . ." He is aware of the young woman's interests and for her benefit mentions the potential groom's good looks, but the matter is clearly seen as one for family discussion, since it will have an impact on the family for generations to come.[12] Apart from the stress on generations past and future, the letter reads rather like a standard *commendatio* for a political candidate or a young man suitable for attachment to a governor's retinue. Romans saw it as quite reasonable that friends of the family would offer up such suggestions, arguing the credentials of the candidate, to be considered by the members of the other family.[13]

This public and rather communal approach to the arrangement of marriage contrasts greatly with the modern Western norm, which is pervaded by the ideology of young romantic love, in which two people after courtship decide to marry and announce their decision to their families. It is usually at this stage that families become involved and, if the marriage transgresses the understood marriage groups (class, age, ethnic, or religious), it is borne upon the couple that the decision does have ramifications for families. If it is acceptable, the match is welcomed (though often with a certain ritual grumbling or conflict symbolically played out over wedding arrangements, timing, or gifts from the parents) and the families of the engaged couple accept that they are now linked in some way.

Roman matches were clearly arranged by the older generation. The partners probably had some say in them, depending on their own age and status within family and society. A young upper-class girl, married in her early or mid-teens,[14] might barely be consulted, and someone like young Quintus, Cicero's nephew, would be pressured by his parents and the older generation generally to accept their choice.[15] Widows and widowers and the divorced tended to be involved actively in the process, but it was still a communal one, a matter of discussing candidates with their supporters. One of Cato the elder's lower-class *clientes* assured him that he would not dream of arranging his daughter's marriage without consulting Cato, and Cicero lists finding a husband for a daughter as one of the problems on which an orator's advice might be sought.[16]

Legally, the *paterfamilias* arranged a match. His consent was essential for its validity. So, in theory, was the consent of the bride and groom, but jurists' quibbles make it clear that this was assumed, and even express refusal could be discounted, particularly in the case of the bride.[17] As we saw in chapter 2, the mother of the bride (or groom) assumed the right to be actively involved in the process, although she had no legal basis for this social assumption.[18] The decision was usually celebrated by an engagement party, at which agreements (*sponsalia*) and gifts were exchanged.[19] Unfortunately, we do not know whether the couple then courted in the style familiar in modern societies practicing arranged matches, in which the groom conventionally woos the bride in a romantic way. It is logical to assume that matches lower down the social scale were more amenable to individual decision making, but this is not certain.

We know a little more about the marriage ceremony and the dowry arrangements, although neither dowry nor a ceremony was a legal requisite of a valid marriage.[20] Parties and general hilarity attended the wedding rites, which probably began in the home of the bride, who then processed, attended by torchbearers, to the home of the groom. Small boys would dance around the procession making ribald jokes and grabbing at nuts thrown in their midst. The groom probably awaited the bride in his home, and on her arrival they joined in a religious rite to mark her entry into her new home. A small image representing her *Genius* would be placed on the symbolic conjugal couch in the *atrium* (the *lectus genialis*). Some aspects of the ceremony would vary according to personal preference, wealth, and the age of the partners. Probably the first marriage of a young girl was more elaborate than that of a mature widow or divorcée. Many funeral sculptures show bride and groom at the wedding grasping right hands symbolically, with figures in the background bearing torches. It is indeed interesting that Roman men whose sarcophagi were decorated with scenes of their military and public achievements should also have chosen their wedding and in many cases the common domestic scene of husband and wife reclining to eat dinner as images to be passed on to posterity (as in the Balbinus sarcophagus, for example). The famous Aldobrandini frieze shows the bride in the bridal chamber, wearing the special bridal clothes, including saffron shoes, her saffron-colored veil cast on the bed. She is clearly nervous but is comforted by a mythical figure, perhaps the goddess of marriage, while a handsome and rather lecherous-looking Hymenaeus gazes at them, and a veiled female figure off to the left makes a sacrifice of some kind at a domestic altar (see plate 1).[21]

In chapter 2 we looked in some detail at legal landmarks concerning dowry, from the establishment in 230 B.C. of the legal action for its return on the dissolution of marriage (*actio rei uxoriae*). Rules gradually arose about the timing and mode of payment and return of dowry. It seems to have been generally assumed that after an initial transfer of real property—a piece of land or a house, for example—the cash component would be paid over in annual installments and that this basic arrangement would be followed by the husband in repaying the dowry at the end of the marriage.[22]

Such rules constituted a kind of safety net for people who had not made specific arrangements or could not agree on the terms. It seems to have been usual to draw up contracts (*pacta dotalia*) stating the rules for payment and return. Few original contracts survive from Roman Italy, but there are many from Roman Egypt, and the *Digest* contains references to such contracts, real and hypothetical.[23] In statues and relief sculpture of marriage ceremonies, the groom is commonly represented as holding a papyrus scroll which probably records the marriage, the dowry agreement, and any special conditions (see plate 2). Roman Egyptian contracts, which drew on Ptolemaic conventions, sometimes specified that the wife would not spend a night away from the husband without his permission or that the husband would not take a concubine.

In the event of the husband's death, the dowry was normally returned to the widow fairly speedily. If the wife died, in the absence of special conditions the dowry was returnable only if it had been given by her father.[24] If the marriage ended in divorce, the wife and her father had a right to sue jointly for its return, but they probably did not do this unless the usual mechanisms broke down. We have some information about the repayment of dowry on the divorce of Cicero from Terentia and on the divorce (and subsequent death) of his daughter Tullia. This information suggests that negotiations about the dowry were conducted through intermediaries and that there was some flexibility in adapting the original agreement.[25] The legal sources, for example, imply that a wife who initiated a divorce without cause might forfeit the right to the return of dowry and that the husband's right to retain part of the dowry for the maintenance of children was dependent on the wife's misconduct.[26] In practice, however, the notion of fault seems to have been of little significance in late republican divorce. The arrangements were determined by the social assumption that children were entitled to part of the mother's dowry for their maintenance (or a daughter's dowry, which perhaps amounted to the same thing) and that a divorced mother (like a widow) needed a dowry to remarry.[27] The provision of dowry (and, by implication, marriage) is explicitly seen as a matter of public interest:

> It is a matter of state concern that women should have secure dowries which enable them to marry. (*Dig.* 23.3.2 [Paul])

> A case involving dowry takes priority at any time and in any place for it is actually in the public interest that dowries be preserved for women, since it is of the utmost necessity that women are dowered for the purpose of bringing forth progeny and replenishing the state with [citizen] children (*liberi*). (*Dig.* 24.3.1 [Pomponius])

The tablets or papyrus scroll in which the dotal agreement was recorded did not constitute a marriage contract or a wedding certificate in the modern sense, but it could be used to demonstrate that a marriage had taken place, and it would be invoked in the reassignment of property and money on the dissolution of the match. This forethought again conflicts somewhat with modern romantic notions of marriage. It is not clear whether the Romans were more materialistic than moderns or simply more realistic and efficient about their materialism. The common law tradition encouraged the presumption that the property of husband and wife was held in common. Perhaps as a result of this tradition (or because the law reflected an entrenched social assumption), Anglophone married couples today, regardless of their legal claims, still tend to treat their property as joint for the duration of the marriage. Divorce or death then forces a decision on them at a time when they are least likely to be capable of rational decision making. The trauma of divorce is exacerbated by the modern perception that it constitutes a personal failure to measure up to society's ideal of a lifelong partnership. The Romans also had an ideal of marriage as a lifelong union, while in fact they practiced remarriage (on the death or divorce of spouses), very much as modern Western cultures do. They seem to have been more pragmatic about their solutions, and the custom of bargaining through intermediaries (a general feature of Roman social relations) apparently worked fairly well. In the modern world, negotiation tends to be carried out directly by the parties or through lawyers. Prenuptial agreements and that most recent innovation, mediation, are closer to the Roman system, except that Romans began the process of mediation before marriage, then renewed it at its end.

I stated at the outset that the purpose of Roman marriage was the production of legitimate citizen children. It is from this that so many other consequences flow for subsequent generations. The production of legitimate citizen children is perennially the basis of any state's concern with marriage. When the Roman census was held, it was traditional for the censors to put to men of the equestrian and senatorial orders the question, "Have you married for the purpose of creating children?"[28] This formula, with slight variations in wording, recurs in popular literature and in marriage pacts. In Plautus's play *Aulularia*, written in the second century B.C., Eunomia tells her brother that she has a plan for his permanent welfare: "I want you to marry a wife so that you can procreate children—may the gods grant it!"[29] In the *Captivi,* the parasite Ergasilus says of another character, "I gather that a wife has been given to him for the purpose of producing children."[30]

This suggests that the phrase, stilted as it sounds, had some currency beyond the purely formal sphere of the census. A marriage contract from the Augustan period uses a comparable expression, and St. Augustine refers to such phrases occurring in the marriage contracts of his own time.[31] The laws of the emperor Augustus, examined below, might have renewed emphasis on this aspect of marriage, but it seems to be a continuing theme. The story told by Aulus Gellius about the third-century B.C. senator Sp. Carvilius Ruga hinges on his claim that he had sworn to the censors that he had married his wife for the purpose of producing children and therefore felt bound to divorce her because she was sterile.[32] This story has several points of interest. Aulus Gellius took it from a work on dowries by the late republican jurist Servius Sulpicius, who had noted it as the occasion for the establishment of a regular *actio* for the recovery of dowry by the widow or divorced wife and her father. Aulus Gellius and Valerius Maximus pass it on as "the first divorce" at Rome, to illustrate the theme of moral decline which, as we have seen, often characterized Roman literary references to the history of marriage and the family (just as it does in today's mass media). Valerius Maximus elsewhere mentions earlier divorces, and the institution of divorce itself probably dates to the fifth century B.C. or earlier,[33] but the establishment of a procedure for the recovery of dowry suggests that divorce was more usual from the mid-Republic.

Perhaps one of the most interesting aspects of the story is the presumption that Carvilius Ruga behaved badly, not only in failing to repay the dowry but in ending a marriage on such grounds. Aulus Gellius adds that he did truly love his wife but that he thought his oath more important. Valerius Maximus also appreciates his motive as honorable but adds that his action was (rightly?) censured by contemporaries because even a desire for children should not be placed above conjugal loyalty.[34] Such anecdotes and comments imply that the public and private ideology of Roman marriage was continually associated with the desire for progeny but that the concept of marriage included other elements, such as compatibility, partnership, and love. This is more obviously the case from the first century B.C. on, though perhaps it is merely a reflection of the greater quantity and variety of sources available to the historian from that period. It is, however, plausible that there was a change in sentiment, just as there was in marriage preference. For example, anecdotal stories about the earlier period tend to focus on the "external" aspects of married life—the wife's fertility, industry, and chastity—rather than the feelings husband and wife held for each other.[35] It becomes clear that marriage, while still firmly associated with the hope of children, was also expected to produce other satisfactions.

It is interesting that the apparent change coincides with the greater incidence of divorce, which is no longer associated with the adultery of the wife. In his *Life* of the general Aemilius Paulus, Plutarch mentions Paullus's divorce of his first wife Papiria, which seemed inexplicable to his contemporaries. Plutarch then cites a general anecdote about "a Roman" who divorced his wife in spite of his friend's remonstrances that she was fertile, discreet, and altogether a good wife. The man picked up his sandal and said that it looked sound to the onlooker, but only the wearer could tell where it hurt. Plutarch agrees that it is the little everyday irritations that make some marriages unbearable.[36] The old idea that divorce was rare and shameful seems to have passed away by the second century B.C. Probably the husband had to initiate divorce if the wife were in his *manus,* but an agreement could probably be reached in many cases,[37] and gradually the separate marital regime, in which women could also initiate divorce, became dominant. In a society where so much was public, divorce now became a matter for speculation, because the reason for divorces was not known. Aemilius Paullus's divorce was the precursor of the new style.[38]

Partnership becomes an automatic inclusion in discussions of marriage. Livy, writing in the Augustan period about early Rome, creates a portrait of a virtuous soldier symbolic of the simplicity of the past who enjoys a partnership with his wife in his fortunes, his estate, and his children.[39] Such references—usually expressed from the husband's perspective—proliferate. The notion that a wife was a welcome partner in prosperity and adversity was invoked, for example, by the emperor Augustus in Dio's representation of his attempt to persuade the men of the upper classes to marry[40] and by senators arguing that provincial governors should be permitted to take their wives with them on tours of duty rather than be deprived of their companionship.[41] The notion of marriage as partnership and companionship was so established, then, as to be part of the civic rhetoric and the public sphere. The many literary and epigraphic references to companionship, mutual loyalty and support, and the ideal of a happy and harmonious marriage show that this was part of a popular ideal as well as public and imperial ideology.[42]

The notion of *concordia,* or harmony, in marriage was frequently mentioned in literature and in epitaphs boasting that marriages, especially long marriages, had been without discord (*sine discrimine, sine offensione, sine ulla querela*).[43] Ovid has the aged bucolic couple Baucis and Philemon speak of their harmony throughout their long marriage leading to their wish to die together.[44] The elder Arria defends her decision to commit suicide on her husband's condemnation by arguing that she and he had such a long and harmonious marriage.[45] When this ideal was attached to the imperial family, it carried the implication that harmony ensured stable rule and succession. It could also be invoked in the language of jurists, as in the quote from Modestinus at the head of this chapter[46] or the *Opinion* of Paul citing the emperor Marcus's judgment that a father does not have the right to end a daughter's harmonious marriage (*bene concordans matrimonium*).[47]

Later we shall examine the emotional expectations that Romans took to marriage and the extent to which they are likely to have been met—a matter of some controversy. For the present, the point to note is that the *ideal* of harmony was almost as strongly embedded in the Roman notion of marriage as was its reproductive purpose. Like the association of marriage and children, it is reflected in public and private discourse. Marriage was viewed, therefore, as the proper vehicle for continuing the citizenship and serving the state into the next generation, for maintaining an individual family or a particular order. It was also viewed, both privately and officially, as a partnership in which each side supported the other and which was ideally harmonious and long-lasting.

## Marriage, Law, and the State: Historical Trends

At Rome, marriage was essentially a private arrangement, but it had legal implications, and the state occasionally intervened to remedy what were perceived as injustices or anomalies. There are now several authoritative works which state and discuss the rules and conditions governing Roman marriage.[48] It is not the function of this volume to echo such works. Legal aspects of marriage—the capacity to marry, the payment of dowry, its return on the dissolution of the marriage—are set in the context of marriage as a social phenomenon, an important element of Roman family relations embedded in Roman notions of status, sentiment, and economic exchange. It is important to test any legal principles against practice as far as it can be ascertained not only from individual decisions recorded in the *Codices* but from literary evidence (particularly the law court speeches of Cicero and the letters of Cicero and Pliny) and from inscriptions and papyri. We saw in earlier chapters that such an approach has led in other areas of family life to a modification of traditional ideas. This applies also to marriage, for example, in the contrast between the legal and recognized powers of the *paterfamilias* in determining a match, the actual practice of deciding and paying dowry, the effective powers of the husband over the wife, and so on. Some scholars now are more inclined to speak of strategies than of legal rules and make a persistent attempt to plot change over time, relating developments in marriage to other trends in Roman society. This presents a contrast with the earlier tendency to theorize from the *Digest* as if it were timeless and perfectly reflected Roman society.

We have seen that the partners in a Roman marriage were Roman citizens or, more rarely, people with the *ius conubii*, the right to contract a valid Roman marriage with Roman citizens, and that they had to have the *affectio maritalis*, the intention of being married. The contract itself was legally drawn up between two families through the heads of the families. If neither bride nor groom had a living father, the groom would be a *paterfamilias*,[49] and the bride would be a full party to her own contract, with her *tutor* giving his assent to the dotal arrangements and, if applicable, to her transfer to the husband's power or *manus*.[50] Marriage for the most part was governed by customary rules rather than formal law. The legal history of marriage at Rome could be seen as a slow tendency for the state to regulate aspects of an essentially private arrangement.

It is particularly difficult to determine the nature of marriage in early Rome. Later sources are understandably vague or confidently oblivious of the distinction between law and custom, and the picture is blurred by the tendency to mythologize the past.[51] Indeed, reference to marriage in early Rome is almost always part of a moral argument deploring contemporary practice. The traditional extent of the husband's power is a popular theme. Dionysius of Halicarnassus, writing in the time of Augustus, comments approvingly on regal Rome of the eighth century B.C.:

> By passing a single law, Romulus reduced women to modesty. The law was as follows: that a proper wife, who had passed into the *manus* of her husband by a sacral marriage (by *confarreatio*), should have a partnership with him in all his goods and rites. . . . Four relatives would decide the following issues in conjunction with the husband: these included adultery and whether the wife proved to have drunk wine, for Romulus allowed that either of these offences could be punished by death.[52]

This "law" is, then, an affirmation of the power of the family to hold a *consilium* to determine vital issues, including the discipline of family members, and represents a limitation on the husband's power in that capital punishment had to be a group decision. In Livy's account of the traditional story of Lucretia, set at the close of the regal period (late sixth-century B.C.), Lucretia summons a meeting of her husband, her father, and two of their friends to announce that she has been raped, intends to commit suicide, and expects them to avenge her.[53] The presumption here is that the families of husband and wife would be represented at a *consilium*.

Perhaps the most frequently quoted passage on the subject is the statement by Cato the elder in the second century B.C. that a husband had the right to sit in judgment on his wife, even for offenses such as drunkenness, but that she had no such right to judge him, even if she caught him in the act of adultery.[54] Dionysius of Halicarnassus reinforces this picture with the statement that Romulus gave the Roman *paterfamilias* full powers over wife and child,[55] and Plutarch, writing in the second century A.D. in Greece, continued the tradition with the comment that Romulus's laws one thousand years earlier had allowed the husband the right to divorce his wife but she had no such right.[56]

It is very likely that the husband's powers were restricted by custom and the relative interest and power of the wife's relations. It is, however, plausible that divorce, insofar as it occurred in early Rome, was initiated only by the husband and implied a severe marital fault—almost necessarily adultery—on the part of the woman. It is also generally agreed that although there were in archaic Rome two distinct types of marriage, one marking the woman's full legal entry into the family of her husband and the other allowing her to retain her legal status as a member of the family of her birth, most marriages in the early period did involve the transfer of the woman to the husband's family and to his power (*conventio in manum*). This legal transfer could occur by *confarreatio, coemptio,* or *usus. Confarreatio* was an elaborate ceremony open only to patricians and included a joint sacral meal of prescribed foods. Divorce was not possible from this form of marriage, which became very rare.[57]

The "imaginary sale" of *coemptio* remained a common way in which a woman passed into the husband's *manus.* The "sale" resembled other legal ceremonies, such as the emancipation of a child from *patria potestas,* the manumission of a slave, or a Roman will.[58] A woman could also come into her husband's *manus* if she spent a full year under his roof (*usus*) but this consequence of marriage could be avoided if she spent three nights away from the conjugal home. This practice seems to have become obsolete or unusual by the late Republic and certainly by the early Empire.[59] In fact, by the middle of the first century B.C. there seems to have been a general preference for the form of marriage in which the woman retained her natal status and separate property.

In chapter 2 we saw some of the consequences of this development. A woman who had entered her husband's *manus* on marriage became one of his *sui heredes*, or direct heirs, and inherited equally with their children on his death. Any property she owned at the time of marriage or acquired afterwards became part of the joint family holding owned by the husband as *paterfamilias*. In practice, such property seems to have been treated as dowry, which she could recover separately on the husband's death by the second century B.C. The widow of Aemilius Paullus received all her property back on his death in 160 B.C., although this caused some hardship to a small estate.[60]

Valerius Maximus moralizes romantically about the consequences of the death of Q. Aelius Tubero, whose marriage had marked the introduction of movable goods and cash into a family which until then had maintained a simplicity of lifestyle already anachronistic in the middle of the second century B.C. His family had to sell land to repay his widow the value of her dowry—a step (we are led to believe) unprecedented in their history.[61] Cicero tells us that all property of a wife *in manu mariti* was legally classified as dowry by the middle of the first century B.C.[62] This must have been a response to the popularity of the "separate regime" form of marriage, because it virtually restored the widow who had been *in manu mariti* to full ownership of "her" property, which as dowry was now recoverable in its own right rather than being merged with the conjugal holding so that the whole could be evenly divided between herself and her children.

The most significant historical development in Roman marriage is surely this shift from a merged to a separate regime,[63] that is, from the earlier form in which the woman normally entered the husband's *manus* to the later form in which the wife retained her status as *filiafamilias* or, if her father were dead, *sui iuris*. It is frustrating that nobody has been able fully to explain the shift or to plot it precisely. Authors have sometimes called the separate-regime style of marriage "free marriage" and have interpreted the shift as one to greater individual female power. De Zulueta (1953,

2.36—37) writes approvingly of the change but places it firmly in the evolutionary, comparative legal spectrum with a moralizing tone:

> Comparative law shows that all over the world dependent marriage of the type involved by sale-marriage (*coemptio*) goes with a patriarchal organization of the family. . . . But coexistent with sale-marriage are found other forms of marriage. . . . These latter forms Roman jurisprudence, by a feat of abstraction of which it alone was capable, brought under the single concept of consensual marriage, of marriage as such, distinct from lordship or ownership. Marriage so conceived respected the personality of the woman; it was the progressive type of marriage; the future belonged to it. But it must not be forgotten that its very freedom opened the door to grave abuses.[64]

Certainly, the wife was not in the husband's formal control and had greater freedom to manage her own property and to initiate divorce. The problem is in determining how the *ancients* viewed the different marriage styles and, therefore, what moved them to alter their preference over time. It was probably a corporate decision based on corporate interest. At first glance it seems to be in the interest of the bride's family to defer the final division of the patrimony in any generation until the father's death.[65] The dowry seems to have represented a smaller share of the family holding than a daughter's intestate (or testamentary) portion. This must be offset against the likelihood that so many women would be *sui iuris* at the time of marriage or within a few years of it because of the death of the father.[66] The shift might have conferred on the woman's brothers greater control of her fortune, but as we saw in chapter 2, the tendency was to view a woman's property as destined eventually for her children, and even brothers who were *tutores* must have given permission for their sisters to make wills in favor of the brothers' nephews and nieces. In time, the *tutela* of male relations over women was abolished, surely because the men of the family had no particular interest in it and did not see it as a means of keeping property in the family or under their control.[67]

The Roman sources do not discuss the shift explicitly. The change could well be linked with economic transformations in

Roman society, for the attitude towards wealth, particularly landed wealth, altered significantly from the third century B.C. Without reverting to Roman myth about the simplicity of the past, we can still acknowledge that after the second Punic War and the subsequent expansion into the eastern Mediterranean, Romans of the elite class became more involved in conspicuous consumption, such as the building of elaborate private homes and gardens and public buildings such as temples, and less tied to the concept of maintaining landed holdings within the same family. The preferred early system of marriage, like the ideal system of inheritance enshrined in the rules on intestate succession, seems to have been posited on a more static society in which a woman moved physically from the holding of her father to that of her husband and remained there for life, sinking her own property into her husband's and identifying with his family and therefore with the children of the marriage (who necessarily belonged to his family).

From the second century B.C., this scenario was no longer followed by an aristocracy that treated land as a commodity to be exploited in any way offered.[68] In spite of legislation directed against the concentration of wealth in female hands,[69] we hear increasingly of wealthy women such as Aemilia and her daughter Cornelia (mother of the Gracchi) in the second century B.C. In the first century B.C. women such as Caecilia Metella, Servilia, Clodia, and Fulvia seem to be characteristic of the political elite, prominent for their wealth, their patronage, and, to an extent, their public activity and image. The establishment of an *actio rei uxoriae* for the return of dowry to a woman after divorce or widowhood slightly precedes these other developments and suggests that divorce and the departure of the widow from her marital home had already become more common than in early Rome. Even allowing for the recurrent historical problem of the greater abundance and reliability of sources for the later Republic, it is difficult to avoid the conclusion that the changing character of upper-class wealth and spending, the greater public profile of upper-class women, and the change in marriage preference and frequency of divorce are all somehow linked.

The affiliation of married women seems also to have changed

from the early stress on the *univira,* the woman with one husband who came to him as a young *filiafamilias* and died as his *mater-familias.* The term was extended to the widow who declined remarriage out of loyalty to her husband's memory.[70] From the time of the late Republic at least, widows were likely to remarry, and divorce became quite common and casual. The relative instability of marriage might have been tied to the volatility of elite political alliances in that period, but the tendency continued in times of political calm. Perhaps the earlier ideal, elaborated in ritual and sentimental ideology, was actually grounded in the assumption of a static property system in which women moved only once in a lifetime, taking with them their intestate portion, which remained with their conjugal family whether they died in the marriage or not. The presumption of the late Republic is that women will move into other marriages, taking their property with them but on the understanding that their children will eventually share it. Politically, married women of the elite promoted the interests of their brothers and sons rather than those of their husbands.[71] Economically, they favored their children. Emotionally, they showed great affection and loyalty towards their husbands. All of these characteristics are not only displayed by the actions of the elite women best documented by the sources but lauded as the proper behavior of an ideal wife, mother, or sister.

In a general way, the history of marriage and the family seems to be characterized by a very slow erosion of the powers of the *paterfamilias,* both as father and as husband. We have seen that stories about early Rome are typically examples of extreme husbandly harshness, but even they reveal the importance of the *consilium* as a possible check on his arbitrary exercise of power. A story was told of Lucius Annius's removal from the senatorial list because he had divorced his young wife without calling a *consilium* to justify this step.[72] Even the shocking story of the husband who successfully defended his fatal assault on his wife with the excuse that she was a drunkard reveals that he was tried for the murder, however unsatisfactory we might find the outcome.[73] By the early Empire, the *consilium* as a medium for passing judgment on wives seems to have become obsolete, presumably because wives were no longer seen as being in their husband's power and because divorce was a remedy readily available to both parties. This is illustrated by the story of Appuleia Varilla, related to the imperial family and accused of treason and adultery in a politically motivated trial in the time of the emperor Tiberius. Tiberius had deliberately softened the more serious penalty suggested for adultery and determined that she should be handed over to her relations, "following the example of the ancestors."[74]

The trial of Pomponia Graecina in A.D. 57, during the reign of Nero, was similar in some respects. She was also related to the imperial family. She was charged with practicing a "foreign superstition" and given over to the judgment of her husband, who tried her and pronounced her innocent after following the "ancient institution of trying his wife among their relatives."[75] In both cases, there is some stress on the antiquity (and, by implication, obsolescence) of the custom followed. The husband's authority, always tempered by public opinion and the family *consilium,* had been severely eroded over the centuries. The Augustan legislation on adultery transferred much of the power of adultery trials to the public sphere, and such powers as remained tended to lie with the father of the errant woman rather than with the husband, although he had a right to punish summarily a male adulterer caught in the act in his own home.[76]

Approximately one century after the Augustan legislation on marriage and the family, Tacitus wrote that in characterizing the act of adultery as a breach of the religious and legal code Augustus exceeded the more lenient attitude of the ancestors and even went further than his own laws. It is not quite clear what he meant by this, but the gist of his statement is that marriage and offenses against marriage had belonged traditionally to the private realm.[77] Any problems that arose, including adultery committed by the wife, were dealt with by the families involved. The legislation sponsored or actually inspired by Augustus represents a strong and significant incursion by the state into this private sphere.[78]

This statement needs some qualification. We have already seen that the censors regularly put to men the question whether they had married for the purpose of producing children[79] and that Lucius Annius was struck off the senatorial roll for divorcing his wife without justification.[80] There were also times when the aediles had, as public officials, judged cases of adultery and other female sexual transgressions.[81] There had, moreover, been rules limiting intermarriage even between citizens. Until the *Lex Canuleia,* of ca. 445 B.C., marriage between patricians and plebeians could not produce legitimate issue and was in effect invalid.[82] Yet at this time Latins and many Italians had *conubium* with Roman citizens; that is, they had the capacity to contract proper legal marriages with Romans which could produce legitimate Roman citizen children.[83] There is some suggestion that marriage between freed and free-born Roman citizens was either illegal or subject to strong social sanctions, including condemnation by the censor.[84] Such unions were not prevented or punished by the law in the modern sense, but the effect of the law was to invalidate the union, that is, to determine that any children of the union were not legitimate Roman citizens. This issue is discussed further below, as well as in chapter 4.

In sum, the law had always had some relevance to issues of marriage and related questions, such as betrothal, dowry, divorce, and the status of children. Notwithstanding, the Augustan legislation passed in at least two blocks, in 18 B.C. as the *Lex Papia Poppaea* and in A.D. 9 as the *Lex Iulia,* did represent a new development.[85] Augustus saw himself as a moral crusader, one who was bound to restore the pristine virtue of the Roman state. He perceived a failure, particularly in the upper class, to marry and have children, and his legislation was designed to provide incentives in the form of more rapid promotion through the political and administrative ranks and advantages in inheritance for those who married and produced children, with penalties for those who failed to conform to his requirements. In addition, his legislation attempted to formalize divorce by requiring a formal letter of divorce and witnesses and by compelling husbands to divorce adulterous wives.[86] Men were also to be punished as criminals for committing adultery with married women or fornication (*stuprum*) with single women.[87]

The laws were not markedly successful in suppressing adultery or propagating the Roman population. Marriage was probably already popular with those who could afford it and had marriageable partners available; indeed, some made a career of marriage, like their modern equivalents. It is therefore not clear whether there genuinely was a serious demographic and moral problem in Augustus's day. Nor is it entirely clear whether he hoped that his legislation would affect all echelons of society, since the rewards and penalties were largely directed towards the upper class, with significant property to bequeath and with political ambitions to satisfy. The legislation aroused strong protests from men of the upper classes, and Augustus chose to respond to these in a variety of ways. He himself mounted a demonstration of sorts by appearing in public with his grandchildren, in effect presenting a counterexample to errant citizens.[88] He also harangued recalcitrant upperclass bachelors and praised married men in speeches passed on to us in imaginative form by Dio.[89]

The legislation itself has not been well preserved, so we must rely heavily on ancient summaries of the laws. The provisions on adultery were retained in the sixth century A.D. *Digest,* but Justinian finally eradicated many references to rewards for marriage and parenthood because of the new Christian regard for celibacy and theoretical dislike of the remarriage of widows. From what can be pieced together we get a sense of Augustus's moral purpose. He seems, in part, to have aimed at providing a eugenically sound ruling class for the empire, furnishing Italian soldiers for the imperial army and ensuring the survival of the great estates of the aristocracy. His methods were not successful; overall, their greatest significance is for the violence and extent of his intrusion into the private sphere. Henceforth, adultery was a criminal offense which could, moreover, be prosecuted by anyone moved by moral outrage, malice, or the hope of gaining a percentage of the confiscated wealth of convicted miscreants.[90] This ensured the persistence of accusations and trials, and the legislation, slightly modified from time to time, was maintained by subsequent emperors. Pliny passes on the sad story of the high-ranking provincial woman who had committed adultery with a centurion. Once the man was banished, the husband wished to drop charges and have his wife back, but when the governor referred the case to Rome in A.D. 107 the emperor Trajan insisted that the husband must divorce her and pursue the matter legally or he would himself be charged with pandering (*lenocinium*).[91]

Augustus also introduced an element of regulation into the processes of marriage and divorce by requiring witnesses and other formalities and established a system of registration of legitimate citizen births. These measures do not seem to have been observed widely. The imperial insistence on a letter of divorce (a common but not automatic feature of republican divorce) would only be invoked when someone challenged the legality of a divorce after the event. Since the Augustan legislation compelled a husband to divorce an adulterous wife, the provisions were designed to provide evidence in the case of a husband prosecuted for complaisance or pimping, who might claim in his defense that he had divorced the wife.

Just as marriage continued to consist of two Romans with the capacity and desire to marry cohabiting, so divorce continued to be a matter of mutual agreement or unilateral repudiation, instantaneous in its effect in either case and requiring no recourse to state authorities unless the parties failed to agree on the restitution of dowry.[92] In many respects, then, Roman marriage was more "private" than many of its modern equivalents. The theory and practice of marriage was monogamous, but there was no equivalent to the penalties of some modern states for bigamy as a crime.[93]

It was to be expected that Christianity would have some impact on Roman marriage, but in fact the legal and social impact was less immediate and less strong than one might have imagined, given the early theological decision that marriage was a sacrament. Divorce by mutual consent remained straightforward even under Justinian's legislation, but it became more difficult for one partner—especially the wife—to institute divorce even in the face of clear hardship.[94] Among themselves, Christians imposed social penalties on those who remarried or who married out of the proper groups, and in time they formulated many complicated prohibitions on marriage between quite distant relations or between people related only by marriage or betrothals (or even by relations of godparenthood).[95]

In earlier Roman law, marriages between close kin had been subject to sanctions, but it is not clear that it was ever illegal in the sense that it was a crime.[96] There was a tradition that cousin marriage had been illegal or discountenanced in archaic Rome,[97] but it seems to have been acceptable from an early period. Livy has the long-serving and highly decorated old citizen soldier Sp. Ligustinus, a model of antique virtue, speak of his marriage to his undowered cousin, apparently towards the end of the third century B.C.[98] Authors of the late Republic and early Empire certainly seem to find nothing worthy of comment in the marriage of cousins.[99] Cousin marriage has some obvious advantages for the preservation of estates in families and is in many societies a favored mode (given the usual prohibition on marriage between siblings). St. Augustine claimed that cousin marriage was rare in his day,[100] and the Christians did introduce bans against it, but it is by no means certain that these have ever been particularly effective in preventing it in regions or social groups where it is preferred.[101]

New prohibitions were introduced from time to time in the imperial era. The prohibition against a provincial governor marrying somebody within his province, against a *tutor* or his son marrying a *pupilla* (ward), against senators marrying freedwomen or actresses, and so on,[102] all show a certain tendency to intervene in the private sphere of marriage, which by modern standards is surprising only in the emphasis on status. In general, then, it can be said that marriage remained an essentially private affair on which the state intermittently intruded, particularly where there was some economic advantage to be gained from the imposition of penalties. In other cases, the state tended to impose as rules accepted community norms. It is, for example, improbable that a great number of senators were ever given to marriage with freed slaves, and such rules (like the earlier prohibition on marriage between patricians and plebeians in an era when the distinction was meaningful) reflected the actual marriage groups. Subsequent legislation prohibiting marriage between Jews and Christians reflected the ideology of the official religion.[103] It is not clear how strictly such rules were applied at any stage. They could have been enforced by recourse to the Julian laws on adultery, since people living in such relationships were actually committing adultery or fornication in legal terms, but as we saw in chapter 2, and as will be made clear below, there was considerable acceptance of certain types of *de facto* marriage, e.g., soldier marriage or unions between slave and free partners.

The ground was certainly laid in the classical period for the harder line eventually followed by Christian rulers, who saw marriage as a matter for public regulation. The earlier trend away from husbands' absolute rights was also undermined in late antiquity, and women, subject to public penalties for adultery, gradually lost their relative equality with the increasing Christian stress on wifely endurance and one-sided virtue in marriage and on the impropriety of widow remarriage.

*Inside Roman Marriage: Feelings between Husband and Wife*

> No Roman thinks it shameful to take his wife to a dinner party. At home the wife, as mistress of the household, takes first place in it and is the center of its entertaining. Things are very different in Greece, where the wife is never present at dinner, except for a family party, and spends all her time in the Women's Quarter, separated from the rest of the house—an area broached only by close male relatives.
> —Cornelius Nepos, Preface, *de Vit. Ill.*

Lattimore (1942, 277) notes the greater wealth of detail in the many Latin epitaphs by husbands and wives to each other and the usual Roman epigraphic tendency to give greater biographical detail about the deceased than was usual in Greek equivalents.[104] Williams (1958) also makes the point that the Roman matron held an honored social position. We have seen that partnership and harmony were Roman marital ideals. The relative social visibility of Roman women and the fact that men such as Cicero and Pliny had women friends, their references to the literary interests of such women (e.g., Juvenal's savage attacks in the Sixth Satire on women who talk incessantly about politics, literature, or philology) all suggest a society in which a married couple might have interests and activities in common that give some meaning to the ideal of partnership beyond a community of interest in their children and the family generally.

There are serious problems in attempting to analyze relationships and feelings even in a contemporary society, where taped interviews and questionnaires give a more solid base to speculation. The evidence of attitudes within Roman marriages is difficult to interpret. The comedies of Plautus and Terence are based directly on Greek models and, like modern equivalents, find more humor (especially in the case of Plautus) in quarreling couples.[105] Similarly, satirists such as Horace, Martial, and Juvenal emphasize the horrors of wives and marriage (as they do those of other human types and institutions). Epitaphs, on the other hand, are almost exclusively laudatory and frequently degenerate into clichés. Famous stories of married love and loyalty abound but are somewhat larger than life. Then we have the proverbial and philosophical generalities about women and marriage—why the wise man should not marry or the famous censor's speech beginning, "If we could manage without a wife, Romans, we would all avoid that nuisance; but since nature has laid it down that we cannot live peacefully with them but not at all without them, we must consider the long-term benefit rather than immediate satisfaction."[106]

In assessing these varied sources (and more) we have also to bear in mind other aspects of Roman marriage. We know that matches were commonly arranged by the older generation with an eye to material and political advantage, that divorce was easy and common, that many marriages ended fairly soon with the death of one partner and subsequent remarriage. Scholars have argued that Roman marriage, especially within the political elite, therefore engaged little of the partners' emotions and that there was scant likelihood that affectionate feelings would develop in such a milieu.[107] Yet the four surviving letters from Cicero to his wife during his exile 58—57 B.C. reveal his dependence on her emotional and practical support. Consider, for example, *fam.* 14.4:

If these misfortunes are permanent, I truly desire to see you, light of my life [*mea vita*], as soon as possible and for you to remain in my embrace, since neither the gods whom you have cultivated so virtuously nor the men whom I assiduously served have rendered us our proper return.

He ends his letter with the following:

Take good care of yourself, as far as you are able, and believe me when I say that I am more desperately perturbed by your wretched position than by my own. My Terentia, most faithful and best of wives, and my most beloved little daughter and our one remaining hope, Cicero—farewell.

Letters to Terentia are replete with expressions of longing for her and terms of endearment: "most faithful and best of wives," "light of my life, my longing," "my own life," "dearer to me than anything ever."[108] Ovid, exiled to the Levant a generation later, uses the same or similar expressions to his wife: "dearest," "light of my life," "best of wives."[109] The author of the long *Laudatio 'Turiae,'* horrified at his wife's altruistic suggestion that they divorce so that he could marry a woman who could give him children, exclaimed that (unlike Carvilius Ruga) he would not put even the desire for children above their bond (*fides*). Elsewhere, he laments the fate that has left him, the older spouse, alive, full of longing for her and despair.[110]

The recital of "Turia"'s heroic acts in saving her husband's life during the civil war and protecting his interests in his absence puts this inscription in the same category as the stories of exemplary wives who show their mettle in adversity—war, opposition to the emperors, or fatal illness within the family. Arria the elder was famous for following her dissident Stoic husband into exile and taking the lead in showing him how to commit suicide heroically. Pliny noted that she had also committed other brave acts which were less well known. She had, at one stage, attended her husband and son, who were both critically ill. The boy died, but she kept the sad news from her husband until he recovered. Pliny preserved her deeds for posterity:

Indeed, that was a glorious act of hers, to draw the blade, to plunge it into her breast and to pull out the dagger and offer it to her husband, to utter besides the immortal, almost divine words, "It does not hurt, Paetus." But fame and posterity were before her eyes when she did those deeds and said those words. How much more glorious it was for her, without the incentive of immortality and fame, to hold back her tears, to suppress her grief, to go on acting the part of a mother, when she had lost her son.

There was a *genre* of such inspirational tales.[111] The account of "Turia"'s behavior during the time of danger and the husband's absence contains echoes of the letters of Cicero and Ovid from exile. The eulogy of "Turia" could also be classed as a much longer and more detailed version of the standard epitaph commemorating a most beloved (*carissimus/a*) or well-deserving (*bene merens*) spouse and referring to the length or happiness of the marriage in a few lines.[112]

We have already seen the great popularity of the tombstone formulae celebrating marriages without discord. There was another, somewhat less common formula, used more by wives and typically following a statement of the length of the marriage, that the only unhappy day in that time was the day of the husband's death. Sometimes these briefer epitaphs also give sufficient detail to make it clear that the sentiments are no empty convention. Such is *CIL* 6.29580, where the bereaved husband follows his recital of his wife's virtues with the statement that he has added these details so that people reading the epitaph would understand how much they loved each other. Consider, too, the woman whose husband had befriended her as a young slave girl, bought her out of slavery, and married her.[113] This suggests that even the most conventional formulae, far from being "essentially loveless,"[114] might represent a shorthand for much stronger emotions which could not be spelled out for reasons of custom and economy.

It has also been claimed that Roman men did not expect to gain sexual satisfaction from their wives but sought this with mistresses.[115] Certainly the tradition of passionate attachment is associated with mistresses of a lower social group, but the literary conventions are adopted by authors speaking of married love. This is the case with Sulpicia's love poetry to her husband, with Ovid's yearning for his absent wife, with Statius's claim that he had been struck as by a thunderbolt with love for his wife, and with Pliny's letter to his young wife lamenting her absence and stressing his longing for her:

> I am seized by unbelievable longing for you. The reason is above all my love, but secondarily the fact that we are not used to being apart. This is why I spend the greater part of the night haunted by your image; this is why from time to time my feet lead me (the right expression!) of their own accord to your room at the times I was accustomed to frequent you; this is why, in short, I retreat, morbid and disconsolate, like an excluded lover from an unwelcoming doorway. The only time free of these torments is time spent in the forum and in friends' law cases. Just imagine what my life is like—I, for whom you are the respite from toil, the solace of my wretchedness and anxieties. Farewell.[116]

There are probably elements of literary conceit in all of these, but all see it as appropriate to adopt the language and imagery of passionate, romantic love when speaking of married love.

Cato the elder's famous punishment of the senator who embraced his wife passionately before their young daughter, Seneca's insistence that men should not make love too ardently to their wives, Lucretius's contrast between the modest immobility of a wife and the unseemly coital gyrations of a prostitute, and Plutarch's caution against the use by wives of aphrodisiacs on their husbands all imply a dominant ideology of moderation and decorum in married relations, particularly as displayed in public behavior.[117] Yet the very fact that these warnings are seen as necessary is an indication that married couples did show the symptoms of sexual infatuation celebrated by the lyric poets. Plutarch's contrast between the heady, obsessive attachment of newlyweds and the stabler and more profound love between long-married partners is a modern commonplace. The references in Catullus 61 to burning passion and jealousy between the bridal pair imply that such references are stock elements of wedding songs and other ritual.[118] Tacitus's account of the murder of a woman by her husband after a stormy night of alternating reconciliation and quarreling and the references to the well-known passion of the Stoic Seneca himself for his young wife remind us that this decorous ideal was not always realized (and that we should not take philosophical generalization too seriously?). Consider Seneca's own words:

> This is what I said to my Paulina, who tells me to watch out for my health. Because I know that her life is inextricably bound with my own, I begin to be considerate of myself as a way of considering her. And although old age has made me brave in many respects, I am losing this advantage of my state of life. . . . Sometimes, however pressing the reasons are for ending it, life must be maintained for the sake of our loved ones even at the cost of extreme pain. . . . He who does not think enough of his wife or friend to hang on longer to life but is obstinate in choosing death, is effete.[119]

In the end Nero gave him no choice about the suicide.

There is no doubt that men did have extramarital sexual relationships with women of their own class—Augustus's laws against adultery did not, after all, stop the practice!—and with others who were not seen as marriageable. Such phenomena are hardly unknown in the modern world, where sexual satisfaction is a highly publicized expectation of the partners. A dual sexual standard certainly prevailed—again, this is hardly unique to Roman society, upper-class or otherwise. In the ancient world, sex outside marriage might even have been seen as a means of limiting the legitimate family, and gratification of male sexual whims was easy in a society with an abundance of slaves of both sexes lacking any rights. Many men probably did find casual and adulterous sex an exciting variation from sex with a respected and even beloved wife of many years' standing. I have no difficulty in believing that wives might have felt the same. Yet this scarcely justifies a firm statement that Romans saw sexual satisfaction as entirely distinct from marriage. There is enough contrary evidence to give us pause in making absolute pronouncements on the subject.

It will be apparent by now that most of the examples of legendary married love and heroic conjugal *fides* concern women. It is also true that wives are overrepresented in epitaphs.[120] This reflects the generally masculine orientation of the sources and probably the notion that men should be identified primarily by their jobs or public offices, and women by their position in the family. There are, to be sure, husbands known for their extraordinary love, such as Tiberius Sempronius Gracchus, who virtually chose to predecease his young wife Cornelia when faced with an omen in the form of two snakes, one male and one female, and husbands who killed themselves on the death of a wife.[121] The usual trend, however, is to laud the courage and loyalty of wives. Given the historical tendency for women to retain their status after marriage as members of their own natal families and the acknowledged identification of elite women with their brothers' interests rather than their husbands', the ideal and reality of wifely loyalty in an age of frequent divorce is quite striking.[122]

Another curiosity already noted above is the persistence of the ideal of the *univira,* the woman with only one husband. This soubriquet was applied originally to the woman who had come to her husband as a young virgin in her father's power, transferred to the husband's *manus,* and died before him. By the late Republic it came to be applied approvingly to widows who chose to remain single out of loyalty to their husband's memory and their children's interest. The ideal is celebrated in tombstones and literature against a background of frequent remarriage occasioned by divorce and spousal death.[123] The law, as we have seen, acknowledged the right of widows and divorcées to the full or partial return of dowry so that they could marry but increasingly applied safeguards for the children of the earlier marriage against the designs of a stepfather.[124] How did the ideal manage to persist, then? Because, like many ideals, it was sometimes met, and because people accepted it as part of their culture. This paradox (if it is a paradox) is perfectly paralleled in modern states, where people promise to marry until parted by death and plan their happy life together as if unaware of the statistics that give them such a high chance of divorce and widowhood. The ideal of romantic love— once only and for life—is active today, promoted by literature, the visual media, and pop songs, all produced by industries not distinguished by great individual adherence to the ideal. But hope springs eternal. Perhaps it is not so ironic that Augustus, himself scarcely chaste, should have promoted moral legislation and the ideals of marriage and family, for he and Livia were known for their devotion to each other and, once they had contracted the "right" marriage, stuck with it.

It is worth repeating that feelings are very difficult to reconstruct historically. It is possible to argue both ways about Roman marriage. Evidence of cold-blooded political marriage and divorce abound, and it could be maintained that tombstones and tales of model marriages are empty conventions against a background of arranged matches and frequent remarriage. This is the sort of evidence that influences scholars such as Hallett, Bradley, Veyne, and Lyne to characterize Roman marriage, especially within the elite, as emotionally unrewarding. Yet the references to the ideal of happiness or harmony, the relative trouble taken to comment on marriages and the dead spouse in tombstones, and the popularity of stories of overriding conjugal love all suggest that these matches, arranged by the older generation for reasons of material and political advantage, were expected to yield affectionate, companionable relationships and that this happened in numerous cases.

*Irregular Unions*

It was once standard practice for scholars to deplore the proliferation of *de facto* relationships in Roman society as symptomatic of "moral decline," a view fostered by Meyer's (1895) and Plassard's (1921) long works on concubinage. The tradition has been reversed by Rawson's careful (1974) examination of inscriptions in the environs of the city of Rome, which revealed that many of Meyer's alleged cases of concubinage between freeborn Roman citizens could not be sustained by the evidence and that in every case in which such a cohabiting couple had the legal capacity to marry, they did so.[125] Slaves who had no legal right to marry and few inducements to maintain stable relationships formed couples and commemorated each other after death in much the same wording as legally married citizens, save that they usually referred to the dead spouse as *contubernalis* rather than *coniunx*.[126] If any moralizing is called for, it is surely more appropriate to applaud the indomitable spirit that creates human comfort and affection in the appallingly inhuman state of slavery, where spouses or parents and children could be separated without notice by sale.[127]

Romans were restricted legally from making certain marriages. The prohibitions included close kinship and other relationships of trust or status, such as that between *tutor* and *pupilla* or governor and provincial. The effect of the restriction was that such unions were void at law and the usual consequences of marriage did not flow from them. That is, the children were not legitimate, were not *in patria potestate,* and had no rights of intestate succession to their father. Any dowry was treated as a gift between strangers and therefore was not subject to the dotal rules of payment and restoration.[128] Bigamy was not so much forbidden as assumed to negate or terminate one of the "marriages."[129] From the time of Augustus, members of the senatorial class were not permitted to marry freed slaves.[130] People who were not Romans could not contract proper marriages with Roman citizens unless they had the *ius conubii* (right of marriage). This was conferred on many Latin and Italian peoples in the days of Rome's early continental expansion, but by the end of the Republic most free Italians (and freed slaves in Italy) were Roman citizens. The Augustan *Lex Aelia Sentia* placed limitations on the number and type of slaves who could be manumitted by an owner. Slaves manumitted in contravention of the rules were deemed to be Junian Latins, whose free status ended with their death. Junian Latins could, however, gain Roman citizenship by producing a child and presenting the child at the end of its first year of life for official registration as Roman.[131] Unions with foreigners (*peregrini/ae*) were not Roman marriages, and the children were neither citizens nor legitimate. By universal custom, illegitimate children were deemed to take the status of their mother until the *Lex Minicia* of ca. 70 B.C., which ruled that they should take the status of the "lower" spouse.[132] In the case of free foreigners, this law ceased to be of such significance after A.D. 212, when the Edict of Caracalla dissolved the fundamental distinction between Roman and non-Roman citizens within the empire. It was eclipsed by the distinction between *honestiores,* the very small, very wealthy minority increasingly favored at law, and the *humiliores,* or everyone else.[133] The distinctions between freeborn and freed and between slave and free remained, but these groups did frequently intermarry or form unions which they regarded in effect as marriage.

Roman soldiers beneath the rank of centurion were not permitted to marry during their term of service, and it is probable that any marriage a soldier had legally contracted beforehand was void for the lengthy period of his service.[134] This law probably originated with Augustus and sits oddly with his general promotion of marriage. In practice, soldiers did form stable relationships, and the epigraphic and archaeological evidence suggests that women and children were regularly to be found in and around camps.[135] The law was probably revoked by Septimius Severus in A.D. 197.[136] In the meantime, "wives" of serving soldiers lacked the full rights of legal wives and sometimes suffered hardship—they could not, for example, reclaim dowry from the estate of a deceased soldier unless he had made provision for it in a will—but it seems to have been common to grant soldiers on discharge the right legally to marry a foreign woman (*peregrina*) and produce legitimate Roman children.[137] In most cases this would have amounted to legitimizing an existing union, which would then be transformed legally from a *de facto* relationship to one acknowledged for status purposes as a binding and respectable marriage, while in other respects the relationship was unchanged. In this it would resemble slave unions or unions between a slave and a freed person in which both partners, having formed a union that could not be classified legally as marriage, became free and capable of contracting a legal marriage between Roman citizens. The many inscriptions to soldiers as fathers and husbands and by soldiers to wives and children are difficult to date precisely, but many of them certainly precede the change in the law.[138] The problem would remain that Roman soldiers, like other citizens, could not contract legal Roman marriages with foreigners (*peregrinae*), and many clearly did form unions with women in the provinces where they were stationed. This difficulty, met in the past by special privileges granted individually to veterans on discharge, would have been alleviated by the Edict of Caracalla, of A.D. 212, which extended the citizenship widely.[139]

A woman who lived with a man fulfilling the role of wife without being married to him was properly termed *concubina* (concubine),[140] a word which (as in English) had no masculine equivalent. In epitaphs, *concubinae* are described in the same terms as wives and use terms of affection and respect towards their partners. Treggiari (1981a, 59) sums up the trend neatly: "They are expected to have the virtues of a wife but not her pretensions." In the great bulk of cases, concubinage represents a union between people of differing status, such as a freeborn man (*ingenuus*) and a freed woman. Usually the status of the male was higher than that of the female, and in most cases marriage between them was either legally impossible or socially unacceptable. Treggiari's analysis of Italian epitaphs shows that not one single *concubina* was freeborn but that the male partners sometimes were. As we have already seen, Rawson (1974) challenged Meyer's (1895) claim about the pervasiveness of concubinage as a wilful avoidance of marriage by freeborn Roman citizens. Her findings have since been modified slightly by Treggiari (1981a, 61) and Shaw (1987b, 37 n. 149), who argue that concubinage within the lower classes was sometimes a viable alternative to marriage for reasons that are not quite clear. Treggiari cites a guild in which provision is made for commemoration of members and their wives and concubines; one man kept his options open by erecting a funeral monument to himself and to his wife *or* concubine. It is difficult for us to determine why freedmen would have freedwomen as *concubinae* rather than wives. There may have been social niceties that are not clear to us.

Concubinage also existed in the higher social echelons. From the time of Augustus senators (and their children) were not permitted to marry freed slaves.[141] This probably reinforced an existing social prejudice. *Concubinae* are seen explicitly as an honorable alternative to remarriage for widowed men of high status who have children.[142] The emperor Marcus took a *concubina,* we are told, to avoid setting a stepmother over his numerous children.[143] The presumption is that a *concubina* would not have children, a presumption supported by the near-absence of children of such unions in epitaphs.[144] Saller (1987, 76—79) points out that concubinage thus served as an elite strategy to limit the fragmentation of inherited wealth. The *concubina* was seen as deserving respect from her partner and his friends; indeed, the emperor Domitian is criticized by a hostile source for a cool response to his father's *concubina* in public.[145] A man of high status who lived with a slave *concubina* was thought to have an obligation to free her, and she was deemed to have a modest claim to his property.[146]

It was necessary for jurists to determine what constituted concubinage in order to prevent people from using it as a defense against charges of *stuprum* (fornication), which was a legal offense from the time of Augustus. Broadly, they did this in terms of status; a liaison with a woman of "low birth" or of disreputable life, such as a prostitute or actress, did not count as *stuprum*.[147] A man who married was expected to end concubinage; there is virtually no evidence that the two relationships were maintained simultaneously. It was essentially a monogamous union, characterized by companionship, affection, and mutual respect, with someone who could not be seen as a proper mother of the partner's children but in other respects performed the offices of a wife. Sexual satisfaction was clearly part of the presumption, whether for the young man before marriage (the stereotype of Plautine comedy and the reality of St. Augustine) or the widower with a proper eye to his children's interests.

The senatorial decree passed in the rule of the emperor Claudius, the *SC Claudianum,* of A.D. 52, forbade free women to cohabit with slaves without the knowledge of the slaveowner. Even if the slaveowner agreed to such a union, the children were slaves, and the woman, if freeborn, was reduced to freed (*libertina*) status.[148] This sounds like a strong disincentive, but the reaffirmation and partial amendment of the ruling suggests that it did happen, and Weaver's (1986) study has found that in many cases the penalty was not applied. In particular, he argues that male slaves of the imperial family frequently had such unions with freeborn women (*ingenuae*) and that the emperor imposed his rights very selectively, probably in cases where he wanted to make use of talented children of these alliances.[149] The jurist Ulpian makes the point that it is unworthy but not illegal for a woman to free a slave in order to marry him (a practice deemed quite proper for a man of the appropriate station).[150] I doubt that in such a case it was seen as an honorable alternative for her to keep him as a male concubine, but these unions are in effect examples of women—not very high on the social scale, to be sure—forming liaisons with men of lower legal status. They do not properly equate with concubinage, because such unions did produce children. As in soldier marriage, *contubernium,* and concubinage, the partners used the language of affection and harmony in commemorating each other and, indeed, sometimes adopted the language of "proper marriage" by referring to each other as *coniu(n)x.*[151]

Irregular unions seem, then, to have occurred in Roman society chiefly because people were unable to marry or because it was deemed more acceptable socially for them to have a concubinage relationship. Legal and social status were the determinants. The status of children of the union was one of the major differences between such matches and "proper marriage" (*iustum conubium, iustae nuptiae*). In other respects, slave unions, mixed matches, and soldier "marriages" completely mirrored legal marriages in their stability, in the partners' expectations of economic sharing and emotional support, and in the ideal of harmony and affection. Epitaphs make this much clear. Such relationships must have alleviated the trials of slavery and military service. Much of the earlier scholarship on concubinage seems now to have been based on a misconception and dominated by a presumption that Roman morals, marriage, and religion were in decline. On the contrary, those who could marry seem to have done so—repeatedly, in many cases—while those who could not imitated all aspects of the marriage state and commemorated their spouses with the same dutiful and sometimes tender epithets that "real" husbands and wives used. This suggests that marriage was seen as desirable. The main disability of the alternative unions was the lack of status of any children, who were illegitimate and in most cases had no claim to Roman citizenship.

## Conclusion

Roman marriages, undertaken for the purpose of producing legitimate citizen children, performed legal and emotional functions.

The legal aspects involved the status of the partners and the children of the union and, to an extent, their economic rights and obligations. Such considerations would have loomed large in people's lives, but marriage was also viewed ideally as a source of comfort and happiness. Scholars have questioned whether these ideals could have been achieved against a background of arranged matches and casual divorce, but there is sufficient evidence to suggest not only that the political elite often formed loving and loyal conjugal partnerships but that slaves and soldiers, their lives subject to so much external disruption and control, also sought and sometimes fulfilled these ideals even when denied the full legal benefits of marriage.

Those studies of marriage (or concubinage) which were not entirely concerned with legal detail have often been dominated by the view that Roman marriage showed all the symptoms of the Roman moral decline so beloved of popular films and novels. This picture of decline probably owes much to the legislation of Augustus and the writings of the early church fathers and it has been fleshed out by the satirists' racy accounts of adultery and grossness. Augustus's assumption of resistance to marriage is difficult now to assess, and Christian distaste for concubinage and divorce have given an impression that is difficult to sustain in face of the evidence that Romans generally wished to marry and that they hoped for and often found harmony and comfort in marriage. Some also committed adultery, some divorced, and many remarried repeatedly on the death or divorce of spouses. The overall picture does not seem to be one of depravity or disregard for marriage. On the contrary, epitaphs proclaim the virtues of spouses (and, by implication, of the married state), and dramatic stories circulated of model spouses, especially wives, whose love and loyalty gave inspiration and sentimental gratification to a wide audience.

It is frustrating that we cannot adequately explain the changes which did take place in Roman marriage. These changes rest in the alteration of preference whereby women (or their fathers or families for them) chose to retain their status as a member of their own natal families after marriage. These women fully acknowledged their obligations to the children of the marriage and were encouraged to do so by the community, including their own relations, so it is not entirely explicable in terms of retention of family holdings. Husband and wife seem to have looked to each other more for emotional than for financial support; this is reflected in the inheritance laws giving low priority to succession between them and the custom limiting their gifts to one another. Yet there are so many exceptions to this tendency that it is difficult to make too much of it beyond the statement that a married woman owed great loyalty to her husband but that that relationship, which could be severed, was probably not perceived, if it came to the crunch, as being on quite the same level as duty to children and close natal kin.

Scholarship on Roman marriage continues and has been enriched by the legal and demographic expertise of authors such as Treggiari, Saller, Shaw, Gardner, and Corbier, as well as their sensitivity to relationships of power and affection within marriage. The close analysis of ideals and of texts and inscriptions describing actual marriages continues to yield important material which is changing our conception of Roman marriage and might eventually enable us to make sound statements about class and regional differences. In the meantime, it is clear that marriage, beset by the mortality patterns of the preindustrial world and the oppression of economic demands and a hierarchical social structure, yet provided comfort and some measure of material and emotional security for many and remained a desirable ideal for those whose circumstances excluded them from it.

# Four

# Children in the Roman Family

*Ancient Attitudes towards Young Children*

The twentieth century is notoriously obsessed with the young child. The mental health of the young child is a Western preoccupation, but most countries now have laws making elementary education compulsory and censuring parental violence. Governments are committed, at least in principle, to providing or encouraging basic health education. In the West, this universal commitment to children as the future hope is strongly reinforced with sentimental concern for young children as such—witness UNICEF, the use of young children in advertisements for famine aid, and the new media outrage at child abuse within the family. Children are seen as appealing, vulnerable, and entitled to protection.

These attitudes are relatively new, historically speaking, and in practice the rights of parents, especially fathers, to beat, indenture, betroth, or even sell their young children are still acknowledged in many parts of the world. A brief perusal of the history of childhood reveals that this has been the norm. Demause (1974, 1) goes so far as to say that "the history of childhood is a nightmare from which we have only recently begun to awaken." Historians of childhood and the family continue to take sides in the "indifference debate," which was sparked off by Ariès's (1960) suggestion that the very idea of childhood as a separate stage of human life was a recent invention. Stone's (1977) book, *The Family, Sex, and Marriage in England, 1500–1800,* plotted the change from the formal relations between English children and parents to the relatively affectionate style of the eighteenth century. Authors such as Macfarlane (1979), Lambert (1982), and Pollock (1983) have strongly opposed the suggestion that children in the past were uniformly treated with indifference and cruelty. They counter this picture with indications that parents did demonstrate care and concern for their children from an early age.

The picture is equally confusing for the ancient world, and we lack the testimony of children themselves. The question is linked to ancient demography and the relatively poor life chances of infants and young children. Stone (1977, 70) argued that parents in earlier periods could not afford to make too much emotional investment in children who might not live. Sepulchral inscriptions are a vital element in our knowledge of family relations in classical antiquity, so the indifference debate often focuses on the commemoration of young children at death as evidence that their loss was genuinely lamented. This type of commemoration was relatively common in Italy, especially the region around Rome, but not elsewhere.[1] Even in Rome, there was a tradition, dating from the regal period, that the deaths of the very young were not to be marked by the same mourning practices accorded young adults, a phenomenon with many cross-cultural parallels,[2] and letters of consolation make it clear that Romans considered excessive mourning of the very young to be in bad taste.[3] Cicero stated that the deaths of babies were not normally mourned, and he himself, a fond father, showed little personal interest in his short-lived grandchildren.[4]

There are many difficulties in putting together the diverse material to form a coherent picture of attitudes towards young children within society as a whole and within the family. For one thing, formal commemoration need not be a perfect reflection of feeling: people might feel strongly about the loss of a child but neglect to mark the child's death because of social pressure or lack of money.[5] Conversely, people might feel obliged by family or social expectations to organize elaborate funeral rituals for relations whom they disliked when alive. Certainly, the very young do not figure as much in tombstones as older children, and the typical focus of tragic or untimely death is the young adult—apparently about 16—30—with a socially recognized role, who had survived long enough for parents to form expectations that the child would outlive them.[6] This is implicit in Cicero's philosophic ridicule of the notion of "untimely death," the death that was mourned most bitterly: "That old wives' absurdity, that it is an evil to die before one's time, should be rejected. . . . The same people think that the death of a young child should be borne calmly and, indeed, if it was a baby still in its cradle, that its death ought not even to be mourned. . . . Has not old age, 'just now pressing from behind on boys, now on youths still running life's race, overtaken them all unsuspecting?'"[7]

On the whole, the young child seems to have been of minor interest to the Roman literary class. Adults reminiscing about influences on their own development were more likely to focus on adolescence as the formative stage, as in Horace's recollection of his father's moral training or Agricola's recollection of his mother's intervention in his philosophical studies or the emperor Marcus's enumeration of the relations and teachers who had earned his gratitude.[8] Childhood is occasionally invoked in a detached and general way by adult authors as a symbol of the uneducated or innocent human, but literary references to children and childhood are relatively few and often vague, revealing little interest in the activities of young children for their own sake.[9] Medical writers, too, neglect the young child in spite of the fact that children were particularly subject to accident and serious illness. Étienne (1973, 43 and *passim*) argues that this stemmed in part from indifference, an acceptance that that was the way things were (akin to some modern attitudes to geriatric ailments), and in part from the assumption that babies and young children were the concern of midwives and women in general rather than the more prestigious (predominantly male) doctors.

It need not follow from this that Romans failed to distinguish childhood as a separate stage of life, the approach Ariès described as typical of traditional societies. The ritual connected with birth and other *rites de passage* are themselves indications of Roman awareness that childhood and its stages were distinct from other stages of life. The newborn child, once pronounced fit to live, probably by the midwife, would then be placed on the ground for the *paterfamilias* to raise up ritually as his indication that he accepted his paternity of the child and wished to rear it.[10] As on other festive occasions, the doorway of the house would be wreathed with flowers, and a sacrifice would be made to the family deities. On the *dies lustricus* (the eighth day after the birth of a female child, the ninth after a male) a party would be held for family and friends, who came bearing presents. A sacrifice would be made, and the child would be given a name and the apotropaic necklace, the *bulla,* which marked her or him as freeborn.[11]

There is no record of any puberty ceremony for girls at Rome, although it is quite possible that the occasion was celebrated by women but not mentioned (or perhaps even known) by male authors. Puberty is, after all, clearly marked in the female sex by menarche and unequivocal secondary sexual characteristics, and most cultures have folklore surrounding menstruation and different codes of behavior for pre- and postpubertal young girls and for males interacting with them. It is usually assumed that marriage marked the formal transition from girlhood to womanhood,[12] and first marriage could be accompanied by traditional ceremonial such as the sacrifice of girlish toys, a special bridal coiffure arranged with a spear blade, slippers and a veil of a color to suggest hymeneal blood.[13] The male transition from boyhood to manhood, which takes longer and is more nebulous, tends for this reason and for reasons of cultural emphasis to be marked by specific, fairly public ritual, since it marks above all a change in boys' relationship to the state. At the age of about fifteen a boy would undergo a ceremony at which he set aside the *bulla* and the tunic (*toga praetexta*) of his childhood and took on a man's dress (*toga virilis*).[14] This could occur in a private ceremony or on the Liberalia, on 17 March, when young boys, accompanied by their fathers

This sentimental interest in young children and enjoyment of their childish qualities is, I believe, part of a general ideological stress on the domestic comfort of the conjugal unit which emerges in Latin art and literature from the first century B.C. and is to be related to the ideal of conjugal happiness discussed in chapter 3, above. There are similarities with the nineteenth-century European *topos* of the family as a "haven in a heartless world." Consider Cicero *Att.* 1.18.1, where Cicero speaks in a maudlin vein of the shallowness of his relations with alleged friends and supporters and claims that his only satisfying times are those he spends with his wife and young children: "I am so deprived of all companionship that my only unguarded time is what is spent with my wife, my little girl, and sweet Cicero."[21]

Lucretius cites (for philosophical criticism) the common lament of mourners for a man struck down in his youthful prime: "No more, no more will your happy house welcome you, nor will your excellent wife. No more will your sweet children run to greet you with kisses and cling to your chest in sweet silence."[22] In such cases the use of diminutives and affectionate epithets for young children are linked to the idea of intimacy and comfort within the nuclear family.

It is difficult to provide comparable examples from a period before the first century B.C., but Bradley cautions against concluding from this that the ideals necessarily arose in this period.[23] Be that as it may, images from childhood and affectionate language for small chidren appear in the literature and tombstones of the late Republic. This does seem to reflect both a notional appreciation of the domestic unit and an interest in children which is associated primarily with parents but also with dependents, family friends, and society at large. Some of the literary images of childhood cited above come from celibate or childless authors, such as Catullus, Horace, or Pliny. Inscriptions such as *CIL* 6.18086 to two-year-old Flavius Hermes or 6.34421 to three-year-old Anteis Chrysostom include references not only to parents and other relations such as uncles and grandparents but also to neighbors and to dependents involved in the child's upbringing. Indeed, the exigencies of Roman life—the death, exile, or patriotic travel of one or both parents, divorce, even remarriage on widowhood—often separated children from a parent or parents or served to bring a child into closer contact with an aunt, grandparent, or stepparent. The aristocratic child tended from birth by nurses and others, then pedagogues and the slave child or *alumnus/a* in a large household was exposed to the care and company of a great variety of people other than parents. It is touching that in a society where status was so important, tombstones do at times cross these boundaries because of common attachment to a young child.[24]

It is nonetheless true that Latin displayed a certain vagueness in describing children and the stages of childhood or youth. The term *infans*, literally "not-speaking," is not confined to infants, and Manson (1983: 151—53) points out that there is no specific word in Latin for "baby." Catullus (61.209) uses *parvulus Torquatus*, "a teeny little Torquatus," to describes his friend's imagined baby. *Liberi* (the term for freeborn Roman citizen children), like the abstract *progenies*, meant issue of any age, as did *filii*. *Pueri* and the feminine *puellae* commonly denoted children as distinct from youths, but the context does not always make this clear.[25]

Such vagueness need not imply total indifference to children or unawareness of the distinctions between babies, toddlers, older children, and adolescents. It is worth noting, however, and the vagueness makes it very difficult for the historian of childhood to assemble a coherent body of data about childish behavior and treatment or attitudes towards young children. Erikson's (1963) scheme of childish stages is not universally fashionable, but modern educational theory does view children in terms of developmental stages (e.g., Piagetian), physically and intellectually. More popularly, each culture has certain expectations of "typical" behavior in children of various ages, and it can be confusing to the modern reader to encounter a description of a child of a specified age whose behavior seems quite out of keeping with it.[26] It also makes it difficult to make confident guesses about the probable age of children based entirely on the described characteristics.

One striking feature of many ancient descriptions of children is the way in which they are praised for being like adults. Carp (1980) and Eyben (1986) have documented the Roman tendency to favor mature qualities in children—the *puer senex,* or "old child," phenomenon. Bereft of his nine-year-old son, Quintilian reminisced about the boy's seriousness and studiousness. Pliny, writing of the newly deceased Minicia Marcella, spoke of her "elderly sense of discretion, her matronly dignity, her girlish charm together with her maidenly modesty." Both children were commended particularly for their gravity. The boy Quintilian was judged as a gentleman-scholar in training, the girl as an apprentice matron.[27] This reflects the reality of parental expectations. The boy would soon have embarked on the pursuit of "higher studies,"[28] while the girl was due to be married; Pliny adds the pathetic detail that the money put aside for the girl's imminent wedding was spent instead on her funeral rites.[29] Even the cute two-year-old Titus Flavius Hermes had the manner of a sixteen-year-old.[30] Biographies conventionally included a section on childhood, showing that the famous person had demonstrated striking qualities from infancy, sometimes of leadership or evil moral tendencies, but sometimes magical and premonitory characteristics. It is therefore interesting that the *puer senex* motif is less in evidence in these works than it was to become in Christian hagiographies, where saints as children had invariably shown adult indifference to play, as if childish characteristics were an aberration.[31]

Some of the definitions of childhood and youth to be found in the dictionaries are derived from the law,[32] which was concerned at different stages to define the limits of criminal culpability and the financial responsibility of the young. The young were often grouped with *furiosi* (the insane) or *prodigi* (those who recklessly wasted the family fortunes), and some of the measures adopted are analogous to those applied to women.[33] In most cases, the guiding principle is the protection of property, which is conceived as an eternal family concern even when it is technically owned by an individual. Judicial rulings and the judgments of jurists are, however, sometimes accompanied by explanations which include specific observations and assumptions about the young, apparently reflecting Roman views on childhood and youth.

The institution of *tutela impuberum,* guardianship of children below the age of puberty, dates at least from the Twelve Tables of the fifth century B.C..[34] It concerned children whose fathers had died and were therefore *sui iuris*, independent at law but too young to manage their estates. Within this category a distinction was gradually drawn between *infantes*, below the age of seven years, who could not conduct their own affairs at all,[35] and *impuberes* between seven years and the age of puberty (usually taken to be twelve years in the case of girls, fourteen in the case of boys),[36] who could manage certain acts but were protected by the interposition of the *tutor's* permission (*auctoritas*). Once the child *in tutela* (the *pupillus* or *pupilla*) attained puberty, the *tutor* was obliged to render accounts, and a legal action lay against him (or them) if the estate had been mismanaged.[37]

With the passing of time, *tutela* assumed importance as a moral obligation, and the protective responsibility of the *tutor(es)* was emphasized,[38] but originally *tutela* was associated more with the protection of the family estate. A *tutor legitimus*, or statutory *tutor*, was the nearest agnatic relation of the *pupillus/a* and therefore the heir on the child's intestate death. Since children below the age of puberty had no capacity to make a will, this meant that the *tutor* would succeed to the estate and had an interest in maintaining it. A father could also appoint a *tutor* to his children in his will, and in the absence of any *tutor*, the mother of young children *sui iuris* was obliged to apply to the praetor or the provincial *praesides* to appoint a suitable man.[39] *Tutela* did not involve any protection of the child's person, and children did not normally live with the *tutor*, so it should not be confused with modern notions of guardianship.[40]

Other legal acknowledgments of childhood and youth included the *Lex Plaetoria* (or *Laetoria*) of about 200 B.C.,[41] whereby a person over puberty but under twenty-five, if sued for a contracted debt, could claim an *exceptio* on the ground that his (and, later, her) youthful inexperience had been exploited by the other party. People contracting with young property holders could guard against this possibility by ensuring that a *curator* was present at the transaction to certify that the young person was not at any disadvantage.[42] This was on the model of the *cura furiosi*, the special care of an insane person, and was really a safeguard for those dealing with young people, but it became a common practice, and by the second century A.D. imperial rulings made it virtually compulsory for people between puberty and twenty-five years to have a *curator* present for most transactions.[43] This virtually extended the institution of *tutela* under another name and seems to show a more protective approach to the young than the traditional Roman system, which awarded independence to the fatherless at a very early age.[44]

The *SC Macedonianum,* enacted in the time of Vespasian, was directed, not strictly at the young as such, but at sons (and, by extension, daughters) in power, *filiifamilias*. The ruling prevented them from borrowing against their expectations. The motive assigned to this ruling was protective not of children but of fathers and seems to have been associated with fears of parricide.[45] Such fears were probably not very rational, but they reflect a certain suspicion between the generations—more specifically, between fathers and sons—which colors Roman literature and even law, as we shall see in chapter five. I mention the ruling here because it belongs in the general category of legislation affecting the young and should check any temptation to view the legislative trend as wholly benevolent and increasingly protective towards the young, although there were undoubtedly moves in that direction. The statements surrounding these customary and legal practices again make it clear that the young were subdivided into categories, with young children, older children, and youths perceived as having distinctive characteristics which might make them suspect or vulnerable.

All of this suggests that ancient attitudes towards young children were complex. Romans did distinguish between children and adults and between the different stages of childhood and youth for various purposes—civic, legal, personal, and ritual. They showed at times a delight in childish characteristics such as playfulness and childish speech patterns, and some parents deeply mourned the loss of particular young children as individuals. At the same time, there was a tendency to accept the deaths of the very young with impassivity and even a certain disfavor towards those who showed "excessive" pain at the loss of babies and young children.

Literature and art reveal an observation of childish activity, but the literary imagery tends to be incidental to a more general argument. There are linguistic and ritual means of marking off the different stages of childhood and youth, but these are not always observed in everyday description, and idealizing accounts of dead children tend to praise them by emphasizing their adult qualities. It is therefore possible to refute the suggestion that childhood was not perceived as a separate stage of human development, but the argument must allow for these qualifications. The separate but related argument that people in a society with high infant death needed to protect themselves from attachment to small children continues to generate debate. Certainly the young child in the Roman Empire, whatever his or her social standing, assumed none of the importance of the modern counterpart in Western society, with its massive production of toys, books, and visual entertainment for young children and literature, conferences, and media time devoted to the study of the welfare and development of the young child.

## The Function of Children in the Family

The expectation that children will provide their parents with support in old age and proper commemoration at death is a deep-seated one. It was frequently explicit in the ancient world.[46] Macfarlane (1986) argues that "market societies" like those of modern England have broken from this "peasant" mentality and children are viewed, particularly by the prosperous, as relatively individual creatures who can be cherished and supported for their own sake rather than for any eventual return (cf. Wiedemann 1989, 26), rather as horses and dogs are in the developed world today. There is much to be said for this argument, although long-lived moderns with their own savings or state welfare schemes probably still hope that their children will be buffers against the loneliness and physical dependence associated in many minds with old age. In the ancient world, even the wealthy—who could afford lavish care from a mass of slaves and dependants—valued the support of their social peers in old age[47] and hoped that their children would see to their funeral and proper commemoration after death. Ovid's portrait of the old age of the peasant couple Baucis and Philemon is intended to show how pitiable old age could be for those with neither children nor the material resources to hire others to perform the daily round.[48]

The basic office of burial would not be performed by very young children (although they would be expected to perform rites in subsequent years), but the expectation would have been part of the wish to have children and could have affected attitudes towards young members of the family. Those without children of their own might hope that their nephews or nieces would perform these offices, which tended to be associated in Roman culture with the duties and privileges of inheritance.[49]

The maintenance of the very young would represent a significant drain on the resources of the poor, and it is not surprising that the elite literary sources take for granted that the poor commonly exposed children they were unable to rear.[50] Those children who were reared must have been viewed in part as an investment in the future, for their labor would be of use on a farm from an early stage, and if the parents could afford specialist training through apprenticeships, they could bring some income to their families once they became skilled.[51] Slaves were trained by wealthy owners from an early age and might even have been in a position to benefit their parents and other relations if they were able to accumulate money and prestige through their skills.[52]

The children of the elite might not have faced the same necessity to bring in an income from the earliest possible age, but it was equally vital for them to learn the tasks appropriate to their station and, in their own way, to contribute to the maintenance or improvement of the family's status. The Roman senatorial class was one to which membership had to be re-earned in each successive generation. The young man of a senatorial family had to see to it that he was elected to senatorial office and that he maintained the family's fortune at the requisite level to avoid exclusion from the specific census category. The young senatorial woman was obliged to marry within her class and to foster by her own activities the political ambitions of her brothers and sons.[53] The younger gener-

ation needed to acquire a range of skills that affirmed and perpetu-
ated membership in this elite during the period of extended economic dependence characteristic of the children of the wealthy in
all epochs. Thus Cicero spoke of his willingness to spend lavishly
on his son's studies and lifestyle in Athens because this reflected on
his own standing. He wanted young Marcus to be seen to be living
as well as the sons of the old noble houses.[54]

The maintenance of social standing and family honor was a
function of children in other classes as well. Roman sons and
daughters literally bore the family name and could bring glory or
discredit on it by their behavior. With all its strict social divisions,
Roman society had a surprising potential for social mobility. Senators had to put some effort into maintaining their status; the Roman emperors chose to replenish the fortunes of some noble
houses to prevent them from becoming déclassé, and we know of
at least one example in which children allegedly caused this ca-
lamity.[55] The poet Horace was the child of a freed slave who could
afford a good education for his son.[56] Cicero had elevated the
status of his municipal family to senatorial nobility at Rome.[57] The
baker M. Vergilius Eurysaces began life as a slave in the Republic
and ended it as a millionaire whose spectacular funeral monument
(to himself and his wife Atistia), in the shape of a giant oven decorated with scenes of baking, continues to proclaim the source of
his wealth near the Porta Maggiore of modern Rome. Naevoleia
Tyche, another freed slave, married a member of the local office-
bearing elite of Pompeii and died a wealthy woman, also leaving a
notable funeral monument, which probably illustrates the source
of her wealth in the shipping trade.[58] The poor probably provided
the soldiers of the Roman army, who could, if they survived, retire
as a privileged group with a modest amount of land,[59] and their
noncitizen children could themselves gain Roman citizenship by
enlisting,[60] just as skilled slaves from foreign backgrounds could
be raised automatically to the rank of citizen by manumission[61]
and provincials could sometimes win or buy citizenship.[62]

Then, as now, social mobility could estrange a child from its
parents. Horace punctiliously acknowledged his debt to his father
and showed no shame about his origins in a society in which first-

generation senatorials could be tormented with the arrogant question, "Who was your father?"[63] Yet an imperial librarian refused to be reconciled as an adult with the mother who had abandoned him as a child, although he could have gained the coveted prize of Roman citizenship by allowing her to reclaim him.[64] Even where the bond was acknowledged, the parent might gain only the abstract advantages of the child's status or the prospect of it. Presumably Horace's father labored for his son in much the same spirit in which modern parents emigrate and condemn themselves to years of sacrifice in the hope that life will eventually be easier (economically or politically) for their children.

Above all, children confer some kind of posterity on their parents and on all the preceding generations (not only their direct ancestors). They inherit not only concrete goods such as houses, land, businesses, slaves, and jewelry but also such intangibles as the family name and honor and the obligations that go with them—the continuation of the family cult and the specific, ritual commemoration of individuals such as parents and aunts and uncles whom they remember, as well as the maintenance of family traditions, whether oral stories or *imagines* (ancestral portraits) or records from public office.[65] The mere idea that children outlive one can be a source of comfort and some claim to immortality. This is the sentiment that Dio has Augustus stress in his speech to the bachelor knights: "Is it not blessed, on departing from life, to leave behind as successor and heir to your line and fortune one that is your own, produced by you, and to have only the mortal part of you waste away, while you live on in the child?"[66]

Conversely, it was a tragedy to be predeceased by a child of any age. Apart from any sense of loss, of missing the child as an individual, it represented the dashing of hopes and, to an extent, the reversal of the natural order, in spite of the observed reality that the young, especially the very young, were physically vulnerable. Like Greeks before them, Romans lamented on the tombstones of their children that they were—unnaturally—performing the very office for their children that the children ought to have performed for them. This sentiment is so common as to be abbreviated to a code. Like Medea, they grieved for the loss of the many services the children would in the normal course of events have performed for them.[67]

There were, however, some ways in which Romans could gain the perceived benefits of having children even if choice or circumstance rendered them childless. Adoption was the obvious means of gaining virtually all the benefits listed above as functions of children within the family. Even the notional physical continuity could be gained by adopting a relative; and indeed the majority of attested adoptions, many of them included in wills, so that they were performed posthumously, were of nephews or grandsons.[68] In the case of sisters' sons or daughters' sons, adoption had the effect of continuing the family name, which normally passed through the male line, and of ensuring that the cult that went with it was maintained.

It must say something about Roman attitudes towards children—and about our own—that they usually adopted adults, while we of the urbanized West associate adoption with newborns. There are, to be sure, examples of the adoption of young children in documents from Roman Egypt and some instances of the adoption of females.[69] There is even an attempt by a woman to simulate adoption by requiring her heir to take her name.[70] In general, however, adoption was conducted between males and involved the legal transfer of the adoptee into the agnatic family of the adopter. The distinction between *adoptio* and *adrogatio* rests in the status of the adoptee: if he was in the power of his father, the process was called *adoptio* and must be done with the father's permission; if he was *sui iuris,* it was called *adrogatio* and the adoptee and any people in *his* power were also transferred to the adopting family. Adoption did not sever normal relations with the original family any more than marriage or emancipation from the father's authority would have done and the law still observed certain obligations between the adopted child and his biological father.[71] In general, adoption altered hereditary succession, and the adoptee was subject to the same legal privileges and limitations of a legitimate biological son.[72]

It is now acknowledged that most cultures, however committed to the ideology of a specific form of descent and inheritance, are obliged by demographic exigencies to develop alternative systems, and it has become more usual to speak of strategies than of rules or systems of inheritance.[73] The notorious failure of the Roman elite to reproduce itself meant that other means might be necessary to compensate for the absence of children, and adoption within the elite was clearly an attempt to do this. One poignant example beloved of historians and biographers in the ancient world was that of Aemilius Paulus, a successful Roman general of the second century B.C., whose triumph was marred by the deaths of the two sons of his second marriage after he had already given out his two older sons in adoption.[74]

Interestingly enough, adoption was not used as widely as it might have been. It does not seem to have extended often beyond the ruling class. Romans had other means of co-opting children as objects of affection or as heirs and tenders of their old age and posterity. Young slaves sometimes held a privileged position in the Roman household. The sale of very young slaves and their separation from their parents, especially their mother, implies a pervading callousness,[75] but other literary and inscriptional references suggest that some slave children could also be petted and become the focus of genuine affection. Seneca's essay on old age reminds us that this relationship might not have survived the slave's appealing cuteness in early childhood, and other references show that the relationship could be based on sexual abuse,[76] but some of the young home-bred slaves or foundlings lamented in poetry and tombstones might have lived to fulfill the role of children in that, although socially subordinate, they could alleviate the harshness of old age and attend to funeral rites.[77]

The surviving tablets from the town of Herculaneum include depositions from a court case concerning the status of the girl Petronia Iusta and provide an intriguing glimpse into just such a relationship. The prosperous couple who had owned the girl's mother had taken Petronia in and apparently become fond of her. When the mother wanted to reclaim her, the couple argued that the girl had been born before the mother's manumission and was therefore their slave, not freeborn. They clearly wanted to continue to treat the dependent girl as a daughter and were prepared

113

to insist on her servile birth as a means of keeping her from her mother.[78] The dry legal records, with their reported speech and affidavits, echo the intense emotions involved in the situation, the type now associated with cases for custody of the children of divorced parents or *causes cèlébres* such as the "Baby M" case.

Slaveowners without kin could and often did include their freed slaves in a commemorative plot, on the assumption that these freed slaves would maintain the rites and pass the duty on to their own descendants—all of whom would perpetually bear the name of the deceased owner/patron, a kind of posterity. This ritual entitlement was often added to an epitaph. Sometimes provision was made for the expenses of tending the monument, and explicit instructions could be given about seasonal funeral rites.[79] In this way, family dependents gained the security of a place of proper burial and in return saw to it that their patron had proper rites. Again we are reminded that free Romans lived in continual contact with certain specialized slaves and formed relationships with them that in some ways resembled kinship, even if the slaves were always in the position of poor relations.

Friends were frequently included in Roman wills, even by testators with children of their own. They might name friends as heirs in the second or third degree, to prevent failure of the will and to honor these friends publicly. It was possible to go further and to make them joint heirs with children or even to bypass unsatisfactory children in their favor, for the Roman testator possessed great freedom in theory. In practice, the social expectation was that people with children would favor them and perhaps include friends as legatees. It is important to note that the Roman ability to leave estates to non-kin gave rise to a mass of literary references to fortune hunters who cultivated the childless for this purpose and even the presumption that some people chose childlessness in order to be courted by such people.[80] It is difficult to extract the reality from the moralizing. Pliny the younger, who condemned *captatores* (inheritance or legacy hunters), was delighted to be named in the wills of friends and even accepted an inheritance that excluded the son of the testatrix.[81] Friends could thus take the place of children in the sense that their attentions and affections would ease the later part of life, they would share in one's possessions after death, and they would observe the duties of commemoration and any particular trusts, such as looking after favored dependents and in other ways honoring the wishes of the deceased.

The poor and the servile could also have recourse to friends and associates to perform similar offices by forming kinlike associations among members of the same *familia* or members of burial clubs.[82] In both cases, friends virtually take on the role of kin, presumably for those who had no family at all. In both cases, we historians have found out about the relationships because of written commemorations (or inscribed club charters), but this was just one aspect of friendship. Even the funeral clubs were social clubs that gathered regularly and showed an interest in members' general welfare in their lifetime, celebrating with them if they were freed from slavery or had a birthday.

Life could be harsh in the ancient world for those with no kin, and the common human expectation is that the nearest kin— spouse and especially children—will be of an age to provide support at the crucial stages. Human history is full of examples of un-filial children and of children who predecease the parents, but that fundamental hope remained: that children would survive to bring pride, prosperity, and material and emotional support to the parent in due course, to produce children in their turn and thus confer a kind of immortality. Only children could fulfill these myriad requirements, and children were the focus of hope, frustration, and affection in ancient Rome, although the expression of interest in children in their early years was probably rather different from what we regard as usual in modern urban cultures. Young children could be petted and valued, but they were seen primarily for their potential: their full usefulness, and perhaps adult interest in them, began to flower in adolescence, and it was the child who died in its prime who was mourned most.[83] The options available to the childless were probably seen as second-best, but it was possible for Romans of some means to preserve the family name, to ensure support in old age and commemoration after death, to acquire affectionate dependents or friends who would fulfill some of the roles normally associated with children even if they could not give the full gratification of physical parenthood: "And is it not a delight to rear a child who shows the endowments of both parents, to nurture and educate it, at once a reflection of your own physical and mental character, so that in its growth another self lives again?"[84]

## Relations between Parents and Children

Modern parents are bombarded with advice on child rearing. Mothers of babies and young children are the main targets of books, articles, special radio and television programs, and oral advice from relations, health professionals, and strangers at bus stops. Parents in the ancient world doubtless gained instruction and advice from elders and peers, but apart from odd pieces of recorded folklore, this has not survived as well as the prescriptive literature of philosophers and moralists.[85] It could be the oddities of survival that leave the modern reader with the impression that Roman parents and Roman society were more concerned with the moral and practical training of children than in their cognitive, physical, and emotional development, but the surviving literature does support the conclusion that educators and medical writers were not as interested in the young child as their modern equivalents are.[86]

To be sure, literature on rhetorical training sometimes invoked the idea that significant learning might occur in the early years and that it might therefore be hazardous to hand over young children to servants of dubious morality and syntax.[87] Quintilian explicitly argued that the first three years were important for intellectual development (*Inst.Or.* 1.1.16—17) and elsewhere noted the need for the budding orator to be surrounded as a child by good speech models, whether parents or servants (1.1.6). But such statements are isolated and theoretical, not to be compared with modern commonplaces about the "needs" of infants for emotional security and intellectual stimulation.

Yet the Roman ideal entailed intense parental involvement in children's upbringing. Cato the elder, Cornelia (mother of the

Gracchi), Augustus, and his mother Atia were among the figures praised for their close supervision of children and even grand-children.[88] This sometimes involved direct teaching, as in the case of Cato writing out the history of Rome in large letters for his young son, or Augustus insisting that his grandsons (who were also his adopted sons) imitate his handwriting, or the mother teaching her daughter to spin and weave.[89] It could, however, con-sist of arranging for teaching in the home by a tame philosopher or rhetorician or sending the child off to school and actively check-ing on the results of the education.[90] When elite boys reached ado-lescence, they could be entrusted to experts—relatives or friends of the family—to learn by example the gentlemanly skills of ora-tory, the law, or the military.[91] The men to whom the youths were attached were very different from professional teachers. Their so-cial standing was similar to that of the youth's father, and the rela-tionship was explicitly likened to father-son education.[92]

Wiedemann rightly points out that Roman military training—and, by implication, much of Roman elite education—was "decid-edly amateur" in its practical and relatively unsystematic charac-ter. Even in an age when the wealthy did send their sons abroad to learn certain liberal arts from professional teachers, they prized those skills which were transmitted in traditional fashion on the model of home-based, practical learning. In this they resembled lower-class parents, who trained their children in agriculture and trades or apprenticed the children out to those who could teach them such skills. Slave children would also be taught useful skills within the household or, if necessary, by a craftsman or contract teacher.[93] The nine-year-old Viccentia was commemorated by her parents as a worker in gold.[94] Free children were expected to do housework and wait on the adults in the home, something they would learn by example from an early age.[95]

Roman parents were also expected to teach their children moral values, and severity in this process was generally regarded with some favor by the ancient sources. The *paterfamilias* had wide-ranging theoretical powers over children and grandchildren (children of sons). Even if they seldom exercised these to their full extent, cultural approval was extended to legendary fathers who had even executed adult sons and mothers who had successfully remonstrated with sons; the legal expert T. Manlius Torquatus and Coriolanus's mother Volumnia were both admired for putting the public interest before their parental preference.[96] Yet this very admiration is based on the assumption that parents would normally favor their children and that such patriotism was exceptional.

It is not difficult to assemble texts to show that ancient authors saw the parental role as vital to the development of a child's character.[97] Statements commonly take the form of deploring modern trends that impose insufficient discipline on the young child or youth or of praising the parents of a famous man for instilling virtue in him from his earliest years.[98] Even so, the idea that parents were entirely responsible for their children's adult character was not as consistently argued or as firmly entrenched as it is in the postpsychoanalytic West. Cicero made a point of denying that fathers could be blamed for sons who went wrong, and biographers tend to write on the assumption that character is revealed little by little rather than formed by education.[99]

Yet such generalizations are common in so many societies as literary or conversational commonplaces that it is difficult to know whether they bear any relation to everyday practice. The imagery of childhood—usually invoked, as we have seen, incidentally, to make some other point—does refer routinely to parental discipline: children punished for behaving inappropriately in a household in mourning or Eros beaten by Aphrodite, a popular visual motif.[100] Demause argues that parents in the ancient world casually employed great violence against their children, but Saller modifies this somewhat by his insistence that whipping was deemed inappropriate for people of free status in the Roman Empire and that this moderated paternal styles of discipline.[101]

Literary sources do indeed associate great physical coercion of children more with teachers than with parents. Even Cato the elder was said to have taught his own son rather than have him beaten about the head by a Greek slave, that is, a professional teacher.[102] This reminds us that the elite delegated many child-rearing functions to servants and professionals—nurses, attendants, pedagogues, and teachers. The philosopher Favorinus argued against wet-nursing because it could divert the affections that belonged properly to relations between parent and child,[103] but it was clearly usual for elite children to grow up surrounded by a variety of such caregivers, especially in early childhood. Slave children, too, might be assigned to nurses or other *educatores* to release their mothers for work, and the free poor seem also to have used foster parents and babysitters to some extent.[104] Parents (except perhaps slave parents)[105] still supervised these relations and took overall responsibility for the children, as do modern parents who send their children to schools and consult child health clinics. It is, however, likely that children often associated the most violent and persistent forms of discipline with people other than their parents. As I have argued more extensively in *The Roman Mother,* the relationship between parents and children was viewed in its totality in Roman society, with the emphasis on relations with the adult child, in contrast with the modern cultural emphasis on the parents and the very young child. Within the political elite, there were good reasons for family solidarity as the young men approached the age for political office, but other levels of society also show a continuing, albeit dynamic, relationship between the generations. Ideally, "children" retained their respect for parental guidance well into their adult years, a phenomenon examined in the following chapter.

### Deliberate Childlessness in Marriage

I argued earlier in this chapter and in chapter 3 that the late Republic saw an idealization of family life and a concomitant sentimental interest in young children. We have seen, too, that Roman marriage was undertaken for the express purpose of producing legitimate children, a purpose reflected in public and private media, and that the common expectation was that these children would perform a number of vital social and economic roles in the lives of their parents. And yet there was a perception by imperial times that Romans were avoiding parenthood.[106] The emperor Augustus sponsored two blocks of legislation in 18 B.C. and A.D. 9 to address what he clearly saw as a pressing social issue,[107] but more than a century later it was a literary commonplace that the upper class avoided procreation[108] and that childlessness was rewarded socially, even if it continued to incur penalties from the Augustan legislation.

This legislation apparently consisted of a *Lex Iulia* and a *Lex Papia Poppaea,* although even this basic information and the full content of the laws is uncertain because they were not well preserved in the Christian compilations of Theodosius and Justinian.[109] It was probably the Julian law of 18 B.C. that prohibited senatorial men from marrying freed slave women (*libertinae*) and laid down penalties for adultery and fornication as criminal offenses that could be tried on the initiative of an injured spouse or father or of any third party who could benefit materially from a successful prosecution.

The *Lex Papia Poppaea,* sponsored by the consuls of A.D. 9 (who were both bachelors), penalized those who had not married by a certain age (men between twenty-five and sixty, women between twenty and fifty) and rewarded those who produced legitimate children. The penalties were chiefly in the area of inheritance. Single people (*caelibes*) were ineligible to be heirs or legatees of any significant wealth by testament except from near relations, and those who were married but childless (*orbi*) could take only half the amount left to them.[110] This restriction applied even to wills between husband and wife. The restrictions did not apply to people with any surviving child; for example, a widow or divorcée who had had one child could remain unmarried, but if she was childless, she would attract the usual penalties unless she remarried within the specified period. The full privileges of the *ius liberorum,* however, were secured by producing three, four, or five children, depending on the status of the parent. The privileges included earlier candidacy for political office for men and freedom from *tutela* (quasi-guardianship) and the restrictions of the testamentary *Lex Voconia* for women.[111]

The purpose of the legislation is not entirely clear. There was a vague moral aim evident particularly in the strictures on adultery. Like the religious revival of Augustus's rule, it reflected an attempted return to the imagined morality of the Roman past.[112]

There was some suggestion that it was designed to replenish the native Italian stock to avoid its being outnumbered by citizens from freed slave (and predominantly foreign) backgrounds and to fill the army.[113] In practice, the Roman population in Italy was stabilized by immigration and the importation of slaves as well as by the reproduction of these groups. Dio has Augustus remind the Roman knights of this in ethnic terms: "It is sacrilegious and distasteful for our people to come to an end and the name of Romans to cease with us and our city to be handed over to others—Greeks and even barbarians."[114] If this was the intention, it was not well executed, for in spite of the privileging of the Italian freeborn population, most general incentives were available to the freed and to Romans of provincial origin. Moreover, the mass of rewards and penalties, concerned as they were with considerable inheritances and incentives for a political or public career, were not directed at the people at large so much as at the upper classes,[115] and it was the men of these classes who showed their displeasure by public demonstration.[116] Dio has preserved a version of a speech given by Augustus on such an occasion. The text is doubtless Dio's own, but the arguments show something of the official ideology promoting marriage and parenthood, while acknowledging the well-known problems associated with them.[117]

The laws themselves remained in force, with occasional emendations, for centuries. Many of the penalties and privileges mentioned above had to be balanced against other laws and customs (such as the traditional rights of *patroni* over the estates of freed slaves), and this meant continual changes to the workings of the laws, often decided on a casuistic basis. The sources are agreed that the laws failed in the aim of compelling Romans to marry and have more children[118] and were no more successful in eradicating adultery. The probable cause of family limitation by the poor was not systematically addressed, although later emperors instituted public programs—and encouraged private ones—to endow freeborn children of the Italian poor with basic subsistence. Such plans, usually termed alimentary schemes or foundations, were never on a massive scale but did demonstrate an official interest in encouraging the poor to procreate.[119]

This raises the question whether the Roman population, especially that of Italy, was indeed declining, and if so, why. From time to time people have theorized about the possibility of general sterility from the lead in Roman pipes or upper-class sterility from the lead used in certain processes.[120] There were certainly people who wished to have children and did not—Pliny the younger is a well-known example[121]—but the general assumption is that people deliberately limited their families to one or two children at most. Upper-class families who had more ran the risk of becoming déclassé with the successive partition of estates in each generation.[122] The poor were often incapable of supporting more children and apparently aborted them or, more likely, exposed them at birth.[123] Exposure was the usual fate of deformed children and was taken for granted as a general means of family limitation.[124] Contraception was known, but the combination of spells and bizarre ingredients (the heart of a lion killed in the arena formed part of one) inspire little confidence in its efficacy.[125]

The right of the father to expose a newborn baby, particularly if he suspected its paternity,[126] remained the strongest aspect of his "right of life and death" (*ius vitae necisque*) over his children and, like the rights of a master or mistress over the children of slaves, gave way only gradually to the changing ideology of Christianity. Laws against infanticide and exposure were introduced in the fourth century, but their confirmation by Justinian in the sixth century shows the persistence of the economic pressures and social assumptions behind the practice.[127]

Yet family limitation, even by means now regarded with abhorrence, does not imply a blanket dislike of or indifference to children as such. In modern countries, extensive contraception and abortion go hand in hand with an unprecedented emphasis on the welfare of the individual child.[128] There were a number of stock Roman sayings about the trials of parenthood, as there are in many contemporary cultures. Some were consciously adopted from Greek originals, like the comic poet Caecilius's

> Unlucky indeed is the poor man who brings
>    forth children to destitution![129]

The rich also noted the anxieties and uncertainties attendant on rearing children. The Stoic Seneca was drawing on a Greek tradition of a different kind (probably Theophrastus) when he composed his attack on marriage, which has come to us in scattered quotations via the Christian Hieronymus (St. Jerome). He argued that parenthood was a distraction from philosophy and its accompanying equanimity, since parents worried about children's health and safety and the children might end up being unsatisfactory and causing more worry.[130] This is clearly the kind of thing that the speakers have in mind in the senatorial discussion of A.D. 62 about legislation to prevent the childless from using a bogus adoption to gain equal status with a parent who has had all the usual worries and burdens of that state.[131]

Such parental grumbles, proverbial in so many cultures, seem to bear little relation to preference for family size or feelings for children who are reared. They become formulaic, and it is difficult to tell whether those who utter them mean them literally or see them as related to behavior. The Roman population did not die out, nor did the upper class as such disappear, although it showed a poor ability to reproduce itself socially and physically over many generations (Hopkins 1983; Corbier 1985). Large families, in the sense of many children born to the one marriage, do not seem to have been typical either before or after the Augustan legislation, but those children who were reared appear to have been the focus of parental affection and expectation. It will never be possible to determine what proportion of the Roman population did remain childless or how many chose that state rather than limitation of the family to their perceived economic capacity.

## Children of Varying Status

We have seen that the avowed purpose of Roman marriage was the production of children—that is, legitimate citizen children. Yet the Roman Empire contained vast numbers of slaves and foreigners incapable of having such children. Legal status was an important matter even in the Republic and early imperial times, before the formal hardening of categories that occurred in later antiquity.[132] In chapter 3 we looked at the rules governing *matri-monium iustum* or *iustae nuptiae* (a "proper marriage" between two people with *conubium* who could produce a freeborn Roman citizen child) and at some "irregular unions," that is, unions which did not fall within that definition but resembled marriage in their permanence and the reciprocal obligations and affection shown by the partners. Here we shall look at the implications for children of the range of options and at the differing status of children within the kinship group and within the residential group, both family and *familia*. In some cases, "status" rests not only on the formal legal standing of the child but on special relationships the child might have with other members (slave and free) of the wider household.

The complexity of the Roman law of status is a reflection of its liberality. In most contemporary Greek states (as in some places today), illegitimates probably could not be full citizens, and it was extremely rare for foreigners or slaves to gain admission to citizenship. Roman citizenship was therefore a relatively accessible and dynamic concept. It was possible for a child at birth to be a free Roman citizen but illegitimate; this would be the case for the child of a senator and a freed slave or of a soldier and a Roman woman, for example.[133] Illegitimacy as such was not a serious stigma in Roman society, although some disabilities were associated with it, such as exclusion from the imperial alimentary foundations designed to aid the children of the poor.[134] Children who were neither legitimate nor citizens suffered greater disadvantages, while slave children, by definition illegitimate, had virtually no rights. The child of a slave woman was necessarily a slave; the child of foreigners (*peregrini*) or of a Roman and a foreigner was a foreigner.[135] By universal law, illegitimate children normally took the status of the mother (Gai. 1.80), but the *Lex Minicia* of ca. 90 B.C. determined that the child must always take the lesser status in such cases, presumably to prevent foreigners and others from gaining citizenship for their children by liaisons with Roman women.[136] In any case, the socially approved norm was for women to marry men of their own or a higher social level, the exception to this being the marriage of free women with imperial slaves.[137]

Augustus's attempts to encourage procreation seem to have been aimed in part at increasing the ranks of the Italian freeborn citizenry. Although most of his "family legislation" would have affected the governing classes, he did engage in intermittent public relations exercises to indicate his desire for a general population increase. Apart from his address to the knights and his pointed appearance at the games with his own grandchildren, Augustus's public gestures included occasional distributions of largesse to the urban poor who could display freeborn children to him on his tours of the voting districts and singling out for personal praise an old man with numerous descendants.[138] His restrictions on the unlimited manumission of slaves (which would otherwise have swollen the citizen ranks) seem to have been intended to balance the servile and freeborn elements. Since the slaves commonly were of foreign origin, this might show an ethnic bias.[139]

Augustus also instituted a system of birth registration for citizen children which excluded illegitimate children, presumably as an inducement to citizens to marry fellow citizens and perpetuate their status. Yet the measures were not consistently applied, and it was even possible for those who had not been properly manumitted and had Latin status to gain full citizenship for themselves and their children.[140] Freed slaves had to have more children than the freeborn to qualify for the full privilege of parenthood (*ius liberorum*), but they could and did gain it.[141] Perhaps the most puzzling measure is the ban on the marriage of career soldiers, which made it impossible for a considerable body of male citizens to produce legitimate citizen children for a significant part of their adult life. Children who did not share their father's Roman citizenship were not in his power (*patria potestas*). This might not strike us as a disadvantage, but its association with citizenship meant that it was seen as a privilege—witness Gaius's lengthy discussion of ways in which *patria potestas* could be acquired by new citizens over their children.[142] Children not in the father's power had scant right to inherit from the father if he died without making a will. Moreover, a Roman testator or testatrix could not legally name a foreigner as heir or legatee.[143] This stricture was formally relaxed in the case of soldiers, probably under Nerva or Trajan,[144] and was important because the children of their unions with foreign women would be *peregrini*. Although disinclined formally to revoke the ban on soldier marriage until its apparent abolition under Septimius Severus ca. A.D. 200, successive emperors progressively relaxed the effects of the ban, and it became common to issue soldiers on discharge with the right to marry a foreign woman and produce legitimate Roman citizens from the mixed marriage. Children born "in camp" (*castris*), that is, during the father's term of service, probably were not covered by the usual postdischarge dispensation, but even they were permitted to acquire citizenship by themselves enlisting in the legions.[145] Quite apart from their legal position, they described themselves on epitaphs as the children of soldiers.[146]

We have already seen that one of the functions of children within the family was to perpetuate or raise the status of the whole group. Consider Cicero, who brought his own family from the municipal nobility into the political elite of Rome. He is said to have insisted on retaining the humble cognomen Cicero (meaning chick-pea), asserting that he would make it as famous as the names of the great figures of Roman history.[147] In the next generation, young Marcus Cicero hobnobbed with the children of the great political families.[148] The descent line of Cicero's equestrian friend Atticus eventually became absorbed into the imperial family.[149] It was even possible for the freeborn son of a freed slave to aspire to municipal or senatorial office.[150]

Other examples of social mobility over one or two generations are less well known but reveal themselves in tombstones, where the nomenclature sometimes allows us to reconstruct the gradual rise of a family to freed, then freeborn, status. In her study of lower-class Roman families, Rawson cites the example of Aelius Aelianus, who appears to have been a slave when his freed wife Claudia Zosime bore him a freeborn but illegitimate daughter, Claudia Dioscoris. His subsequent manumission would have enabled him to have legitimate children with Zosime.[151] They would then have taken his name instead of the mother's (as Dioscoris had done). The gentile name signified the family—in this case, the name Claudia (the masculine being Claudius)—while the additional, Greek name was probably the one by which each woman was normally known and might indicate a foreign slave origin. On manumission, a person took the gentile name of the former owner. A freeborn Roman boy had a *praenomen* (e.g., Marcus, Gaius, or Titus), followed by the gentile name, or *nomen* (Claudius, Iulius, Caecilius), and the *cognomen,* making up the full *tria nomina,* for example, Marcus Caecilius Secundus. A freeborn girl would bear the feminine form of her father's gentile name and sometimes the *cognomen,* for example, Caecilia Secunda. A freeborn citizen was also entitled to include filiation—for example, Marci *filius/a* (son/ daughter of Marcus), commonly shortened to M. *f.*—whereas a freed slave might indicate the former owner—Marci *libertus/a,* abbreviated to M l or M *lib*—and the current owner could even be recorded with a slave's name—Marci servus or Marci s. Although these rules were not followed consistently,[152] they have sometimes provided a means of marking the status of people recorded in tombstones. Rawson, Weaver, and others have used tombstones with such indicators to expand our knowledge of lower-class unions.[153]

The issues raised by such scholars have varied somewhat according to their interests. Some have concerned themselves primarily with technical aspects, such as the light the inscriptions throw on Roman law and practice regarding mixed (i.e., slave and freed) unions.[154] Others have assembled such information for numerical analysis with a view to reconstructing social aspects of family life in these circles. Thus Treggiari concluded that freed male slaves in the republican period were less inclined to commemorate (and presumably to acknowledge or care for) children born before their own manumission, while Rawson emphasized her finding that certain family members of varying status somehow maintained a common family life.[155] A number of inscriptions to parents who are characterized as mother or father and *patrona/us* testify to the fact that parents sometimes bought their own slave children and freed them, and in some cases children were able to perform this service for their parents.[156] Bradley looks also at contracts of sale, which reinforce the impression that owners were quite prepared to divide slave families (including separating mother and child) even when children were very small.[157]

This separation of mother and child was probably imposed by owners in order to maximize the productive and reproductive activity of slave women. Different types of evidence suggest that slave children, even if retained by the mother's owner, might have been assigned to wet-nurses and childminders who specialized in these activities. As early as the second century B.C. we hear in Plautus of a nurse who suckles the slave children born in the household (*vernae*),[158] and the legal sources refer incidentally to slave children being sent from an urban household into the country "to be nourished."[159] An inscription to fifty-year-old Licinius Meropnus refers to him as a *nutritor* of the dedicator's own children and of her *alumni*.[160] *Vernae* and *alumni* are interesting groups that recur tantalizingly in the inscriptions and other sources having to do with slave children. Although the precise nature of these classifications is open to argument, it can be assumed that they roughly equate to slave children born within the *familia* and to foundlings brought up as foster children (sometimes free, sometimes slave) within the household.[161]

Such children seem often to have occupied a relatively privileged position in the household in spite of their low formal status. Owners commemorating their early death often employ affectionate terms and diminutives on the epitaphs.[162] Martial has left a charming poem on the death of a *verna,* a little slave girl who died at the age of five, and the slave Felicio reminds Seneca in their mutual old age that he had once been treated as a pet (*delicium*) and given dolls on festival days.[163] Such children would sometimes have had a special relationship, such as foster brother of a free child, a relationship probably manifested by playing together as young children and observing a patronage link in later years.[164]

People without children of their own might sometimes rear a slave child—born in the household or taken up from where it had been abandoned—with the specific intention that the child should see to their proper burial and commemoration. The frustration of this wish by the premature decease of the child is sometimes lamented in epitaphs, as in the case of Turrania Polybia, regretting that seven-year-old Turrania Prepusa, a "sweet, delicate spirit," has been snatched away by the wickedness of fate and cannot perform the expected obligations for her *mamma,* a term used in a number of fostering and childcare relationships.[165] Genuine affection and self-interest are both evident, as they are in inscriptions by parents. The privileged position of some *vernae* is evident from their high incidence of early manumission and their occasional mention in wills.[166] *Alumni* might also be reared as heirs or with a view to serving in some specialized capacity—such as the heirs of Coelia Palaestine, who dutifully commemorated her death, or the famous teacher of rhetoric, Antonius Gniphus, who, though free-born, was abandoned as a child but was rescued and trained in literature.[167]

In some cases, the children born to slave mothers might have been fathered by the owner, which could explain their favored status,[168] but there is no real evidence that this was always the case. Augustan law restricted the number and type of slaves who could legally be manumitted by an owner (the *Lex Aelia Sentia*), but imperial jurists admitted exemptions in certain cases, such as cases of slaves who had saved the life of the owner or stood in a special relationship to the owner. The exemptions include slaves who were closely related, or a foster brother/sister or foundling (*alumnus*), although Marcianus thought it more appropriate for women than men to manumit foundlings. Ulpian attempted to formulate the general rule that any honorable relationship of affection should qualify the slave for manumission.[169]

Such exemptions must have been rationalized in response to applications based on these grounds. We need to remind ourselves, however, that these happy relationships were not necessarily the norm, for as we have seen, many slave children were simply treated as chattels or as potential income and separated from their parents by sale or even deliberately disabled to aid beggary.[170] Even Seneca's slave Felicio, petted as a child, is treated with contempt once his age makes him unattractive and unproductive.[171] The term *alumnus* and its cognates are less likely to be employed of an adult than of a child, which suggests that the special relationship might vary over the life cycle.[172] This also reinforces the argument that Romans did see childhood as a special stage of life, with an appeal of its own. It is also encouraging to note the occasions when affection and reciprocal obligation created bonds across the boundary between slave and free and that relationships formed within slavery could be maintained as family members gained freedom.

Status considerations could be overcome or supplemented by links of kinship or quasi-kinship and patronage between owners and slaves, for example, or between fellow slaves. Even the law, which tended from the time of Augustus to harden status boundaries, with restrictions on manumission and intermarriage between the categories, was softened in practice by the acknowledgment of family ties which transgressed the legislation. Neither slaves nor soldiers could have a proper marriage, and their children were not technically related to them in the strict legal sense as *agnati.* Yet Hadrian acknowledged the right of a soldier's children to succeed to his property, and the jurists allowed that an owner had a right to manumit his or her own children even where this transgressed the restrictions of the *Lex Aelia Sentia.* There was a certain tolerance of relationships crossing the formal status boundaries—even in the case of free women cohabiting with imperial slaves and bearing their children. In addition, relationships resembling kinship but based on affection and early child rearing were acknowledged socially and legally, so that children could sometimes gain benefits as *alumni, collactei,* and even *vernae* which their formal status might seem to preclude.

## Conclusion

It seems clear that childhood was acknowledged as a separate phase of life by the Romans, even if they were sometimes vague about its stages. In art children are depicted with the physical characteristics of their particular stage of life and, usually, in characteristically childish activities such as play (or being beaten). There was certainly a sentimental interest in children as such, and some parents were desolate at the death of small children (see plates 19—24). Nonetheless, infant mortality was high and by and large an accepted and expected part of life. Most children who died young were not formally commemorated, and parents who did openly grieve for them were commonly rebuked by their peers (even by the other parent) for such excess. The great cultural emphasis was undoubtedly on children as progeny who were able to continue the family name and cult, supply labor, inherit and maintain the family estate, support their aged parents, and supply them with proper funeral rites. Children outside the family structure, especially slave children, could be absorbed into the network of sentiment and patronage but were also treated as a straight economic investment, to be developed or sold in most cases. Those who took up exposed children to rear usually did so with a specific gain in mind: economic exploitation or personal services, including burial rites.

The modern concern for child welfare had no real equivalent in the ancient world. Depending on their social standing, young children were routinely apprenticed, put to heavy labor, sexually exploited, or beaten by schoolteachers. Roman law made certain concessions to youthful ignorance and the need to provide guardians for orphaned children, but the main emphasis was on the preservation of family estates rather than the protection of the individual child.

The Roman *paterfamilias,* whether father or paternal grandfather, had few legal checks on his treatment of his own children, but there is no indication that this power was regularly exercised to its full extent. Relations between parents and children were probably rather different from the usual expectation in the modern urbanized West, where parents, especially mothers, are intensely involved with their children in the early years. In many Roman families, young children would be cared for by nurses and babysitters (see plates 18 and 23), but the parents were closely involved in their later upbringing. Both parents were expected to give children moral training and oversee their formal education, and the deference to parents extended notionally well beyond childhood and even youth. There was still the possibility of strong emotional bonds between parents and children, and letters and tombstones alike leave us with the impression that relations were usually affectionate. This could be a built-in source bias, but it does suggest that overt expressions of affection for children were culturally acceptable. There is a contrast, for example, with the ways in which seventeenth-century puritans routinely wrote of their children.

Oddly enough, the best evidence for Roman parental emotions comes from the frequent statements about the problems of raising children, in particular the anxieties that parents typically suffer over their children's health and development. Such statements are relevant to the whole question of conscious family limitation in Roman society, where abortion and contraception were known and exposure was always an option. It is, however, extraordinarily difficult to establish whether childlessness was as extensive as the moralizing sources imply. It seems more likely that families were deliberately limited to one or two children and that this, combined with ancient living conditions, condemned many families to extinction. Augustus's legislation on marriage and the family certainly did not achieve the aim of boosting the Italian citizen population (especially the elite population). Ironically, his legislation encouraged informers (against adultery) and fortune hunters (*captatores*). Even these texts imply that many of the elite did have children, for *captatores* could not otherwise have qualified under the Augustan legislation to accept legacies and estates from the childless whom they allegedly courted.

The history of Roman childhood and relations between parents and children through the life course are still being reconstructed. The great bulk of the work has been done in the last twenty years, and more remains. Research in other disciplines on such aspects as wet-nursing practices, demographic patterns, and affective relations has had an impact on Roman scholarship, which has in turn provided valuable insights into the history of European childhood. As in other areas, the earlier preoccupation with prescriptive legal statements has been superseded by a more historical approach, which treats the law as one of a number of sources, each requiring its own kind of assessment. The implications of the parent-child relationship in Roman society were often explicitly different from those expressed in modern literature on the child (usually the young child), but many generalizations and attitudes will strike readers as familiar.

# Five

# The Family through
# the Life Cycle

*Family Ritual and the Life Stages*

I t has been said, off and on throughout human history, that one of the primary functions of the family is the protection of the dependent young and old.[1] Whatever the residential arrangements, the family usually spans several age groups, and its members perform certain basic offices for each other. All human infants are helpless, needing to be fed, cleaned, and physically protected by older members of the family—parents, grandparents, older siblings, aunts and uncles—or family dependents. The elderly can become, if not incapacitated, incapable of earning a full livelihood or even of feeding and cleaning themselves. We have seen that it was a stock view in the ancient world that children were in part an investment, an insurance against these common hazards. The benefits received by children from parents were explicitly linked with the solace they should provide for their parents in their old age and even in death.[2] Thus the generations were perceived as eternally linked in this reciprocal exchange.

This represents a fairly basic level of family obligation and solidarity which has its parallels in most societies. Progress through the stages of an individual's life would typically be marked by ceremonies grounded in the family; the festivities marking birth, coming of age, engagement, birthdays, and marriage would also consolidate the family unit, which would gather for these cheerful ritual occasions, as well as for the sadder ritual attendant on the death of a family member or its annual commemoration.[3] Family members would also assemble, in whole or in part, for occasions leading up to these rituals—discussions of suitable marriage candidates, consultations about coming business or political ventures, a party to mark the signing of a will by a family member—and in the face of crisis (divorce, debt, an impending lawsuit, political threats, unemployment, the mortal illness of a family member).

Literature contains passing references and more detailed descriptions illuminating these occasions and their role in consolidating the sense of kinship and reminding the individual at each stage of life of membership in the unit. The bias, as always, is in favor of the upper class, especially the political elite, but celebrations of birth, marriage, and death surely played their role in lower-class life, too, where such ceremonies often loom larger in the stark relief they provide from the daily grind of subsistence.[4] Pliny describes his attendance at such functions in the role of family friend as part of the normal social round at Rome: "For if anyone asks, 'What did you do today?' one might answer: 'I took part in the ceremony of assuming the *toga* of manhood, I attended engagement or marriage ceremonies, someone invited me to the signing of a will, another to legal representation, another to an advisory meeting.'"[5]

Ceremonies, parties, and sacrifices marked the progress of life for the freeborn. Once a new baby had been ritually raised up from the ground, the family would probably mark the occasion of the safe delivery by decorating the front door with flowers and making an offering at the family altar.[6] When the child was eight (if a girl) or nine (if a boy) days old, the parents would hold a party to mark the purification ceremony for mother and child and the naming of the child. This was the *dies lustricus* (day of ritual purification).[7]

The assumption of the *toga virilis,* the adult dress of the Roman male citizen, like the marriage ceremony and the funeral, was conducted partly in public, with a procession (*deductio*) and sacrifices conducted outdoors, and there were celebrations in the home of the boy as well.[8] Cicero mentions that even distinguished men were expected to attend this long procession, beginning early in the morning, for the sons of their poorest dependents (*clientes*).[9] The more public sacrifice in the forum was probably followed by a family party in the boy's home.

The customary ritual and festivities associated with weddings are described in chapter 3. As noted there, the formalities of a particular marriage form—the special meal eaten by the rare people who married by *confarreatio* and the ritual sale, *coemptio,* which marked one type of transference of the bride to the *manus* of her husband[10]—are to be distinguished from the religious and social ritual which would accompany virtually any wedding: the preliminary sacrifice by the bride of her childhood tokens; a procession by the bride, dressed in special clothes, to the home of the groom; the antics and jokes of young boys; the customs of lifting the bride over the threshold and adorning the doorway; special sacrifices at the conjugal home; and a feast with family and friends.[11]

Death was a less happy occasion for family gatherings. Members crowded around the deathbed, marking the perceived moment of death by crying out the name (*conclamatio*), kissing the dead person, laying flowers around the couch, and marking the doorway of the home with cypress for the duration of formal mourning. The body would be attended by mourners, especially women, and flanked by torches. The funeral procession to the burial ground, family tomb, or pyre would also be characterized by torches and by people showing their grief in ritual fashion, tearing at their cheeks and chest, hair disheveled, crying out laments (especially at untimely deaths), and dressing in mourning as shown by color or by the lower social standing of the dress.[12] Members of the family (like the physical house) were marked out by the need for ritual purification after the funeral.[13] This ceremonial, like the grouping of family remains in tombs or of the names on memorial tablets, marks the family as a unit and reminds all kin that kinship is an affiliation that cuts across other social groupings and transcends divisions between the generations and even between the living and the dead.

It was probably customary for the family to assemble not only to observe the ceremonial attached to the life stages of individual members but also to celebrate annual festivals marking the agricultural or state religious year. Many modern religious occasions have become such family celebrations even in very secular societies.[14] Festivals such as the annual feast of the ovens (Fornacalia) and the agricultural Terminalia might well have fallen into this category.[15] There were also other fixed, annual ceremonies specifically related to life stages and to the family unit. The Lemuria, in May, drew attention to the need to appease the dead as a group, but particularly family.[16] The dead were also remembered with offerings of flowers, wine, and prayers on the Day of Roses (11 May) and the Day of Violets (22 March).[17] The Lar or Lares of each household were closely associated with the welfare of the family unit and especially with the *paterfamilias*. The image was probably honored daily by the pious and given special attention on holidays with flowers, food, and libations. Similarly, the Genius was accorded special offerings when the *paterfamilias* celebrated a birthday or marriage.[18]

The Lemuria was a general festival of the dead. While people certainly commemorated dead friends on these occasions, or distant ancestors and kin, the concentration would have been on family members still recalled as individuals by surviving kin. The Parentalia, celebrated 8—21 February both publicly and privately, specifically linked the family and the dead. Unlike the more sinister Lemuria, it was, on the whole, a festive occasion in which the dead might be regretted but were not feared.[19] In many respects, it repeated the ritual of the individual funeral rites which were commonly renewed on the anniversary of the death of key family members—marked by a funeral meal at the gravesite, linking living and dead family members, regular offerings, and circumscribed behavior and culminating in a family party specifically for the living members of the family, the Caristia or Cara Cognatio ("beloved kindred"), on 22 February.[20]

This party involved a large feast, with contributions from all participants. Like Christmas or Thanksgiving, it was characterized by a notional family harmony, a deliberate dispelling of feuds.[21] Doubtless, like modern equivalents, it was in fact characterized by the reenactment or invention of such feuds, which seem in practice to stimulate the family unit as much as the idealized form of harmony that often coexists with them. Ovid lists the wicked family members who ought to be excluded from the happy feast: the bad brother, the mother who detests her own children, the father who lives beyond his family's patience (one assumes it is the impatient heirs who are deemed immoral), the child who is waiting for the mother's death, the nasty mother-in-law who persecutes her daughter-in-law. This is probably a poetic way of saying that these unpleasant sentiments should be banished, rather than that offending individuals should be excluded: a condition that, if implemented, or even contemplated, would greatly increase the scope for new feuds and alignments!

Ovid is specific about the rites to be performed: incense should be offered to the gods of the family line (*di generis*); the Lares dressed and given offerings of food; and at the end of the day, libations offered before the party retires, with a prayer and a blessing on the emperor, followed by a speech.[22] What he does not provide is precise information about the family members who would constitute this idyllically harmonious unit. It sounds as if it would be the wider, extended family. The term *cognatio* includes virtually any relations, and Ovid speaks of assembling the living blood relations and totting up the surviving degrees.[23] This is not definitive, for marriage involves two families with competing claims. The *sacra* might be taken to extend, like the *gentilicium,* through the male line, but that would still leave the question whether brothers (and possibly sisters?)[24] would eventually split into their own three-generation units as family size increased or the older generation died. This dynamic process is often witnessed in the modern world: thus the cousins who had played at the Caristia each year as children would gradually be sectioned off in parental groups as they grew up and had families of their own. February is not an ideal time for an outdoor gathering (even allowing for the shifting character of this month over Roman history), and even Italian families must acknowledge some limitations of space indoors in crowded homes.

### Change and Conflict within the Family

The ceremonies and different terms (*infans, puella, puer, liberi, adulescens, mulier, iuvenis, anus, senex*) for the life stages of the individual could also signal gradual changes in that individual's role(s) within the family group. In general, people gained in authority within the family and the outside community as they grew older. This extended to children, whose careers and opinions were taken more seriously as they progressed from childhood to youth, then to the duties of adult life, which might take them out of the parental residence but leave them within the family circle of influence and honor. The duties of children remained much the same throughout their advance: they were expected to respect their parents, defer to them, support them (materially and otherwise) in their old age, and see to their proper commemoration after death. These duties could even fall to a fairly young child, depending on the health and mortality of the parents. The difference would lie in the child's relative maturity and economic capability, which would affect that child's standing in the world outside the family—in the eyes of the law, dependents, social peers, social superiors—and would have some bearing on the individual's ability to protect and support parents and other relations.

We have seen that ritual bound the family group and regularly reminded its members of their links with each other across the living generations and with earlier generations of dead ancestors. The *paterfamilias* was, in a sense, the public representative of the family unit, interacting between its members and the law or the state. He managed the family estate, which was viewed as a continuing trust, although the law classed it as his personal property.[25] In theory, his rights over the person of his child *in potestate* were absolute, but we have seen that they were in practice tempered by custom and gradually by law. By the second century A.D., a *paterfamilias* who killed an adult child could be charged with murder unless he had carried out this action with the advice of the family *consilium*.[26] The *consilium* was an institution which represented family opinion and corresponded (and perhaps overlapped) with the *consilium amicorum,* the meeting of friends which could be called by a Roman to discuss or announce any important step.[27] It was a committee convened for specific purposes. We tend to hear about the gravest occasions, such as the traditional tale of the noble Lucretia, who summoned her father, her husband, and their friends to hear her account of her rape by Tarquin and to entrust them with the task of defending the family honor.[28] This is closely related to the function of the *consilium* as a family court and organ of discipline.[29] Tacitus refers twice to trials of noble women by their families on criminal charges (adultery and foreign superstition) as if this were an archaic revival in imperial times,[30] but the imperial legal presumption that a *paterfamilias* would normally take disciplinary action on the advice of a *consilium* implies the continued existence of the institution.

We have already discussed the family *consilium* for which we have the most detailed account. It was held at Antium (Anzio) in June 44 B.C., during the turmoil following Caesar's assassination in March. It was attended by Brutus (a leading assassin), his mother Servilia, his wife (and cousin) Porcia, his half sister Iunia Tertulla, and her husband Cassius. It was also attended by friends of the family—the circumstance to which we owe Cicero's report.[31] The situation was urgent and extraordinary, but the composition of the *consilium* was probably the core unit of the family, which formed the basis of any *consilium* called for more everyday purposes, such as decisions about marriages or gatherings to celebrate births or to rally support for political office in more stable times. This core unit seemed, then, to include different age groups and half-relations as well as both sexes. It also included more than one *paterfamilias* (Brutus and Lepidus), and Servilia, apparently the oldest member of the family, seems to have presided over proceedings. We have no way of determining the age at which "children" were included in the decision-making group. It could be that it was a gradual process, with no fixed age and stage markers, much as it is in modern families.

The composition of the Antium council reminds us of the major change in family relations brought about by marriage, which increased the number of people linked by kinship and affinity and introduced new possibilities of solidarity and conflict between the generations and the extension of the family into a new generation, which linked the marriage groups further. Marriage highlights the fact that people fulfilled different roles within families—the same person is daughter, mother, sister, aunt and has varying duties and authority in each role. The married daughter visiting her mother might seek and provide advice. A mother, no matter how wealthy and influential, might need the daughter's solace in widowed old age as much as an indigent widow needs the material support of her adult children or a young woman in childbirth needs the help of *her* mother.[32] This sort of shift is not unique to the Roman family, but we need to remind ourselves that any picture we form of family relations is but one snapshot from a changing series of pictures.

As we saw in chapter 1, crisis was often the cue for a show of family solidarity, but the more common disruption caused by changes in married status could also remove people from their central role in the family unit. Thus a widow or divorcée who remarried ceased to be part of the household and in most senses of the family of her husband, but she retained kinship and its reciprocal obligations with her children. Similarly, a widower or divorced son-in-law might maintain certain duties towards his in-laws, but these would not be the same as they were during the marriage.[33] Although the marriage link was invoked, the relation was more like that between family friends than between kin. If there were a child of the dissolved marriage, this would represent a continuing link between families, but the death of the child would virtually end any kinlike connections. This could be what happened in the case of Cicero's infant grandson Lentulus, child of Dolabella and the dead Tullia.[34] The most dramatic example of such an alteration in family relations is perhaps the rift between Caesar and Pompey following the death of Caesar's daughter Julia and her baby.[35]

Within the Roman political elite, the need to amass support and fortune for gaining political office reinforced the lengthy dependence of the younger generation. Fathers, mothers, aunts, and uncles all had to pool their patronage and influence for the purpose.[36] Marriage increased the number of kin who could be called upon for routine and critical help and who could call for such help in their turn.[37] This probably accounts for the relatively early age at first marriage for the elite, in which women typically married in their mid or late teens and men in their early twenties.[38]

Yet marriage, with the introduction of new family and even household members and a reallocation of family roles, also increased the possibilities of conflict. The post-Freudian assumption of the modern West is that conflict occurs between children and the parents of the same sex. If this is so, it could be less for reasons of sexual rivalry (simplistically defined) than for the material goods and status associated with the position of the parent. Father-son conflict has been represented historically as competition for control of the family goods or power within the family circle and plays an important part in Roman conceptions of ideal and feared family behavior, as we shall see below. There is very little suggestion in the sources of mother-daughter conflict,[39] but this could reflect masculine interest, which would be more directly involved in father-son conflict and in conflict between in-laws. Cicero's letters to Atticus about the marriage of Cicero's brother Quintus to Atticus's sister Pomponia are interesting. One letter, clearly written in response to a complaint by Atticus about Quintus, provoked an angry account of a scene which Cicero witnessed. It has a very familiar ring—both the pettiness of the reported behavior of husband and wife and the highly partisan nature of the accounts which invariably follow such incidents are familiar features of family quarrels in all periods: "As soon as we got there, Quintus most politely said, 'Pomponia, you ask the ladies and I'll invite the men.' Nothing, as far as I could see, could have been more agreeable than his manner and expression, let alone his words. But she retorted (within our hearing), 'I am a guest here myself!' Then Quintus whispered to me, 'You see! I have to put up with this sort of thing every day!' . . . What more do you want? Nothing, in my view, could have been more conciliatory than my brother, nothing more objectionable than your sister; and I'm leaving out a lot of things that got up my nose more than Quintus's."[40]

There is a considerable anthropological literature on the proverbial disruptiveness of women, particularly in systems which prize the solidarity of coresident brothers and view women as interlopers in the domestic group, whose competition with sisters-in-law for the priority of their own children (and husbands) is often the trigger for separation of goods and households into conjugal units.[41] Although the admired ideal Roman family was traditionally the joint household of married brothers, the norm in Italy of the late Republic and early Empire seems to have been separate conjugal households.[42]

If sisters-in-law did not share a common residence, this reduced some of the possibilities for conflict. The Roman custom of partible inheritance might have reduced competition for different shares of the family wealth, another common cause of conflict. It is perhaps significant that the main conflict we hear about concerns the imperial family, which had wealth enough to go around but only one supreme office, with no established form of succession to it. The common perception was that there was rivalry between the imperial princes Drusus and Germanicus and their wives, that they vied for general popularity but particularly for marks of favor for the men and their male children in competition for the imperial succession.[43] One need not take this too seriously—it is unlikely that the Princess of Wales and the Duchess of Kent are as interested in this sort of thing as the modern media imply—but it is suggestive that Augustus's sister Octavia was reputed to have spent her life mourning the death of her son Marcellus and being particularly resentful of her sister-in-law Livia, whose sons and grandsons thereby became eligible for consideration for the supreme office.[44] The women are represented in these stories, as in the more common stereotypes from other cultures, as jealous guardians of the rights of their own children against those of the husband's siblings, but as we have seen, much of this competition was precluded by the nature of Roman inheritance, while competition between brothers-in-law was relatively easy to end by means of divorce in a system in which married women identified with the interests of their natal kin.[45]

Modern studies of Mediterranean households sometimes locate

particular conflict between mother-in-law and daughter-in-law when the two live in the same house. The relationship typically begins with the young daughter-in-law being subordinate to her mother-in-law, but as the young bride becomes a mother, then a matron with mature responsibilities, she might eventually eclipse her husband's mother in authority. Roman literature provides few examples of an older mother living in the same household as her married son. Caesar's mother Aurelia is presented by Plutarch as a stereotype of the watchful and suspicious mother-in-law of a flighty young bride—an image which suits her role in the Bona Dea scandal, in which she and her daughter testified that the reckless noble Clodius Pulcher, dressed as a woman, had gate-crashed the all-women's state religious festival in Aurelia's home, in the hope of gratifying his passion for Caesar's young wife.[46] Whatever the reality of that specific situation, it could have been building on a stock image transferred from lower in society, where it would have been more common for a young married couple to live with the husband's mother. In the second century B.C., Cato the elder's daughter-in-law lived in his home.[47] Ovid's reference to the mother-in-law who persecutes her daughter-in-law might suggest joint residence, while Juvenal seems to assume that some daughters-in-law lived in a two-generation household.[48] These passing references are insufficient basis for any strong argument, either for residence or for stock notions of conflict. As we shall see below, the image of the stepmother—and to a lesser extent, of the step-father—as a cause of conflict and injustice within the family was the predominant prejudice. These passing references might indicate a certain popular presumption of conflict, but separate residence, stock inheritance practices, and ancient patterns of mortality would all have affected the intensity and likelihood of in-law conflict between women. The possibility that a daughter-in-law might defy a father-in-law does not even seem to arise.

Indeed, if Roman folklore was weak on tales of the scheming or lazy daughters-in-law and wicked mothers-in-law, it was rich in suspicion of the stepmother, a common figure in a society of easy divorce and fairly frequent maternal mortality. It is easy to cite examples of stepmothers who had good relations with their children: Octavia made a public relations exercise of her benevolence; Seneca's mother apparently lived happily with her stepmother from early childhood; Fannia was a model substitute mother to Helvidius Priscus in the tight circle of the Stoic opposition; and the emperor Galba actually took the family name of his stepmother Livia.[49] Yet Tacitus referred to the *novercalia odia* (stepmotherly hatred) of Livia for Augustus's daughter and grandchildren.[50] The suspicion of murderous impulses and undue testamentary influence rest on the assumption that a stepmother would do all in her power to advance her own children over those of her husband's earlier marriages.[51] It must have been difficult to avoid tension in families, given this kind of expectation, but concrete examples are sparse in the sources.[52] In the modern European folklore tradition, the wicked stepmother typically maltreats helpless young children, but in many Roman cases the conflict might have originated with adult children of the former marriage jealous of their property rights. The decision by some men to take a lower-class concubine rather than a second wife was applauded as a sound and respectable way of avoiding such conflict.[53]

Stepfathers, too, were perceived as a possible threat to the interests of their stepchildren. Although there are examples of beneficent stepfathers,[54] legal means were eventually adopted to prevent their inroads into the estates of stepchildren.[55] In his surviving *Apologia,* Apuleius assured the North African jury that he had done his utmost to heal the breach between his wife and her sons but his stepson brought charges of magic against him.[56] The Bacchic scandal of 186 B.C. was sparked off when the youth P. Aebutius reported the alleged crimes and obscenities performed in the rites followed by his mother and stepfather. The stepfather, says Livy, did not want to have to give accounts of his management of the boy's estate and sought to have a sinister hold over him by initiating him into the allegedly perverted cult.[57] This was obviously a family with conflict. The details will not stand factual examination, but the image of the wicked stepfather with his hands itching to grasp the rightful fortune of his stepchild is the constant and corresponds to the recurrent image of the murderous, scheming stepmother. The sketchy anecdotal and conventional evidence makes it difficult to form a clear picture of what actual step-relationships were like. The portraits do not allow for variations at life stages, although such variation is typical of conflict within families. The accounts might represent fears and fantasies more than reality. But, as we shall see below, this can often be said of the perception of relations between the generations.

We have seen that the Roman political system imposed on its members the need for a certain degree of kinship solidarity and a prolonged dependence by the young on the support of the older generation. Yet the time might come when the younger generation grew impatient of this relationship. Elite sons sometimes turned against their elderly mothers,[58] and Roman fathers certainly suspected that undutiful sons might wish to supplant or even murder them.[59] The theoretical extent of *patria potestas* was almost unlimited in the early Republic and modified very slowly within the legal system. The ancient sources reflect the paranoia of fathers or perhaps the guilt of grown men remembering their own youthful resentment of these wide-ranging paternal powers and the daunting fact that they normally ended only with the life of the *paterfamilias*. Both the paranoia of fathers and the tendency to dwell on and repeat the revolting tales of fathers who executed their sons reveal a strong cultural stress on father-son conflict.[60] Predictable sentiments accompanied the passing of the *SC Macedonianum*, directed against loans made to sons *in potestate* who borrowed against the expectation of paternal inheritance, and the law was traditionally assumed to have followed a parricide by a debtor son.[61]

The fact that children *in patria potestate,* whatever their age, had so few rights could well have created tensions which erupted from time to time throughout the life cycle. Veyne argues that Roman sons were able to endure the situation only because so many fathers died before their sons reached adulthood. Computer simulations of Roman demographic trends suggest that fewer than two-thirds of Roman men had a living father by the time they were in their twenties. Daube insists that the oppressive system of *patria potestas* applied only to the propertied elite, because lower-class sons would naturally keep whatever small goods they could accumulate.[62] Neither Veyne nor Daube considers the position of

a grim struggle for power between the middle-aged and the elderly. In the end, the middle-aged are more likely to win. Biology, demography, and—moralizing about the aged aside—public opinion are on their side. In many cultures, there is a "hand-over" from father to son in which the aged farmer or craftsman passes on effective leadership of the family household and livelihood to the next generation. In ancient Greece, this seems to have happened on the son's marriage.[68] Mitford amusingly represents this type of process as a means for the landed English aristocracy to evade death duties in the modern world.[69] The more plausible consequence, which she represents elsewhere in fiction, is the eternal battle of wills whereby the old lord is constantly crying out against the methods of the young successor.[70]

The institution of *patria potestas,* while tempered by custom, the family *consilium,* and eventually by law, probably made this practice less common in Roman society. The fact that the Romans did not have the standard Greek laws requiring children to maintain their parents could be a reflection of this lifelong authority of the *paterfamilias,* who is assumed to have reigned supreme in his own home, in the fashion of Appius Claudius, Cato the elder, or Augustus himself, well into old age.[71] In fact, the absolute exercise of his authority would have been limited by a number of factors— public opinion, personal inclination, the family *consilium,* the particular domestic economy, his own health, and patterns of residence which allowed apprentices, married daughters, scholars and aspiring politicians of the upper class, soldiers, and farm laborers to live apart from their parents. It is surely true that some Romans yearned for the death of their father and that some fathers were tyrannical and brutal, but we need to separate fear, fantasy, and moralizing from the likely pattern of everyday life.

Roman imperial rescripts and opinions contain relatively little on the neglect of aged parents by middle-aged children or disputes about the management of family estates by parents. Children had some recourse after a parent's death against an unfair disposition of the patrimony or the maternal inheritance, but it was incumbent on the child to demonstrate that exclusion had not been merited.[72]

In his treatise on old age, Cicero refers to the (probably apocryphal) Athenian case in which the sons of the famous tragedian
Sophocles had taken him to court in his old age to have him de-
clared incompetent. The main character of the treatise, Cato the elder, refers to a similar Roman rule: "quem ad modum nostro more
male rem gerentibus patribus bonis interdici solet" ("whereby it is
customary after our tradition that a legal restraint is applied to fathers mismanaging their affairs"), but this seems to be a general
rule for anyone whose irresponsible spending habits or unstable
mentality endangers the future of an estate that he has inherited
on intestacy.[73] The rule is fairly limited in application and does not
presume that older men become financially incapable. It is similar
to the general provisions against abuse of a family estate and based
on the assumption that the current owner of the estate is in effect a
trustee for life. The threat of disinheritance against disobedient
children does not figure as much in Roman literature as it does in
nineteenth-century English novels, where it plays a stock role in
the representation of generation conflict. As we shall see, the
elderly often felt neglected in Roman society, but the emphasis is
on the public sphere and the attitude of younger men as a group
towards older men, as in the common lament: "They would continually complain . . . that they were shunned by those by whom
they had once been assiduously cultivated."[74] Similarly, there are
many stories about generation conflict in which the impetuous-
ness of senatorial youth revolts against the slower ways of the established statesmen and generals.[75]

On the whole, then, there is a strong literary tradition of generation conflict at Rome but a dearth of attested examples. Old fathers and young rakes are pitted against each other in comedy.[76] In
his guide to authors, Horace argues that old men are properly
characterized in literature as criticizing the young and comparing
them unfavorably with the youth of their own day.[77] There are leg-
ends and personal reminiscences of such processes. Compare
Cicero's comment as an old man, "For I recall the hopeless prog-
nostications of those who were old men when I was a youth. Perhaps I am now following in their footsteps and indulging in the

vice of my stage of life." There is also ample evidence of paternal suspicion of sons' motives, but there are few genuine examples of the parricide that obsessed Roman fathers and has apparently fascinated some modern authors.[78] The family in any society is typified by change, a process often accompanied by conflict. Young wives and husbands, fathers and sons, in-laws and cousins, will often spend time adjusting to new situations (notably marriage) before equalizing into a pattern of relative tolerance. Some modern commentators have even represented the family as a permanent battleground for power between the sexes and the generations.[79] Certainly the common human stress on kinship solidarity is an attempt to check the tendency of kin to conflict,[80] but solidarity *is* also a characteristic of families, and the Roman family is no exception to either of these trends.

## Attitudes towards the Old in the Roman Family

It is frequently assumed or stated that traditional societies typically show respect for the aged. It has also been said that retirement is a relatively modern concept.[81] While both beliefs can to an extent be justified from the ancient evidence, they require modification. After all, ancient literature is full of the lament that contemporary youth lack the respect of the previous generation for the wisdom and experience of their elders, so it could well be a universal fantasy that we once respected our elders (especially our parents) more than our children respect us and that earlier generations showed progressively greater regard for age and experience.

Before examining the situation of the old in the Roman family, we need to establish what the Romans considered to be old in a society in which the median life expectancy was about twenty-seven years for women and about thirty-seven for men and relatively few people lived to see their grandchildren.[82] Romans are not always precise about what they mean by *old,* and some have even argued that there was no ancient perception of old age as a distinct stage of life. This view has rightly been refuted by Eyben,[83] and it is clear from the ancient texts that there were conventional literary stereotypes about old men (*senes*) and old women (*anūs*) which in part reflected society's view of the aged and sometimes the anxieties and regrets of the elderly themselves.

Macrobius (*Sat.* 2.5.2) introduces his jokes about Augustus's daughter Julia with the statement that she retained an unsuitable girlish frivolity at an age when most women are accepting their elderly status: her age was thirty-seven! This is not, however, typical. Cicero's mind was turning in this direction when he wrote *de Senectute* at the age of sixty-one and dedicated it to his sixty-four-year-old friend Atticus to alleviate the impending "burden" (*onus*) of old age.[84] Like Seneca's work on the same topic, it seems to take the age of sixty as the approximate beginning of old age. The fact that retirement from the Roman senate customarily dated from that age reinforces the view that this was the accepted marker, and it conforms to the examples given in Cicero's text, although there are scattered applications of the terminology of old age to people in their forties and fifties.[85]

This is not so different from our own concept of old age, which is also a little vague and elastic but is defined in terms of retirement custom, pension benefits, and other social markers as beginning at sixty or sixty-five. The great difference is surely that a much smaller proportion of the ancient population attained this age. The Roman domestic group, characterized in its own mythology as a three-generation household dominated by an aged patriarch, would seldom have included grandparents or great-aunts and great-uncles, resident or otherwise. The other difference is that many households would include aged dependents having an intimate association with the family and a status conferring claims of patronage very close to those of kinship.

Did the ancients respect the aged and look after them? Certainly Roman society paid some institutional marks of deference to age. Cicero notes that in the political sphere, the senate's name had a semantic connection with age and seniority was literally a determinant of precedence in giving one's opinion in the senate or on other magisterial boards.[86] The laws and practices of the ancestors were described in the reverential expression *mores/mos maiorum*, which could be used to justify steps in the public sphere.[87] Within the family, the supremacy of the older generation was enshrined in the institution of *patria potestas,* which gave such far-reaching powers to the oldest surviving male ascendant. Cicero has Cato look back with admiration on the example of the aged, blind Appius Claudius, who managed to tyrannize over his family, household, and *clientela.*[88] Women had no formal position corresponding to that of the *paterfamilias,* but in practice a woman tended to accumulate authority within the family as she grew older, although this would be affected by factors such as maternity and widowhood, which enhanced her status in Roman society.[89]

We hear most of the expectation of care in old age when this expectation is frustrated by the death of children or grandchildren. The long inscription *CIL* 6.18086, to the two-year-old Flavius Hermes, reproaches him for failing to live up to his claim that he would be his grandmother's support in her old age.[90] Seneca, consoling Marcia on the death of her adult son, imagines her expressing the conventional lament at the loss of a son in his prime (*iuvenis*), the "support and glory" of his parents, and crying out, "There will be nobody to protect me, to shield me from contempt."[91] He reminds her that she has daughters and grandchildren to comfort her in her old age and that the grandchildren need her guidance.

Such references convey a benign impression of relations between the generations, especially between parents and children or grandchildren. It is to be expected that commemorations of grandparents and other elderly relations on tombstones should emphasize positive feelings. But hardheaded counts of surviving tombstones show that relatively few people did commemorate grandparents, and even parents were not commemorated as often as one might imagine.[92] The nobler genres of epic, oratory, and history propagated that much-discussed Roman ideal of *pietas* by prescription, example, and denunciation.[93] The stress tends to be on the duty to older generations, but it is important to note that *pietas* was a reciprocal quality, owed also by the older to the younger.[94]

The genres of comedy, satire, and even erotic poetry, however, often reveal a different attitude towards the aged, one of contempt, ridicule, and disgust. The old men, the fathers of Plautus, are almost uniformly ludicrous figures and conform to Horace's prescription about the proper comic characterization of someone at this stage of life: fearful and hesitant, inactive, greedy and miserly, querulous, constantly praising the past and criticizing contemporary youth.[95] Juvenal mocks the commonplace wish for long life with a long description that is probably more pitiable than he intended: an old man is physically repulsive, a burden to his wife, children, and other relatives, incapable of sex and even of eating with dignity, his mental faculties so deranged that he cannot recognize his intimates. Even if he has not decayed, he experiences the horror of surviving his own children, wife, brothers, and sisters, living out his overlong existence in perpetual mourning.[96] These descriptions draw on a literary and probably a popular tradition about the trials of old age as reflected in specific descriptions of individuals[97] and in serious treatments of old age in general, as when Cicero passes on the stock laments of old men (that their enjoyments are curtailed, that the young avoid them) and the usual complaints *about* the old (that they are foolish, forgetful, garrulous and irascible).[98]

Not all literary treatments are concerned with the position of the aged in the family. Most are about the stages in the life of a citizen male, especially a senator, in its more public aspects.[99] The stock figure of the old woman, perceived in these literary forms from the masculine perspective, is sinister, repellent, and even dangerous. The women who figure in Horace's works as objects of passion in their youth (particularly lower-class women) become objects of men's contempt in their old age. The representation of older women in prose sources and epitaphs, where they are seen as individuals in family roles, is generally much more positive.[100] It is in the more impersonal group portrait that a certain primal hostility emerges.

The avowed aim of Cicero's *de Senectute* is to help him and Atticus confront this stage of life, on the assumption that it is a hardship.[101] Seneca's shorter work on the same subject, which argues that old age is in some ways the culmination of life's experiences, begins with a personal anecdote. In making the rounds of his country estate, he had been horrified at the poor state of repair of the building and trees and mortified at being told that this was a natural result of their extreme age, for if buildings and trees established in his lifetime were suffering, what did this mean about his own state?[102] This irresistibly leads him to philosophize, but the interesting thing about the epistolary essay is the revealing opening, told at his own expense, about his immediate responses on being forced to acknowledge that he is old. He admits that he took out his annoyance on the farm steward, then on an old man sitting by the doorway:

> "Who is that decrepit creature, all set to be put down?" I asked. "For he is facing the door [that is, like a corpse laid out for the funeral]. Where did you pick him up? Why did it amuse you to take up some strange corpse?"
>
> But the old man said, "Don't you recognize me? I'm Felicio. You used to bring me little dolls. I'm the son of the steward, Philositus—your little pet [*deliciolum tuum*]."[103]

Seneca, unabashed, continued to make cruel jokes about the appearance of this erstwhile favorite, younger than himself, which suggests that respect for the aged did not necessarily cross the status barriers.

This is a reminder that old age could be a burden indeed to the lower classes. We have seen that even members of the upper class, such as Helvia, feared contempt and neglect in old age[104] and that Flavius Hermes' grandmother—certainly from a much lower social group but still able to afford a lengthy, personalized memorial to the child—extracted an explicit promise from the toddler that he would support her in her old age.[105] For the poor, this would have been, not just a playful pact, but an earnest consideration. In his study of apprenticeship contracts and the conditions of child labor in the Roman world, Bradley points out that it was essential for members of this social level to provide children, if they could, with the means of a livelihood that might benefit the parents in their old age.[106] Greek cities often required children, or perhaps only sons, to support their parents.[107] Roman law contained no precise equivalent to this regulation, perhaps because *patria potestas* technically entitled a father of any age to his children's earnings and acquisitions, but the idea was clearly current.

Aged servants might also hope for some protection in old age from their owners or patrons. Felicio, the aged slave of Seneca's essay, did at least have shelter and sustenance, even if he had to bear with Seneca's verbal abuse. He was not cast out, as the cost-efficient Cato recommended for unproductive servants.[108] Plutarch's disapproval of Cato's attitude some four centuries later is encouraging, but legislation passed under the emperor Claudius depriving owners of any sick and aged slaves whom they abandoned reminds us that many Romans took a very hardheaded approach to slavery.[109] There could clearly be diverse views on the proper attitude of an owner towards slaves. There are, however, many affectionate or dutiful inscriptions to slaves, especially those who were involved in the care and education of young children, who would be more intimately linked with the family than were most servants.[110] Ties of affection and obligation—hedged at different stages of life by status considerations—ruled such relationships. Pliny praised the girl Minicia Marcella for having the proper degree of regard for her nurses and other attendants and himself provided his old nurse with a small farm as her pension.[111] But Cicero had pointed out that time alone did not determine the strength of friendship, since this did not happen in relationships with such underlings.[112] The nurse might have good reason to regret her charge's emergence from early childhood,[113] and young men who showed some respect for their authoritative fathers might feel freer to berate a restrictive pedagogue who had once had power over them, as in the situation Martial represents:

> You used to rock my cradle, Charidemus, and you were the constant guard and companion of my childhood. . . . You permit me nothing, but all licence for yourself. You denounce me, you keep close watch, you complain, you heave sighs. . . . Cut it out! My girl-friend can tell you that I am now a man.[114]

In the last analysis, servants were *not* genuinely part of the family, just part of the household. They were dependent on the whims and circumstances of individual owners. If they were lucky, they were thought to merit some upkeep in old age and a place in a family memorial or a commemorative plaque to themselves,[115] as well as some consideration in the patronage process: people were permitted to forgo the restrictions of the *Lex Aelia Sentia* on manumission if the person to be manumitted were kin or bound by special ties, such as a foster brother or sister, or had performed outstanding or intimate personal service.[116]

In the *Dialogus,* one of the speakers condemns the modern habit of handing newborn Roman children over to a nurse and/or some *vilissimus* slave unfit for any other task.[117] One thing that made slaves unfit for anything but childcare in the Roman view was age.[118] This is not an uncommon assumption; there are many societies in which aged relatives or dependents care for young children, which sometimes leads to an attractive alliance between the generations. The childish terms *mamma, tata,* and their diminutives have therefore been associated by different scholars with foster parents, servants, parents, and grandparents, but I am skeptical about our ability to assign definite roles to these expressions.[119] The exigencies of ancient demography also gave some grandparents, particularly grandmothers, the role of rearing their grandchildren, and sometimes commemorations mention this role specifically, as in *CIL* 6.1478 to an "avia carissima educatrix dulcissima" ("most beloved grandmother, sweetest bringer-up").[120] Just to counter this picture, let us add the more severe example of Urgulania, influential friend of the Augusta Livia, who sent her grandson a dagger as a broad hint when it was clear that he was guilty of the murder of his wife. Or the cheering portrait of another *avia educans,* the splendid Ummidia Quadratilla, who sent her youthful grandson off to his studies whenever her personal troupe of mime artistes staged a performance.[121]

The stereotypic laments of the aged reflect the near-universal anxiety that this stage of life would be characterized by neglect and want. The occasional references to the need for protection (*praesidium*) suggest that even the wealthy felt in need of the support of the younger generation, especially children, but the glimpses of the elderly afforded us by the ancient sources some-

155

times show them being tended more by their peers—as in the case of Fannia, who had cared for her ailing relation, the Vestal Iunia, then fallen victim to the same lung complaint. The activities of Ummidia Quadratilla, as described by Pliny, are those of a luxurious and frivolous existence in which she was sought after by friends whom Pliny characterizes as legacy hunters. Occasional glimpses in literature of the old show them enjoying their pleasures in society—for example, the tipsy old couple returning from the large picnic on the outskirts of Rome after celebrating the Anna Perenna festival.[122]

The fears expressed are those of being neglected or burdensome and even disgusting to one's own family and an object of ridicule to the young in general. We have seen that the realities of ancient existence meant that there were far fewer old people. The stock conflict in Plautus's plays between elderly parents and youthful sons, like the recurrent fear of parricide and rumors of an earlier age in which old men had been killed by the community, probably reflected deep-seated fears as much as common domestic situations.[123] The ancients clearly collected examples of those who had defeated old age by maintaining their faculties and proving an inspiration and source of hope to others.[124] Yet as Juvenal rightly points out (10.240—45), this means outliving family members, a fearsome thing in itself. Although it is not stressed by the sources, it also means outliving friends and even acquaintances who share common memories, which perhaps affects personal happiness as much as loss of health might do.[125]

People in the ancient world feared old age for much the same reasons as moderns do. Each hoped that his or her old age would be different—that the retention of physical and mental faculties and the comfort of a caring and dutiful family would shield them from material want and the derision of the world and provide them with a proper funeral. The ancients also hoped explicitly for dutiful personal commemoration after death and incorporation in the group family rites in perpetuity. The poor had particular reason to be anxious and relied on the reciprocal system by which children would care for parents or patrons would extend some help to them in life and perhaps in death. Many people were doomed to have these hopes frustrated: even wealthy family tombs were not regularly maintained beyond a few generations, most of the poor were buried in mass graves, and many old people must have been homeless and destitute for the lack or disregard of family or patronage. But the ideal persisted and was also honored by some. Attitudes towards the elderly (again as now) were a conglomerate of pious generalizations, cruel humor, genuine concern, and casual kindness.

## Conclusion

The recording of the stages of life is affected by the domination of the ancient sources by those in middle life, particularly by men. Generalizations about the role of children, youths, and the elderly tend to be wishful moralizing—that children should respect their elders, that the aged deserve respect and material support—or a pastiche of comic or sentimental stereotypes: the cute baby, the model child (invariably dead) wise before its time, the spendthrift youth, the silly old man, the watchful mother-in-law, the scheming second wife/stepmother, the poisonous old witch, the lovable patriarch or matriarch. Actual practice is, as always, more difficult to gauge but seems on the whole to accord with common human practice, whereby most family members progress through life taking on increasingly responsible roles, particularly after parenthood, then phasing out somewhat as they pass into old age.

*Pietas* laid down certain claims within the family which ideally governed relations between the generations: "It was natural that parents should beget, rear and educate children, and it was natural that children in return should honour and obey parents, give them material and psychological support, including grandchildren, comfort in old age, and burial."[126] Indeed, this would seem "natural" by the ideology of most societies, but as in most societies, it did not necessarily happen in quite that way every time. Fathers feared revolts from their sons, the elderly and those approaching old age feared neglect and derision. Conflict is as much a part of family life as harmony, and some events could fairly predictably spark off confrontations and realignments. In spite of curses and pleas on tombstones, graves were reused or desecrated, and parents were far more likely to commemorate children than the converse. Children were exposed at birth or abused by parents, owners, teachers, and employers. Some of these factors would loom larger in certain families than in others. Most would be a sloppy amalgam of solidarity and conflict, pious intentions and avowals and inconsistent performance.

The essentially Roman institution of *patria potestas* put great theoretical power in the hands of the oldest male in any family group—a power tempered by custom, individual preference, and the fact that so many men were likely to die before their children grew up. In spite of some evidence of conflict between father and son, and recurrent fears of young men by the dominant older men, Roman society furnishes relatively few examples of violent resentment of paternal power. There was a certain ritual clash of opinions between young men and their parents over spending, study habits, marriage choice, and politics, but these seem to have been fairly unimportant in terms of long-term consequences. They produced amusing literary themes and the sort of ritual grumbling which characterizes intergenerational relations in most ages.[127] Attested examples of parricide, disinheritance, severed relations, or betrayal are few. Such conflict as is recorded can best be viewed as redefinition by the young of their position in the family pecking order and of their own individual preferences. The upper-class career structure left little room for serious breaches, and the importance of inheritance, within and outside the kinship network, assured the privileged old of some protection from the capricious callousness of the generation below them. We can only speculate about whether the young of the lower classes were more likely to storm decisively out of their parents' homes, for at that level it was the older generation of parents who had most to gain by maintaining relations.

On the whole the Roman family is characterized by solidarity, in spite of the changes that fairly short marriages and haphazard mortality patterns imposed on relations. Children who grew up in different homes from their mothers, half-siblings, or step-siblings would still rally round parents or relations of dead parents in time of celebration or need. Conflict would certainly occur, particularly at certain stages of the life cycle—the integration of a new son- or daughter-in-law on marriage, competition over a new grandchild, realignment after a death, a shift in family roles once an older member became incapable of maintaining leadership of the family unit. Change, happy or unhappy, universally causes a certain disturbance and rearrangement within a family, yet families survive and continue because of these changes. Families are geared to take sides, then mend differences when conflict occurs; and Roman families had mechanisms for this, not least the family *consilium,* which could resemble a formal court in serious instances or a chatty gathering barely distinguishable from a family party in others. The Caristia or Cara cognatio was an annual reaffirmation of the notional solidarity of the family unit, the necessity of mending rifts, a reminder—after two weeks of public and private celebration—of the links with earlier generations of the family, as well as a reminder that it held living and dead members. The continual regrouping and redefinition that occurred over the individual and family life span was part of the dynamic process by which the family defined itself as a unit (distinct from the household, distinct from legal notions of proper inheritance) and confirmed its importance in the lives—and deaths—of individual members.

# Six

# Conclusion

Old saws about the decline of the family and morality in the Roman Empire do not stand up to close study of the available evidence, which yields a more complex picture. Similarly, the picture of the tyrannical *paterfamilias* meting out death and discipline to wife, children, and grandchildren does not seem to be reflected in accounts of the family as it was. The essence of the Roman family seems to have been adaptability. Strategies were employed to meet the changing demands of the life course and of the circumstances imposed by ancient social organization and mortality patterns. The ideal was that a free couple would marry, have children, live to a happy old age, and be cared for by their children. The reality was that many people were not free and therefore were legally inhibited from enjoying the full benefits of family relationship, that some people did not have children or that the children died in infancy or even early adulthood, that spouses could be separated by death or by military service or slavery, that children could lose one or both parents at an early age. The tombstones and literature make it clear how common all these circumstances were, yet the ideals persisted: of marital harmony and of *pietas* between the generations. Women and men remarried, motherless children were brought up by relatives or neighbors or nurses, childless men adopted nephews, slave families separated by sale did their utmost to preserve their links with one another.

There is great continuity in the history of the Roman family but some significant changes, which were gradually but imperfectly acknowledged by the law. Marriage preferences changed over time, causing many women to be assigned legally to a different family from that of their own children. This caused some difficulties which were met with pragmatic solutions and partial legal remedies. In time, there was even a slight recognition at law of the ties of slave families, which clearly were recognized within the lower classes. Soldiers simply disobeyed the ban on forming marriages and families during service, and successive emperors gradually removed the legal disabilities attached to them. Many problems were not addressed; slaves continued to be separated from family members, for example. The powers of the *paterfamilias,* long restricted by custom, were eventually curbed somewhat by the law.

Many aspects of Roman family life will be quite alien to readers. The demographic setting, the status boundaries governing marriage, the very idea of arranged marriages and frequent infant death, of slave children put to work and subjected to sexual abuse from an early age, seem to militate against anything resembling modern urban family life. Yet literature and tombstones in particular reveal remarkably familiar sentiments between husband and wife and between parents and children. These are not the whole picture: the same Cicero who made playful jokes about his little son seemed unmoved by the death of a prematurely born grandson; Augustus's cool political rejection of his wife Scribonia as soon as she had given birth to their daughter is in contrast to the acknowledged affection and companionship which characterized his marriage with Livia. All of these factors need to be included before we decide whether Romans did perceive marriage purely as an economic and political convenience, and children as an economic investment. But the recurrent themes of parental concern, conjugal affection, and temporary intergenerational conflict strike many chords.

One great difference between Roman families and those of the modern West is the former's readiness to extend relationships. The modern urban family lives in a house or apartment designed for four people in a consumer society which specializes in marketing images of this nuclear family, ideally harmonious and consuming lots of goods. It does not usually have to contend with maternal or infant mortality or the death of a father while the children are under twenty years of age. Partly because of the greater intervention of death (as well as the more familiar disrupter, divorce), and partly because of their very different economy, Roman families were more willing to admit foster parents, servants, apprentices, nurses, and pedagogues to special relationships which closely resembled those of kin. People who were or had been slaves of the same owner acknowledged their relationship to each other and tended to look within that group for marriage and the commemoration of death.

Children were familiar with aunts or grandmothers who reared them in the absence of a mother, slave children were grouped together and brought up by *nutritores,* children at all social levels might have stepparents and stepbrothers or stepsisters, then half-brothers and half-sisters. The focus was not as firmly on the mother-child and husband-wife bond as it is expected to be in "modern" cultures. The effect of this could have been traumatic in individual cases, but it was also very flexible and might have been extremely comforting, at least at times (even the best family relations are not comforting all the time).

The determination of people to form and maintain families is a great lesson of history. There have always been people like Augustus who warn that "the family" is at risk or in decline, by which they mean that they think a particular family form or behavior is changing. It should reassure such people to note that families can contend with the most discouraging circumstances—poverty, separation, legal liabilities, death. The family is a very flexible institution, and change as it may, it seems to satisfy certain constant human needs, especially the need for material aid and the sense of belonging and mutual emotional support. It provides a moral and economic structure from which individuals can operate—not always happily—but the family also withstands constant and cyclic internal conflict.

Family disruption was a fact of life in the ancient world, and as in the modern world, jobs, generation conflict, and divorce could split up the residential unit but kinship remained. Divorced parents would unite to arrange a marriage for a child or, less happily, to commemorate that child's death. At a time of crisis, in-laws and cousins would rally round. On specified occasions, family members would gather to celebrate religious rites and eat and quarrel together to reaffirm their identity as a family. The family is more than a summary of legal relations or moral obligations, more than the focus of constant conflict, more than an economic and reproductive unit and the basis of mutual support. Any picture of family relations needs to take all of these aspects into account to acknowledge the complexity, resilience, and endurance of this basic human institution.

PLATES

*Pl. 1.* Aldobrandini wedding, showing the bride in a tearful and anxious state, being comforted by a supernatural figure, perhaps the goddess of marriage, while Hymenaeus, the marriage god, waits. To one side, a woman offers up a sacrifice. The bride is wearing traditional garb, with her saffron veil cast on the wedding couch.

*Pl. 2.* Wedding ceremony. The couple take each other by the right hand, symbolizing the married state. The groom holds a papyrus scroll in his left hand, probably containing a record of the dotal (marriage) contract. An allegorical child, symbolic of fecundity, holds a torch (a feature of the wedding ceremony). Funeral sculpture often included such scenes, marking the wedding (or married life) as a significant moment in the life of the deceased man or woman.

*Pl. 3.* A wedding ring from Roman Britain. It depicts the joining of right hands (*dextrarum coniunctio*) associated with the wedding ceremony and with the iconographic representation of the married state. Gold, second to third century A.D.

*Pl. 4.* Republican funerary stele of a man and his wife, standing apart in a dignified posture emphasizing the distance between them. Note the realistic depiction of the stages of life and the age differential between them.

DIS MANIBVS
L CALTILI · CALTILIAE
STEPHANI MOSCHIDIS

*Pl. 5.* A funerary altar from Ostia, showing portrait busts of the couple Lucius Caltilius Stephanus and Caltilia Moschis, their names suggesting that they were once slaves of the same *familia*, which is well represented in the funeral monuments of Ostia. Note the depiction of the woman's stage of life.

*Pl. 6.* A realistic funerary relief showing a married couple, both freed slaves, in the style favored by the elite of the Augustan era.

*Pl. 7.* Marble funerary relief commemorating the couple Titus Aelius Evangelos and Gaudenia Nicene and their livelihood in wool-working. Scenes from stages of cloth manufacture decorate the relief. The inscription asks the onlooker to pour a libation for them but to refrain from using the spot for a further burial or commemoration. Late second century A.D.

*Pl. 8.* Republican statue of a man in senatorial dress displaying two wax busts (*imagines*) of his ancestors. The concept of the family extended into the past and the future.

*Pl. 9.*   A shrine in the atrium of the House of the Vettii, Pompeii, in the form of a miniature temple, depicting the Genius of the householder making a libation in preparation for a sacrifice. On each side of him stands a Lar, guardians of the household. The family was a sacral unit, and each family had its own cult.

D · M

M · GAVIVS

SOCRATESCA

VIAECHRYSIDI

MATRIB · M · F ·

*Pl. 10.* Inscription by Marcus Gavius Socrates to his "well-deserving mother" Gavia Chrysis. Most family epitaphs are in this simple form. The son bears the same gentile (family) name as his mother, possibly because he is illegitimate or because his mother was a freed slave from the same *familia* as his father. The tablet was set up in Rome in the first or second century A.D.

*Pl. 11.* Funeral scene depicted on a sarcophagus. The deceased is supine, with torches burning about the bier. Mourners cry out and beat their breasts, and a flautist plays funeral music.

Pl. 12.   Tombs of Roman freed slaves who clearly had become very wealthy. Note the groupings of family members. The deceased were making a statement to onlookers about their status and their family life.

FVRIA ꓛ L · P·FVRIVS·Pl· FVRIA ꓛ L  FVRIA ꓛ L· C·SVLPIC

Pl. 13.   Detailed view of a late republican or Augustan grave relief depicting members of the Furia family, or *gens*. Romans typically showed married couples or individuals on funeral monuments, but particularly in the Augustan age, children were shown with parents, and brothers and sisters might be represented together.

*Pl. 14.* The emperor Trajan depicted giving out donatives to the free poor with children. The alimentary schemes represented the public face of the state's avowed interest in the family. From the passageway of the Arch of Trajan at Beneventum.

D                                    M
IVLIE·V·EVL·PIIENTISS
IME·VIXIT·AN·L·AVREL
MERCVRIALIS·HER·FACI
VNDVM·CVRAVIT·VIVVS
SIBI·ET·SVIS·FECIT

*Pl. 15.* A family meal depicted on the tomb of Iulia Velva in Roman Britain. The children are sharing the meal, but in some depictions it is difficult to be sure whether children are family or slaves, since both might be
serving adults. The memorial was erected by Aurelius Mercurialis, heir to
the fifty-year-old Iulia Velva. His relationship to her is not clear.

*Pl. 16.* Three generations of the imperial family are represented on the frieze depicting the inauguration of the Altar of Augustan Peace in 9 B.C. They serve a propaganda purpose in reminding the public of the stability of the succession, the joys of family, and, to us, a charming indication that Roman artists could depict all stages of the life course. For a state religious ceremony, this gives a remarkably intimate picture of adult-child relations.

Pl. 17. This lovely representation of a mother and children symbolizes the peace, prosperity, and fertility which Augustus has brought to Italy and the Roman Empire. It is on the Altar of Augustan Peace (Ara Pacis Augustae), dedicated to Augustus by a grateful senate in 9 B.C. It is part of the propaganda program promoting Augustus and his attempt to persuade freeborn Italians to marry and produce children.

Pl. 18. A swaddled baby is attended by his nurse, who is depicted elsewhere suckling the child. Many children, elite and poor, were entrusted to nurses or foster mothers at an early age. This is from the funerary altar to the nurse, Severina. Perhaps the family of her charge paid for this expensive monument. Nurses and their children were included in the patronage network of wealthy families.

...9.  The five-year-old boy Aulus Egrilius
...nus is represented with a goat on his
...rary relief from Ostia. Note that he is
...sed as a freeborn child, wearing the *bulla*
...nd his neck. Child death was not uncom-
... in the ancient world, and some parents
...nt have maintained their distance from
...ldren, but some families did commemorate
...ldren who died young. The sculpture shows
...ppreciation of the boy's childish features.
...s sometimes played with chariots drawn by
...s, but this goat might be destined for sacri-
...The inscription is *CIL* 14, suppl. 4899.

*Pl. 20.*  Grave relief for Antonia Threpte
(Threpte being the feminine form of the Greek
word for "foundling," probably equivalent to
*alumna*), A.D. 301, Asia Minor. Antonia was
clearly young when she died (her age is not
specified). She is commemorated by her foster
parents Iulia and Alkipiades, whose names
suggest that they were probably Romanized
Greeks.

179

*Pl. 21.* This unusual grave relie[f] picts a dog, with an inscription t[o] *alumna* (foundling or foster c[hild?]) Helena. It is just possible that this [refers] to the dog, but it is far more [likely] that Helena, "incomparable and [well] deserving soul," was a little girl w[hose] pet dog is shown here. The associ[ation] of children and animals (or bir[ds] is) found in Greek and Roman fun[erary] art. Cf. plates 15, 19, 20, and 22.

*Pl. 22.* A beautiful marble monu[ment] of a girl reclining on a couch w[ith a] small dog. The broken inscriptio[n la]ments that someone so lovely has [died] so young. She is not a little gir[l; she] is depicted as between girlhood [and] womanhood. It is reminiscent of P[liny's] literary portrait of Minicia Ma[rcella] (*Ep.* 5.16), who died at twelve, [just] before her wedding, and had al[l the] best characteristics of childhood [and] womanhood.

*Pl. 23.* This sarcophagus relief depicts the child as a newborn baby being raised up by the midwife at birth, as a boy and a youth, then dying in his prime—the most lamented death. The women mourning him could be his mother and wife. Late second century A.D.

*Pl. 24.* Stages of a boy's childhood depicted on a marble sarcophagus from Trier. He is seen as a suckling infant, a babe in arms, then as a young boy playing with a toy chariot and reciting his lessons. Such depictions display an awareness of the stages of child development.

# Notes

Abbreviations of journal titles are from *L'Année philologique*. Abbreviations for ancient authors are from Lewis and Short, *A Latin Dictionary* (Oxford 1962), and Liddell and Scott, *A Greek-English Lexicon* (Oxford 1948; reprint ed., 1961). The index of ancient authors includes abbreviations.

*AE*  *L'Année épigraphique*. Paris: Presses universitaires de France.

*BGU*  *Berliner griechische Urkunden, Aegyptische Urkunden aus den Königlichen Museen zu Berlin*. Berlin, 1892–1937.

*BMC*  H. Mattingly et al. *Coins of the Roman Empire in the British Museum*. London, 1923–67.

*CIL*  Th. Mommsen et al. *Corpus Inscriptionum Latinarum*. Berlin, 1962–.

*CJ*  *Codex Iustinianus*.

*C.Th.*  *Codex Theodosianus*.

*Dig.*  The *Digest* or *Pandects* of Justinian.

*FIRA*  S. Riccobono, J. Baviera, and V. Arangio-Ruiz, eds. *Fontes iuris romani anteiustiniani*. 3 vols. Florence, 1940–43.

*FV*  *Fragmenta Vaticana*. In *FIRA*, vol. 2.

*Gai.*  The *Institutes* of Gaius.

*ILS*  H. Dessau, ed. *Inscriptiones Latinae Selectae*. Berlin, 1892–1916.

*Inst.*  The *Institutes* of Justinian.

*OLD*  *Oxford Latin Dictionary*.

*P.Oxy.*  B. P. Grenfell and A. S. Hunt, eds. *The Oxyrhynchus Papyri*. London, 1898–.

RE    A. Pauly, G. Wissowa, and W. Kroll, eds. *Real-Encyclopädie der Klassischen Altertumswissenschaft.* Stuttgart, 1983–.

*Sent.*    The *Opinions (Sententiae)* of the jurist Paul.

*SHA*    *Scriptores Historiae Augustae.*

*Tab.*    Twelve Tables. In *FIRA,* vol. 1.

*TLL*    *Thesaurus Linguae Latinae.*

*Chapter 1. In Search of the Roman Family*

1. Extracted *Dig.* 50.16.195. The edict was a statement of the law issued annually by the praetor at Rome (mirrored by a similar statement by each provincial governor), an elected official who served as a judge. On legal meanings of *familia* see also Thomas 1976, 411–12. For the origin and general usage of *familia* see Henrion 1940.

2. Cf. Festus, 87, who connects *familia* with the Oscan word for *slave.*

3. "Because the *familia* is blended and constitutes a single household" ("quia commixta familia est et una domus") (*Dig.* 29.5.1.15 [Ulpian]). This assumes that husband and wife had separate property regimes. Cf. Cic. *fam.* 14.4.4 on Cicero's attempts to secure Terentia's dotal slaves from possible confiscation if they were treated as part of his holdings. If the wife had entered the husband's *manus,* her property would have merged with his on marriage and been treated as dowry (see below, chap. 3).

4. *Dig.* 50.16.195.1 (Ulpian); and see the arguments in Weaver 1972, 299.

5. The sentimental links, like manumission, tended to apply to slaves who had been nurses or pedagogues or had performed some specialist function (e.g., as secretary, hairdresser, or house steward) which brought them into close contact with the owners (Duff 1928, 15–20; Treggiari 1969, 11–20; Vogt 1974, 104–14; Hopkins 1978, 124–29; Bradley 1984, 116–18). Patterns of intermarriage within the *familia* and kinlike groupings are best described by Flory (1978); cf. Weaver 1972, 191–92.

6. See *Dig.* 50.16.195.3 on particular extensions of this. Cf. Crook 1967a, 98; and Solidoro 1981. The term *familia Caesaris,* used as the title of the standard work on the slaves and freedmen of members of the ruling imperial family, is based on this usage (cf. Weaver 1972, 2ff., 229–30. Consider pp. 4–5 on the usual distinctions within a large-scale aristocratic *familia*).

7. *Dig.* 50.16.195.5 (Ulpian). Cf. 50.16.196 (also Ulpian): a woman's children do not belong to her *familia* but follow their *paterfamilias.*

8. *Dig.* 50.16.195.2 (Ulpian).

9. Ibid. Cf. Berger 1953, 472–73; and Kaser 1975, 1.341–45.

10. On *materfamilias* see Cic. *Top.* 14; Aul.Gell. *NA* 18.6.8–9. If she

married without passing into her husband's *manus,* she remained a *filia-familias* as long as her father lived.

11. *Dig.* 50.16.195.1: "Let us consider how the meaning of *familia* is understood. And indeed it is understood in various senses; for it refers both to things and to persons: to things, as in the Law of the Twelve Tables in the words, 'Let the nearest agnate have the estate (*familia*).'"

12. The bibliographies of Berger (1953, 788) and Michel (1979) show some of the trends. Cf. Westrup 1943; and de Zulueta 1953, e.g., 34–37, on Roman marriage. Hallett 1984 (ix–xii, 263–98) contains an excellent summary of collaboration between social anthropology and the classics and discusses some of the early theories. Cf. Humphreys 1978, esp. 17–30; and Finley 1986, 118, where the emphasis is on Greek culture. See now Segalen 1986 on the more recent application of anthropology to French family history.

13. Saller 1984a; Saller and Shaw 1984b; Rawson 1986b, 7–8, 14. Cf. Garnsey and Saller 1987, 129; and Dixon 1988, 20.

14. Cf. Buck's (1949, 93) assumption that the slow development of in-law terms on the wife's side reflected actual relations. Hallett (1984, e.g., 183–87) also uses kinship terminology to assess the cultural significance of certain relationships; cf. Bradley 1987, 51–52. This is an established mode of scholarship (especially in cultural and linguistic anthropology), but it is very difficult to base firm conclusions on it.

15. See Yanagisako's useful critical discussion of the anthropological literature, especially on this point (1979, esp. 162–63).

16. Cf. Pomeroy 1976. And consider the examples of Dixon 1985c, 362–63; 1988, 15, on dual affiliation; and 1988, 221–28, specifically on the ties between Roman mothers and their married daughters. On close relations between married daughters and their mothers in modern societies cf. Young and Wilmott 1957, 28–43; and Walker and Thompson 1983. A wife who takes her husband's name and identifies with his interests will still say, "My family expects us to come over at Christmas."

17. This area is associated particularly with Münzer (1920), Gelzer (1912), and Syme (1979).

18. See esp. Saller 1987a, 33. Saller estimates that only 10 percent of Romans were likely at birth to have a living paternal grandfather and that at the age of twenty only 40 percent were likely to have a living father.

19. Anderson (1980, 27–33) and Stone (1981, 62–64) summarize the arguments against this view of the English household and the criticism of the method and conceptual framework of fixing household composition at any one point.

20. Laslett 1987, 277–78. Cf. Goody 1958; and the paper included in Laslett and Wall 1972.

21. "While the family cycle is limited to stages of parenthood, the life

course encompasses individual *and* family development in relation to each other. The family cycle uses a priori stages that are not always relevant to historical conditions; the life course is concerned with transitions from one stage to the next, or from one role to another, both on the individual and the familial level" (Hareven 1987, xiii; cf. her 1978 book and the article in it by Elder). Others have continued to use the expression *life cycle* (see, e.g., Stone 1981, 63; and Smith 1984).

22. Stone 1981, 62, citing Anderson 1971.

23. See Dixon 1988, 169–70, 222, on adult children visiting their aged mothers; and below, chap. 5, on attitudes towards the elderly in the Roman family.

24. Plut. *Cat.mai.* 24; *Caes.* 7 and 9; Cic. *de Sen.* 37 on Appius Claudius. See also Dixon 1985a; and below, chap. 2, for the argument that the household norm might have changed in conjunction with other economic and social changes in Roman society from the second century B.C. on.

25. Plut. *Aem.P.* 5 and Val.Max. 4.4.9 on the Aelii Tuberones; Plut. *Crass.* 1 on M. Licinius Crassus and his brother.

26. The term *dependent children* is not appropriate in the context of Rome, where children commonly remained economically dependent on their father until he died. Married sons and daughters of the elite normally lived in separate residences but remained dependent in this respect. (This was particularly true in the case of the sons; the dowry might have tempered the obligation of the father to his married *filiafamilias*.) See below, chap. 2.

27. I.e., epitaphs as compared with dedications of statues and goods to temples, for example. Cf. Hobson 1985.

28. Dixon 1988, 141–67; for further discussion see below, chap. 4. See also Bradley 1984, 53–67, on separation of slaves; Bradley 1985a on childcare; Bradley 1986 on wet-nursing; and Néraudau 1984, 281–87, on nurses.

29. See Dixon 1988, 132–33, on arrangements for motherless children.

30. Plut. *Cat.min.* 1. Cato's half sister was even said to have exerted a "maternal influence" (*materna auctoritas*) over her formidable younger brother (Asconius p. 23 St., intro. to Cic. *pro Scauro*), although Hillard (1983) is skeptical.

31. We owe our knowledge of the meeting to Cicero's inclusion as such a friend (Cic. *Att.* 15.11).

32. For other examples see Bradley 1987, 45–46. See also Humbert 1972; and Dixon 1988, 30–31. Kajanto (1970) argues that divorce was less common in the lower classes, but Humbert (1972, 343–44) and Huttunen (1974, 58–59, on widows) suggest that remarriage was a feature of ancient Roman society, as it tended to be of preindustrial cultures in general, even where divorce was not practiced (Stone 1981, 60). For further discussion of this topic see below, chap. 3.

33. Cic. *pro Cluentio* 27. Since Cicero tells the story to prove that Sassia was a classic wicked stepmother who urged the death of her intended husband's children, I should stress that this is not intended as an example of the "positive" side of the blended family. I have great reservations about Cicero's version, but the incidental details are very suggestive. See also Moreau 1983; and Bradley 1987, 46.

34. Cf. Hareven (1987, xvii) on the differences between the pre-industrial (Early Modern) and the modern nuclear family.

35. Technically, slaves and freed slaves had no agnates, i.e., official kin, but even the law acknowledged family connection for the purposes of determining incest (*Dig.* 23.2.8 [Pomponius]).

36. Rawson (1966, 79) has examples of slave children sold and freed at very early ages; Flory (1975, 44) maintains that slave families were split more often by death than by sale, but Bradley's (1984, 53–60) detailed discussion of the effects of sale on slave families is sobering. Cf. Hopkins 1978, 165–66. On children being reared in groups consider the reference to Licinius Meropnus (*CIL* 6.21279A), *nutritor* of his patrona's children and of her *alumni*.

37. See Treggiari 1969, 15–16, and 1981b; and Rawson 1974.

38. Cf. Bradley 1987, 54–62; and Dixon 1988, 150–53. The subject is discussed in greater detail below, in chap. 4.

39. See above all Bradley 1985b and his bibliography n. 18 on apprentices in the ancient world. Wiedemann (1989, 154–56) lists occupations of children, some of them involving movement away from the home. On recruitment into the army see Parker 1928, 45, and Watson 1969, 134; Watson estimates an average age at entry of eighteen or nineteen years. Cf. Brunt 1971, table 11, on conscription. Wiedemann (1989, 114) claims that conscription of boys younger than seventeen years (the legal age) was rare but himself quotes C. Gracchus's 122 B.C. campaign against the practice (Plut. *C.Gr.* 5.1). Cf. the many family letters in Winter 1933, 82–93.

40. Controversy raged around the conclusions of Laslett (in Laslett and Wall 1972)—see, e.g., Berkner 1975 and the criticisms summarized by Laslett himself in his 1987 article and by Anderson (1980, 27–38)—but this has subsided. Cf. Hareven 1987, x: "From a narrow focus on the family as a household unit at one of several points in time, research has moved to a consideration of the family as a process over the entire lives of its members." Saller (1992) suggests that the reason is an awareness of the complexities that affect household size over the life course (see above). Professor Saller has kindly allowed me to see his notes on the papers presented at the May 1989 conference on the history of the family in Italy (held at Bellagio, Italy). See Kertzer 1992.

41. The trend began with Engels (1884), who enunciated the view that the earlier, extended family had been changed by capitalism, which sepa-

rated the home and workplace, specialized the functions of the woman in the household, and contributed to the suppression of women and children with the development of the modern nuclear family, isolated from society at large—a process linked with the alienation of proletarian workers from the product of their labor. Stone's (1977) study took a different approach but tended to reinforce this view, which was greatly shaken by the findings in Laslett and Wall 1972. The literature on the subject is vast. The recent tendency has been to emphasize the continuity of family structures against the effects of industrialization and to argue that the changes were not so great as has been supposed in the past and that the role of the family as a unit was more positive (see, e.g., Medick 1976; Anderson 1980, 75–84, which lists literature on the subject up to that point; Stone 1981, 72–78; and the references in Hareven 1987, x and xix).

42. This is the expression used by Lasch (1977) to describe the Victorian conception of the family.

43. Dixon 1991; see also the section entitled "The Function of the Roman Family," below, and n. 101.

44. See below, chap. 5; and Dixon 1988, esp. chap. 5. The debate arose with Ariès (1962) and continues to rage. Cf. Demause 1974; Manson 1975; the works listed in Karras and Wiesehöfer 1981; Néraudau 1984; Eyben 1986; Segalen 1986, chap. 6; and Wiedemann 1989, esp. chap. 1.

45. Segalen 1972 is typical. Other French examples are Bouloiseau et al. 1962; Lions and Lachiver 1967; and LeBrun 1971. For an English example see Krause 1958. Cf. the English studies of household size, based on census records and parish registers, in Laslett and Wall 1972. On the trend in general see Wheaton 1987.

46. The works of Rawson, e.g., 1966, 1974, 1986c, are typical of both the earlier and the current trend. Cf. Shaw 1982; Saller and Shaw 1984b; and Saller 1987a. The studies of Bradley, e.g., of Roman Egyptian apprenticeship contracts (1985b) and of dislocation in the Roman family (1987), are also statistically based but concentrate on the effect on family relationships. Bradley's 1987 study is statistical, but it is based on family reconstitution techniques and is collected from literary sources rather than from tombstones and inscriptions.

47. E.g., Anderson 1980, 17–18, 36–38; Stone 1981, 55–56; and Wheaton 1987, esp. 296–97. Cf. Rapp in Rapp, Ross, and Bridenthal 1979, 175, on this distinction.

48. This seems to be at odds with Wheaton's claim (1987, 286) that family studies have not usually been linked with political history. English examples include Stone's earlier works, such as Stone 1965. Cf. Davis 1962 on the Venetian nobility; and Duby 1967 on the French nobility. Syme's many studies of elite alliances and prosopographical works cited above represent this kind of interest.

49. Cf. Garnsey 1979; and Garnsey and Saller 1987, 75–77.

50. Cf. the comments in Saller and Shaw 1984b, 124–25; and Shaw's chapter in Saller's forthcoming collection.

51. Rawson, esp. 1966, 1974; Treggiari 1969, 1975; Flory 1978; Bradley, e.g. 1985b. Weaver (1972) discusses the imperial slaves and freedmen, who formed a type of elite and cannot therefore be categorized as lower-class; see also Weaver 1986, 1991.

52. Wallace-Hadrill 1991; cf. Packer 1975.

53. Great advances have been made in this area since the work of Beloch (1886) and MacDonnell (1913). Since Burn's (1953) study, there have been increasingly sophisticated mortality estimates by Hopkins (1966, 1983) and now simulations used by Saller (1986, 1987a) and Shaw (1987a), but the demographic pattern ultimately rests on information from tombstones. See also Kajanto 1968; Huttunen 1974; and Dixon 1988, 30–32.

54. Dixon 1988, 104, and the references given there; Wiedemann 1989, 16–17; Shaw's forthcoming chapter on age and regional bias in the commemoration of children.

55. See Dixon 1988, chap. 6, on the impact of demography on child-rearing practices in Rome. Cf. Stone 1981, 59–60, on the effect of pre-industrial patterns of mortality on parenthood and marriage: "[T]he expectation of a durable marriage in the past was even lower than today, despite our high divorce rate. Divorce, in fact, serves as a modern functional substitute for death. On the average, a seventeenth-century peasant marriage in France could be expected to last only about twelve to seventeen years." Cf. Segalen 1986, 139–58. The Romans also had easy divorce from the late republican period.

56. E.g., Cixous 1970; Daly 1979; Cixous and Clément 1986. Cf. Lacan 1977; and Brennan 1989.

57. *Pace* Degler 1980. Cf. Harris 1976, 159; Rapp, Ross, and Bridenthal 1979; and Wheaton 1987, 290.

58. Étienne 1973; Néraudau 1984, 65–83; Rousselle 1988. Cf. Brown 1989.

59. E.g., Amundsen and Diers 1969 on the age of menarchy, 1970 on the age of menopause. Cf. Durry 1955, 1969; and Bremmer 1987 on aspects of women's experience related to these stages.

60. Frier 1982, 1983.

61. Stone 1981, 55.

62. Wheaton 1987, 296.

63. On criticism of the overly empiricist approach of ancient historians see esp. the comments of Finley (1963, 1986). Saller's remarks were contained in his summary of the conference on the history of the family in Italy, held at Bellagio in May 1989, and should form the basis of his introduction to the forthcoming book.

64. See, e.g., Goode 1963, 1964; Donzelot 1979; Rapp, Ross, and Briden-

thal 1979, esp. 175–81 (Rapp); Hartmann 1981; Stone 1981, 86; Lambert 1982; Mount 1982; Hareven 1987, xvi–xx; and Wheaton 1987, 290.

65. Laslett (1987, 273–74) contrasts familial change, which takes place in "social structural time," with political and economic change in the "wider" social context. Cf. Wheaton 1987, 290, on the persistence of certain kinship norms. Bouchard 1972 is sometimes upheld as an example of *l'histoire immobile*. Kelly-Gadol (1977) queried the usefulness of the concept of the European Renaissance for the history of women. Cf. Rich 1976, 221.

66. This has already happened in the field of economic history, where works regularly include literary and archaeological evidence, e.g., Skydsgaard 1979, on Pompeii; Carandini and Settis 1980, on slave-master relations; Paterson 1982, on maritime trade; Frayn 1984, on the pastoral economy and the wool trade; Purcell 1985, on the wine trade; and Spurr 1986, on Italian agriculture. Those who have written on social history, including history of women, the family, and the life cycle, include the art historians Kampen (1981, 1982) and Kleiner (1977, 1978), who has also looked on the ideology of the family as represented in the funeral sculpture of the Augustan age; Frier (1982, 1983), who has combined juristic and osteoarchaeological evidence; Zanker (1988), who has used iconographic and literary evidence to reconstruct aspects of ideology in the Augustan age, including family ideology; and Wallace-Hadrill (1991), who has examined the use of space in Pompeian homes.

67. Curchin 1982, 1983; Saller and Shaw 1984b; Shaw 1984 and forthcoming. Cf. Packer 1975 on lower-class housing in Pompeii; and Garnsey 1979 on where peasants actually lived and the problems that these authors encounter.

68. See Nicholas 1962, 51–53, for an account of the spread of the civil code.

69. Flandrin 1979, 50–92.

70. Wheaton 1987, 296.

71. See, e.g., Paribeni 1929; and Rawson 1986b, 1. Debates about the status of women that raged in the 1890s and the early part of the twentieth century were often characterized by reference to the position of women in the past, particularly within the family, and contained strong moral arguments that women ought to revert to what was seen as an obsequious model of service within the family sphere and of deference to males such as husbands and fathers.

72. In her reminiscences of her childhood, Susanna Agnelli recalls the difficulties her own mother had in Mussolini's Italy because she was under the power of her father-in-law, who took on the role of *paterfamilias,* directly derived from the Roman law concept.

73. The historian Mount has been enlisted in this particular venture. See, e.g., the review of his book by Sawer (1982).

74. Engels 1884 contains a good statement of this view, which permeates other Marxist and Engelian works of the nineteenth and twentieth centuries and is part of the general assumption of much modern Marxist scholarship, in more sophisticated form. It is, however, important to see this view in the nineteenth-century context of its origins.

75. See, e.g., Reed 1969, 1975.

76. Cf. Liv. *Praef.* 8–9; Val.Max. 4.4.8–9; Juv. 6.286–351; Sen. *Ep. Mor.* 87.41. Cf. Earl 1967, 17–19, on this commonplace among Roman historians; and Courtney 1980, 295, on the *topos* generally.

77. Liv. 1.57–59 (Lucretia); Juv. 6.287–90; Tac. *Germ.* 19–20.

78. See Liv. 2.4 and Val.Max. 5.8.1 on the execution of the Bruti brothers by their father; Liv. 7.3 and Val.Max. 5.8.3 on the execution of Manlius Torquatus by his father; Tac. *Dial.* 28–29 on the rearing of children in the past; and Cic. *de Sen.*, e.g., 37, on Appius Claudius, who ruled over an extended household in his old age.

79. Aug. *RG* 8.5; Hor. *Carm.* 3.6, esp. 33–44 on the past and 45–48 on the corruption of the present age. See also Williams 1962.

80. Val.Max. 4.4; 5.8.

81. E.g., Plut. *Aem.P.* 5, based presumably on Val.Max. 4.4.8–9 and possibly Polybius.

82. *CIL* 6.1527 (*Laudatio Turiae*), 27: "rara sunt tam diuturna matrimonia, finita morte, non divertio in . . . | nobis."

83. Hor. *Carm.* 3.24; Tac. *Germ.*, esp. 19–20 on family life and the morals of women. Horace was writing in the time of Augustus, Tacitus in the early second century A.D.

84. Tac. *Germ.* 19; Hor. *Carm.* 3.24.35–36; Liv. *Praef.* 8–9.

85. Bender 1967. Cf. Yanagisako 1979, 163, 200. Rivière 1971 presents the same argument about functional definitions of marriage.

86. The most famous being Lévi-Strauss (1949, 1967).

87. Rapp, Ross, and Bridenthal 1979. They point out that women and the different age groups have quite diverse interests and that treating the family as a unit of solidarity disguises the constant conflict between these interest groups.

88. Goode (1963, 1964) stresses the dynamic and revolutionary aspects of the family, and Mount (1982) represents the family as a bastion of resistance against state encroachment. See also Sawer's (1982) very critical review of Mount, in which she characterizes his approach as a form of disguised conservatism linked with his role as adviser to the Thatcher government and the reduction of state funding in favor of family-based health care.

89. See Flory 1978 on associations of slaves or former slaves from the same *familia.* Cf. Hopkins 1983 on burial clubs (211–16) and collective tombs (216–17), including the Monumentum Liviae, for the slaves and former slaves of the empress.

90. *Dig.* 40.2.11–14 (Ulpian and Marcianus).

91. Cf. Gai. 3.45–47, 53, on succession rights; *Dig.* 25.3.20, 21, 26 (Ulpian), on the reciprocal duties of maintenance extending through the generations, that is, to the children and parents of *patroni* and to the children of freed slaves.

92. Cic. *fam.* 14.5 (Terentia); *Q.fr.* 1.3.7 (Quintus); *Att.* 3.9.3, 3.11.2 (Atticus); *fam.* 14.4.3–4; *Att.* 3.22.1 (Piso); and *post Red.* 7–8 for many connections.

93. Vel.Pat. 2.67.2. Contrast this with Val.Max. 6.7 on loyal wives and Appian *BC* 4.11–23 for the many tales that circulated of loyalty and the occasional betrayal. Hallett 1984, 224–30, interprets these *exempla* in a different way, as indicative of the rarity of matrimonial loyalty and wifely sacrifice.

94. Val.Max. 6.7.2; Appian *BC* 4.44.

95. *CIL* 6.1527.10–12, 31–33, on her mother-in-law; 42–49 on her generosity to various relations. The edition used throughout is that of Durry (1950).

96. Cf. Plin. *Ep.* 1.14.7 on the support usually expected of in-laws in this circumstance; and Sen. *ad Helviam* 14.3, 19, on the support Seneca gained from his mother and aunt in seeking public office. The references above to the assistance given Cicero in his exile would represent (in direr circumstances) the base of his support for more routine political activity.

97. Aul.Gell. *NA* 12.1.1–5.

98. Quint. *Inst.Or.* 6 *pr.* on the grandmother bringing up the motherless children; and Plin. *Ep.* 4.19.1–2 on Calpurnia's aunt being treated as her mother substitute.

99. *Dig.* 24.1.42 (Gaius) on advancement, 43 (Paul) on a wife's helping her husband if he was at risk of exile, 16.1.21.1 (Callistratus) on a wife's being permitted an exemption from the *SC Velleianum* if her father was at risk of exile. Cf. Plin. *Ep.* 10.4 on the substantial gift made by a mother to her emancipated son and the legal questions this raised.

100. See above on the modern parallel (Lasch 1977); and cf. Mount's (1982) view of the family as a fortress withstanding the bombardment of successive governments.

101. Luc. 3.895–6.

102. Cic. *Att.* 1.18.1.

103. Dio 56.8.2 (Augustus to the knights); Tac. *Ann.* 3.34, set in A.D. 32 in the senate and apparently based on the record of debate.

104. Cf. *CIL* 6.35,536 and 9,810 on marital happiness and 18.086 and 34,421 on feeling for young children. I have written in greater detail on this ideal and on the evidence for its partial practice in Dixon 1991, where I cite the letters of Cicero, Ovid, and Pliny and the correspondence between Fronto and the emperor Marcus as evidence that the ideal did affect

the way in which family members addressed each other in these media as well as in epitaphs. It should, however, be noted that Bradley (1987, esp. 35) disagrees with my view of Roman marriage.

105. Cf. Rawson 1986b, 1–2, for some revealing and contradictory quotations. Cf. Engels 1884.

106. Cic. *Att.* 10.11.3, 10.6.2, 13.37.2.

107. Cf. Saller and Shaw 1984b; Shaw 1987a; Bellemore and Rawson 1990; and Shaw in his forthcoming paper on patterns of commemoration of age groups in Roman imperial epitaphs.

108. Hopkins 1980; Barker 1985; Hobson 1985; and above all Bradley 1984, chap. 2, and 1985b.

109. Gaudemet 1962, 1978; Hopkins 1965a; Humbert 1972, e.g., 304–6, 343–49, 453–58; Lyman 1974; Goody 1983; Shaw 1984, 1987b, forthcoming.

110. Cf. Herlihy 1983, 118–20.

111. Fortunately, the use of the term *primitive* has died out, but Demause (1974) and Shorter (1977) chart *progress* in parent-child relations. Laslett (1987, 268) rightly sees such moralizing generalizations as Whiggish. I have singled out Demause and Shorter because they are clear examples, but I hasten to add that we are all guilty. Is this the point at which to confess that my own approach is culturally relativist, functionalist, feminist, and somewhat *annaliste*?

112. Cf. Stone 1981, 87: "There is thus scarcely any major problem in our lives, or any major dispute, about the nature of change in the past, upon which family history does not somehow impinge." True, even self-evident, but I hope that social historians soon cease to feel the need to reiterate this defensively, in response to the unspoken assumption that the war games and politicking of a minuscule elite are the proper and obvious concern of historians. Cf. Bradley's (1989) review of Syme's *Roman Papers* on the issues of elite history versus "history from below"; and Laslett 1987, 264–95, on the "Obligations of Family Historians to their Own Contemporaries."

113. On the modern belief in the "golden age" of respect and care for the aged see Stone 1981, 69–70, and the debate he documents in n. 25.

114. Rapp, Ross, and Bridenthal 1979, 178.

115. Nor are contemporary impressions and stereotypes necessarily accurate reflections of reality—Wright (1988, esp. 10) and Sherudi (1979) combat in different ways the prevalent image of fond and uncritical grandparents, a stereotype that does have some basis—but reality is always complex. Cf. Laslett 1987, 267: "A casual, intuitive, journalistic knowledge of these circumstances of our own day is insufficient."

116. Contrast Sen. *de Matrimonio* (frag. 58 Haase 1872) with the account of Seneca's death in Tac. *Ann.* 15.63.

*Chapter 2. Roman Family Relations and the Law*

1. Liv. 3.9–57; Dion.Halic. 10.1–60. Cf. Ausonius 11.61–62.

2. They can be found in Warmington 1961, vol. 3; in *FIRA* 1.26–75; and in Bruns 1909, 1.15–40.

3. See Watson 1975.

4. Strictly speaking, a law passed by the senate was a *lex;* one passed by the popular assembly was a *plebiscitum.* On laws and lawmaking see Rotondi 1922, 4–20; Crook 1967a, chap. 1; and Watson 1974, esp. chaps. 1, 3, 7, for the Republic. Cic. *Top.* 28 summarizes the sources of law for the first century B.C., and Gai. 1.2–7 for the early third century, although his statement that certain jurists' opinions had the force of law is thought to be anachronistic (Wieacker 1960, 38, 157). Cf. Jolowicz 1932, 369–72; and *Inst.* 1.1–4 for Justinian's day, the sixth century A.D.

5. In this case, the *Lex Licinia Cassia de tribunis militum a populo non creandis* (Rotondi 1922, 282).

6. See esp. Dixon 1985b, 529–30, on the laws concerning legacies, and 1988, 54; and Thomas 1976, 523–24, on the difficulties of reconciling the *SC Tertullianum* with other rules governing intestate succession, causing a clash of interests between mothers and uncles of deceased children who died intestate.

7. See Lenel 1927, 21–30, on the legislative role of the praetor and the judicial process; Buckland 1932; Jolowicz 1932, chap. 13, on republican procedure; Crook 1967a, 24–25; Kaser 1975, 1.205–7; Watson 1974, 31ff.; Frier 1983, 1985, chap. 2, esp. 44–57, on the development of the praetorian system from its republican origins. Frier stresses the flexibility and creativity of the urban praetor's edict in the 80s and 70s B.C.

8. Crook 1967a, 119. See Gai. 2.147–49a on praetorian attempts to modify the effects of the strict civil law rules governing testamentary procedure; *Inst.* 3.3 *pr.* and Lenel 1927, 355–61, on succession on intestacy. See also Jolowicz 1932, 79–98, on praetorian remedies; Watson 1971, chap. 6, on testamentary succession; and Voci 1982, 413–14, on the historical development. Cf. Cic. *Verr.* 2.1.104 on the decision of a former governor of Sicily to uphold a will instituting the testator's daughter in contravention of the *Lex Voconia.*

9. Lenel (1927, 51–568) has collected these quotes. See also Bruns 1909, 1.211–87; and cf. Watson's discussion (1967, 73–76) of republican procedure for the recovery of dowry as an example of reconstruction.

10. See editions of Cic. *Verr.,* esp. with reference to 2.1.104–58. Cf. *fam.* 3.8.4; *Att.* 6.1.15 on Cicero's own practice as governor; and Berger 1953, 449–50, and his references to the urban and provincial edict.

11. E.g., Bruns 1909, 1.142–46 (*Lex Salpensana*) and the many other laws included in Bruns 1909, vol. 1, and *FIRA,* vol. 1, but note that many

of these *leges* are culled from literary sources and the *Digest,* as well as from inscriptions.

12. *De Confirmatione Digestorum,* esp. lv–lvi, lxv (e.g., Watson 1985, l.lv–lvi, lxv. See also Birks and McLeod 1987, 8–10).

13. On the gradual professionalization of Roman law see Schulz 1946, 49–59, 267–77; Bauman 1983; and Frier 1985. See Crook 1967a, 20–23, on emperors' rulings. On the jurisprudents see Jolowicz 1932, 369–72, and Gai. 1.7, but note that de Zulueta (1953, 2.21–22) and Wieacker (1960, 38, 157) believe that his statement about authoritative jurists' responses (the *ius respondendi*) is interpolated. On republican practice cf. Watson 1974, 134–68; and Jolowicz 1932, chap. 13.

14. E.g., Justinian's *Institutes,* a shorter and more straightforward treatment of the law intended for use by students.

15. Contained in the *Codices* of Theodosius and of Justinian. The *Codex Theodosianus (C.Th.)* dates to the fifth century A.D., the *Codex Iustinianus (CJ)* to the sixth (Berger 1953, 392). The decisions came to have a certain legal force, but the varying efficiency of recordkeeping limited its application (Crook 1967a, 32–33). Sherwin-White's (1966) commentary on Plin. *Ep.* 10.15–120 is illuminating, for it covers correspondence between Pliny and Trajan during Pliny's governorship of Bithynia-Pontus ca. A.D. 109–11. See also Millar 1977, 228–52, 507–66, on the emperor's role in dealing with individual petitions.

16. It is always dangerous to make such generalizations, but I think there is a distinction between the work of the legal historians I have named and that of people such as Watson, Bauman, Cantarella, Gardner, Kaser, Beauchamp, Yavetz, Volterra, and so on, who do consider historical development and social issues but place a more traditional emphasis on juristic reasoning. Other historians, such as Rawson, Hallett, Shaw, Weaver, Millar, Hopkins, and Veyne, often analyze legal material closely in the course of their studies but would not, I think, class themselves as legal historians. The lines are somewhat elastic.

17. And in a sense from conception. Roman laws concerning abortion were based on the assumption that a woman had no right to determine the fate of her husband's child and divert the proper inheritance (cf. Cic. *Clu.* 32, 34, 125; and *Dig.* 47.11.4 [Marcianus]). The unborn child, however, had no legal *persona,* and special provisions had to be made for children who might be born after a will had been made (Gai. 2.130–35, 242).

18. On the powers of the father see Crook 1967b; Watson 1967, 98–100; Rabello 1972, 1979; Thomas 1981, 1982, 1986; and Harris 1986. On release from paternal power see Gai. 1.127–36, esp. 132 on emancipation. Cf. Watson 1967, 100–101.

19. *Dig.* 23.2.2 (Paul). Cf. *Dig.* 23.2.9 (Ulpian); and Corbett 1930, 56–58.

20. Dion. Halic. a.15 on regal law. Hopkins 1983, 225–26. See below, chap. 4, on this practice. The Germans and Jews were unusual in not practicing exposure (Tac. *Hist.* 5.5; *Germ.* 19.5). On infanticide in history generally see Newman 1972; Dickison 1973; and Langer 1974.

21. *Dig.* 28.2.11 (Paul): "in suis heredibus evidentius apparet continuationem dominii eo rem perducere, ut nulla videatur hereditas fuisse, quasi olim hi domini essent, qui etiam vivo patre quodammodo domini existimantur . . . itaque post mortem patris non hereditatem percipere videntur sed magis liberam bonorum administrationem consequuntur." Cf. *Inst.* 3.3, esp. 3.

22. Gai. 2.104–8, 116–17, 123–24; *Inst.* 2.13 *pr.,* and the whole of *Dig.* 28.2 on exheredation, i.e., excluding *sui heredes* from the testament.

23. Gardner 1986, 67–68, summarizes these developments; see also Dixon 1985a, 156–57.

24. The extent and precise timing of this transformation is now very controversial (see, e.g., Brunt 1971, 269–93; Hopkins 1978, 18–64; and Spurr 1986. On the Roman tradition see, e.g., Appian *BC* 1.1.9; and Plut. *T.Gr.* 8–9). For the purposes of this study I am simplifying economic developments in order to concentrate on the effect on family-based practices, especially inheritance and the role of the married woman in the redistribution of property.

25. E.g., Cincinnatus was called from his ploughing to be *dictator* (Dion.Halic. 10.17); and see Liv. 1.57.9 for Lucretia at the loom with her servants.

26. Cf. Friedl 1962, 68, and 1977, 131, on the way men in modern Greece spoke of dowry; and Klapisch-Zuber 1983 on the fifteenth-century Florentine stereotype of the "cruel" widowed mother who remarried, thus depriving her children of her dowry.

27. Gai. 1.144–200. On this see Dixon 1984a, esp. the references, 343–44 n. 4, and below, chap. 4; and Watson 1967, 102–54.

28. For the literary tradition see esp. Plutarch's *Lives* of Cato the elder and of Gaius and Tiberius Gracchus, e.g., *Cat.mai.* 21 and *T.Gr.* 8; and Appian *BC* 1.1.7–9. Cf. Hopkins 1978, 1–11; Dixon 1985a, 148–49, on the property system and legal relations within the family; and Spurr 1986. Some of the relevant texts are collected in translation by Lewis and Reinhold 1966, 227–30 (rev. ed. 1990, 487–96).

29. Dixon 1985c, 359–60, contains some of the stories which contribute to this picture. See also Dion.Halic. 2.25–26; and Hopkins 1978, 4 n. 8.

30. Cic. *de Sen.* 37 on Appius Claudius; Plut. *Aem.P.* 5 on the Aelii Tuberones (cf. Val.Max. 4.4.8–9); Juv. 6.287–90 on the virtuous women of early Rome. Consider also the contrast implicit in Tacitus's admiring account of German customs, *Germ.* 19, and the discussion of child rearing and rhetorical education in *Dial.* 28. It is notable that these authors come

from many different periods and that the golden age they mention varies somewhat from regal Rome, the early or mid-Republic, or even a generation before their own day.

31. Aul.Gell. *NA* 4.3.2 gives the account of the "first Roman divorce"; Plut. *Rom.* 22 gives the grounds for divorce in early Rome; Val.Max. 2.9.2 contains the story of the divorce by L. Annius of his young wife and the censure he incurred for it.

32. See Gardner 1986, 105–8; and below, chap. 4, for the rules governing the return of dowry.

33. Cf. Watson 1975; and Hopkins 1978, 80.

34. E.g., Cicero's wife Terentia rented pasturage and owned woodlands for a quick turnover (*Att.* 2.15.4, 2.4.5); Sassia set up her freedman doctor with a loan (*Clu.* 178). Even Clodia's "loans" to young men were probably the usual type of arrangement within the elite, made at an agreed rate of interest, like Caerellia's loans to Cicero (*Cael.* 31 [Clodia], *Att.* 12.51.3 [Caerellia]). On the decline of *tutela mulierum perpetua* see Dixon 1984a, 348.

35. See, e.g., Parker 1928, 237–38; Garnsey 1970b; Campbell 1978; and the discussion of soldier "marriage" in chap. 3, below.

36. As in the elevation of the *parens manumissor* to *tutor legitimus* of his emancipated daughter or granddaughter, or son or grandson emancipated before puberty (Gai. 1.166. This is discussed below).

37. Gai. 1.55; cf. Aul.Gell. *NA* 5.13.

38. E.g., Plin. *Ep.* 10.11; Sherwin-White's interpretation (1966, 577) is unconvincing. Cf. Gai. 1.93–94.

39. Kaser 1938; Crook 1967b.

40. Gai. 1.132. The ceremony for emancipation of a son required threefold repetition of the *mancipatio*, whereas a daughter was released by a single *mancipatio*, whether for full emancipation or in order to pass into a husband's *manus* (Gai. 1.137).

41. Cf. the story about the marriage of Cornelia to Tiberius Gracchus (Plut. *T.Gr.* 4.3ff.) and the third marriage of Cicero's daughter Tullia (*Att.* 5.4.1, 6.1.10; *fam.* 8.6). *C.Th.* 9.24 refers to the permission of both parents (see also below).

42. *CJ* 5.17.5. Cf. Paul *Sent.* 5.16.5 on Pius; and *FV* 116.

43. *Dig.* 48.9.5 (Marcianus). Cf. Pius's decision not to execute a deserter who had been handed over to the authorities by his own father, lest the father be associated with his son's death (*Dig.* 49.16.6). Yet the law was not uniformly kind to fatherly feeling; a father who disabled his son to keep him from a military levy was exiled by *relegatio* under Trajan (*Dig.* 49.16.15 [Papinian]).

44. Consider the examples of young Quintus Cicero (e.g., Cic. *Att.* 13.42, 14.10, 14.19) and the son of the orator Hortensius (Val. Max.5.9.2 and the discussion of generation conflict in chap. 5, below).

45. Cf. Watson 1967, 76–82, on the father's ritual acceptance of the newborn child; and Wiedemann 1989, 35–38, on examples of rejection. See *C.Th.* 9.13.1 (Constantine) and 9.14.1 (Valentinian and Valens) for Christian attempts to curb the practice.

46. Cf. Crook 1967b, 119: "To understand the true role of *patresfamilias* one must examine what they actually did in recorded examples and what limits were set to their power by the sentiment of society, crystallized in the practice of the courts and ultimately in legislation." See also Harris 1986; Saller 1986, 1991; and Dixon 1988, 26–28.

47. Gai. 1.165, 192. This also applied to an emancipating grandfather. See Dixon 1984a, 348–49, and below on the powers of a *tutor*.

48. Being cuckolded by his son (*Dig.* 38.9.5, cited above. Cf. the ruling *Dig.* 48.8.2 [Ulpian]).

49. *Tab.* 5.3, 5.6. See Dixon 1984a, 345. Cf. *Dig.* 50.17.73 (Q. Mucius Scaevola 1) on the relationship between *tutela* and inheritance.

50. Gai. 1.115a, 2.112–13; Cic. *Top.* 18 on the formalities of the female will; Watson 1975, 75–76, and 1967, 153, on its introduction with the *testamentum per aes et libram;* Gai. 2.101–4 on its history and ritual. Polyb. 31.26ff. describes the execution of the will of Aemilia, widow of Scipio Africanus the elder in the mid-second century B.C. See Dixon 1985a.

51. Cic. *Att.* 12.18.1; cf. 11.16.5, 23.3. Val.Max. 7.8.2, 7.7.4. On all these developments see Dixon 1988, 41–60.

52. *Inst.* 3.3 outlines the historical process. The introductory passage gives the problem which presented itself to the praetor in such a situation.

53. Thomas 1976, 523–24; *CJ* 6.55.1 (A.D. 426).

54. Women no longer had agnatic *tutores* from the time of Claudius, A.D. 41–54 (Gai. 1.157, 171). No women with the *ius trium / quattuor liberorum* had *tutores* at all from the time of Augustus (Gai. 1.145, 194). Hadrian abolished the preliminary *coemptio* for female wills which had marked the separation of women from their agnates (Gai. 1.115a). See again Dixon 1984a for a detailed exposition of the decline of *tutela mulierum perpetua.*

55. See again the second-century B.C. anecdote about the marriage of Cornelia to Tiberius Gracchus (Plut. *T.Gr.* 4.3ff.). Cf. the third marriage of Tullia, in which Tullia and her mother considered candidates and discussed them with Atticus during Cicero's absence abroad (see Collins 1951–52; and the references above, e.g., Cic. *fam.* 8.6; *Att.* 6.6.1). Young Quintus's divorced parents together determined on a match for him (Cic. *Att.* 13.42.1). The wicked Sassia compelled her daughter to have a divorce (Cic. *Clu.* 14).

56. *C.Th.* 9.24.

57. Friedl 1977, 123, for the modern Greek situation; Liv. 38.57.7 and Plut. *T.Gr.* 4 for the Roman examples.

58. Peppe (1984, 65 n. 141) cites Dion.Halic. 2.10.2, concerning a law of Romulus on dowry, as evidence of its early existence. See Watson 1975, 31–39, on the law of marriage and dowry at the time of the Twelve Tables. See Aul.Gell. *NA* 4.3.1–2 and Watson 1965 on the establishment of the *actio rei uxoriae* in 230 B.C.

59. Schulz 1951, 126–29; Watson 1967, 66–76; Gardner 1986, 105–8.

60. Polyb. 18.35.6, 31.22.

61. Val.Max. 4.4.8–9. She happened to be the daughter of Aemilius Paullus. (cf. Plut. *Aem.P.* 28).

62. Cic. *Att.* 5.8.2 (dowry of Fausta, wife of Milo); *fam.* 14.4.4 (Terentia). See the discussion of Dixon 1984c, 80–82, or see Rawson 1986a, 95–97.

63. Plut. *C.Gr.* 17.5, which seems to contradict Javolenus (*Dig.* 24.3.66), who cites P. Mucius Scaevola's view that the damage was the fault of the husband and the wife was entitled to the return of the dowry, presumably its value. Plutarch states that Licinnia lost the dowry. On the controversy see esp. Waldstein (1972), who argues that Licinnia did receive her dowry and that this decision formed the basis of subsequent judgments.

64. See Corbett 1930, 198–200, on *pacta dotalia*. On negotiations after divorce see Dixon 1984c, 97–100 (also in Rawson 1986a, 111–15).

65. Polyb. 31.27.4; Plut. *Cic.* 8.2; *Dig.* 24.3.66 (Javolenus), cited above in n. 63.

66. Gai. 2.63; *Dig.* 23.5.4 (Gaius); *Inst.* 2.8. *pr.* The husband was eventually prevented from alienating it even with her permission.

67. Ulpian *Tit.* 6.8; *Dig.* 24.3.24 *pr.* 1 (Ulpian). Cf. Gardner 1986, 108–9, on special circumstances in which the wife could reclaim the dowry even during marriage, usually because of claims from her own natal family, such as her father's bankruptcy.

68. *CJ* 5.13.1.1b; *Inst.* 4.6.29.

69. Cic. *Top.* 23.

70. *Dig.* 23.3.75. Cf. *CJ* 5.12.30 *pr.*

71. *Dig.* 23.3.2 (Paul), 24.3.1 (Pomponius).

72. Under the Julian law on marriage (Gai. 1.178; Ulpian 11.20).

73. *Dig.* 14.6.7.2 (Ulpian).

74. There are many examples of slave children being separated from their mother by sale at an early age and of brothers and sisters being divided (Hopkins 1978, 164–65; Bradley 1984, 52–63). Bradley points out (1984, 63–64) the effects of inheritance, when estates would be divided among several heirs and the slaves would be distributed among them.

75. *Dig.* 38.8.1.2 (Ulpian), which involves the rights to succession on intestacy, but note that Paul (*Dig.* 23.2.14.2) uses the expression *serviles cognationes* in relation to bans on close-kin marriage.

76. Rawson 1966, 1974; Bradley 1984, chap. 4; Saller 1987b on the slave or slave / freed family; Bradley 1986 on the links between nurse and

nurseling and 1987, 57–62, on the bond between nurseling and the nurse's child (*collactei / collactanei*).

77. *Dig.* 38.2.1 (Ulpian) for the traditional approach; 38.1 for the many rules about the duties owed to *patroni*; Tac. *Ann.* 13.26–27; Crook 1967a, 52–53.

78. *Dig.* 23.2.8 (Pomponius), on freed slaves, explains that this is based on morality (*mores*), not laws (*leges*). *Dig.* 23.2.14.2 (Paul) applies it to slaves after manumission or to a relationship between a free man and his natural daughter, born in slavery. Cf. *Dig.* 23.2.54 (Scaevola) on relations between brother and sister where one is illegitimate. See Corbett 1930, 49 and n. 5.

79. Gai. 1.19; *Dig.* 40.2.11–13, 9–16 (Ulpian). See also Treggiari 1969, 15 and n. 10. Other special services also gave grounds for exemptions, e.g., a slave's having once saved the owner's life. The praetor had discretion to allow them.

80. *Dig.* 40.2.13 (Ulpian).

81. *Dig.* 37.15.1.1 (Ulpian), 21.1.35 (Ulpian). On the *pietas* of a free father to his slave *filius naturalis* see *Dig.* 36.1.80.2 (Scaevola). On these and other applications of the concept of *pietas* in Roman law see Saller 1988, 1991).

82. Gai. 3.41 states that the praetor remedied the *iniquitas* of the earlier law allowing a *libertus* to pass over his *patronus* in his testament; and 3.42 points out that the *Lex Papia* (one of the laws favoring the married and those with legitimate children) allowed *patroni* a large share of the estate of a wealthy *libertus* with fewer than three (freeborn) children. Cf. *Dig.* 38.5.

83. Opinion was divided on whether the former owner could even claim a share of the estate when the *liberta* had made a will dividing her estate among her four children (Gai. 3.47).

84. Gai. 3.43–53, on the succession rights of *libertae* and *patronae* and their children, is a horrifying mishmash.

85. On the Marian army and recruitment see Parker 1928, 45; Carney 1961; Watson 1969, 21ff.; and Brunt 1971, 406–8.

86. The first reference to the ban is in Dio *Ep.* 60.24.3. See Parker 1928, 237–47; and Campbell 1978, 1984, 301–3, 339–45.

87. By Garnsey (1970b, 46).

88. Parker 1928, 237; MacMullen 1963, 126–28, pointing out that the transport of military families was accepted as an official responsibility by the fourth century A.D., long after the ban on soldier marriage had been lifted. Garnsey (1970b) is skeptical about the archaeological evidence. Cf. the reference to women and children in A.D. 9 when soldiers attempted to leave a fort secretly after the defeat of Varus (Dio. 56.22, 26.2 [Zon. 10.37, pp. 452, 453]).

89. Garnsey (1970b) is again the dissenting voice. On this see Macmullen 1963, 126–28; and Campbell 1978, 1984, 301–3, 339–45.

90. Collected in Campbell 1978, 161–63. See also Herodian 3.8.4–5.

91. See *P.Cattavi*, together with *BGU* 114 cols. 3–6, in Mitteis 1912, 2.2.418–25, e.g. 419, lines 11–12; 420 (col. 2), lines 1–2; 421 (col. 4, *P.Cattavi* 3), lines 13–14; 422 (col. 5, *P.Cattavi* 4) line 6.

92. Gai. 1.57 on unions of veterans with Latin and foreign women.

93. Cf. *FIRA* 1.141–42 (no. 76, or *ILS* 9059), referring to a Domitianic edict of A.D. 93 recognizing the "marriages" of the veterans of legion X *Fretensis* and a similar grant to praetorians, *ILS* 1993. On these see Lesquier 1918, 291–332; and Parker 1928, 240–42. Cf. the papyrus examples collected by Mitteis (1912, 2.2.418–25); and *CIL* 16.22 (A.D. 166) granting citizenship to sailors from the Misenum fleet and to their children by women "quas secum concessa consuetudine vixisse probaverint" and with whom they would subsequently have *conubium,* the right to contract a proper Roman marriage.

94. But see Campbell 1984, 439–45, for a different view (based, I believe, on inconclusive evidence). He summarizes the usual opinions on pp. 439–40. His own opinion apparently changed (see Campbell 1978, 156).

95. *Inst.* 2.12 *pr.*; Ulpian 20.10; *Dig.* 49.17.11 (Macer). This led to many special rulings, e.g., concerning the status of a soldier *filiusfamilias* as *patronus* of a woman freed to become his wife (*Dig.* 23.2.45.1–6 [Ulpian]). Cf. *Dig.* 23.2.35 (Papinian) on the need for paternal permission to marry.

96. Gai. 2.109 (*propter nimiam imperitiam*) = *Inst.* 2.11 *pr.*; *Dig.* 29.1.1–2 (Ulpian). See also Champlin 1987.

97. Gai. 2.110–11. *Dig.* 49.17, DE CASTRENSI PECVLIO, includes provisions on wills and other legal aspects of the position of the *filiusfamilias* soldier.

98. Dio. 60.24.3 (A.D. 44).

99. *FIRA* 1.428–30 (no. 78). See Campbell 1978, 158–59, on the legal difficulties that the grant presents.

100. *Dig.* 23.3.3 (Ulpian). See Campbell 1978, 154 n. 19.

101. Although the mother's name suggests that she was a Roman citizen and so the children probably were as well (Mitteis 1912, 2.2.422 [col. 5], lines 1–2). Campbell (1978, 155) gives an excellent account of the hearing of the petition and the increasing impatience of Eudaimon with the veteran's apparent refusal to accept this fundamental problem.

102. Parker 1928, 245.

103. "affectio parentium et adfinium" (*Dig.* 49.16.4.15 [Arrius Menander]). Other acceptable excuses could be health or the pursuit of one's runaway slave. Cf. Campbell 1984, 308–9, on rescripts of Pius concerning other issues of military discipline (*CJ* 16.13.6, 16.4.15).

104. Unless the father is in dire need (*Dig.* 25.3.5.17, based on an edict).

Cf. 25.3.5.14, based on a case in which a mother gained restitution from the father for part of the maintenance of a daughter living with her but the emperor Marcus ruled that she could not get back the full amount because her outlay had been influenced by her natural affection for her daughter (*exigente materno affectu*) and she would have spent some of this even if the girl had lived with the father. The whole of *Dig.* 25.3.5 (Ulpian, bk. 2, *de Officio Consulis*) concerns the duties of maintenance; and need as a determining factor is emphasized in 25.3.5.2–4.

105. *Dig.* 25.3.5.1 (Ulpian).

106. *Dig.* 25.3.5.2 (Ulpian): "et cum ex aequitate haec res descendat caritateque sanguinis, singulorum desideria perpendere iudicem oportet." Mothers and maternal grandmothers and even mothers' *liberti/ae* might also be required to maintain children (25.3.5.2, 5, 21).

107. Cf. the title DE OBSEQVIIS PARENTIBVS ET PATRONIS (*Dig.* 37.15) and the exceptions mentioned above to the *Lex Aelia Sentia,* which privileged not only biological kinship with slaves but foster relationships and the wish to marry a slave (Gai. 1.19; *Dig.* 40.2.11–13, etc. [Ulpian]) or the ruling that allowed a woman to go surety for a third party, in contravention of the *SC Velleianum,* if her pledge was to save her father from exile (*Dig.* 16.1 [Kallistratos], 21.1; *CJ* 4.29, 22–25; *Novel* 13.4.8).

108. Dixon 1985b on the fate of the *Lex Voconia* and 1984a, esp. 348, on the eventual decline of *tutela mulierum perpetua.*

109. Not only within Europe: Roman-Dutch law traveled to the Union of South Africa and to what was then Ceylon (Nicholas 1962, 52).

110. E.g., the much-quoted statement of the elder Cato that a Roman husband (in archaic times?) had absolute powers to punish an adulterous wife but that she had none over an adulterous husband (Aul.Gell. 10.23.4–5). If this had a basis, it was in custom rather than statute law and could certainly have been put to the test by a family *consilium* or praetorian decision. Cf. the case of the husband awarded an insulting one-*sestertius* damages by Marius because the husband clearly had known of his wife's sexual activity before marriage and hoped to use it as an excuse for retaining her dowry (Val.Max. 8.2.3).

111. Val.Max. 7.7.

## Chapter 3. Marriage

1. Gai.1.56. This extends to Latins with the *ius conubii,* the right to have a *iustum conubium* with a Roman citizen. On the importance of the "desire to be married," usually rendered by *affectio maritalis,* cf. Quint. *Inst.Or.* 5.11.32; see also Paulus *Sent.* 2.20.1.

2. Paul *Sent.* 2.19.8; Levy 1925, 72; Donahue 1978. See also n. 20 below.

3. Corbett 1930, 92–94; bibliography, Berger 1953, 578–79. Cf. Lan-

franchi 1936 for a collection of rhetorical and juristic definitions of marriage.

4. In contrast with the Greek situation, in which illegitimates probably could not be citizens or were excluded from the *phratries* (Harrison 1968, 1.161–68; MacDowell [1978, 68] disagrees with this). Attacks on individuals in Greek states commonly took the form of challenging the validity of the parents' or grandparents' marriage (cf. Pseudo-Demosthenes *Against Neaira;* and Isaeus 8.15–16). See below, chap. 4, on the position of Roman children of mixed or uncertain status. See also Rawson 1966, 1986c; Weaver 1986, 1991; and Watson 1989.

5. Cf. Newman 1972, esp. 3, for the idea that "legitimacy" of children is a notion introduced to exclude certain categories from a relatively privileged status in a community.

6. In spite of the notorious difficulty of producing a definition of marriage with universal applicability (Leach 1961, 105; Rivière 1971).

7. On the age of Roman men at marriage and the status differential see Saller 1987. On the ancient notion that history was a dignified medium concerned with the grand events of the battlefield and the senate consider Plin. *Ep.* 5.8.9.

8. Plin. *Ep.* 1.14.

9. Cic. *post Red.* 7.

10. "Cur dicam de tuorum caritate, familiae pietate, cum aeque matrem meam ac tuos parentes colueris eandemque quietem illi quam tuis curaveris?" (*CIL* 6.1527.31–33).

11. Cf. Hunt 1970, 58: "When Jean de Beauvau wanted to marry Francoise du Plessis . . . he penned ardent love letters—to her oldest brother, Henry: 'I want so much to change my relationship to you, my good cousin.'"

12. Plin. *Ep.* 1.14.

13. Cf. Cic. *Att.* 13.28, of a man rejected by "the women" of a family because of his insufficient means, or the lobbying for the position of third husband for Cicero's daughter Tullia, recorded in *Att.* 5.6.1 and *fam.* 3.10. Cf. Collins 1951.

14. Hopkins (1965a) suggested an age at first marriage of early teens for Roman pagan girls, but Shaw (1987a) has argued that it was determined by class and that upper-class girls were more likely to marry in their early or mid-teens, lower-class girls in their late teens.

15. Cic. *Att.* 13.42.

16. Plut. *Cat.mai.* 24.2–3. The man went into shock on learning that Cato was presenting himself for the match, but he soon recovered, and the marriage took place (see Cic. *de Or.* 3.133; and Hallett 1984, 103).

17. Corbett 1930, 2–5 on betrothal, 55–59 on marriage; Treggiari 1982; Gardner 1986, 41–44.

18. Cf. Cic. *Clu.* 14, 179; Plut. *Pomp.* 9.4; Liv. 38.57.7; Plut. *T.Gr.* 4.2;

and Phillips 1978 on the role of mothers in the arrangement of matches, particularly those of daughters.

19. On *sponsalia* see Gardner 1986, 45–47. Pliny lists attendance at betrothal parties as the sort of social engagement which typically take up his time in Rome (*Ep.* 1.9.2).

20. Both were assumed to be a normal part of the match, another reminder that the law, taken in isolation, is a poor guide to practice. After all, neither physical consummation nor cohabitation was requisite at law (*Dig.* 35.1.15 [Ulpian]: "It is not sexual intercourse but consent which makes a marriage" ["nuptias non concubitus sed consensus facit"]; and 24.1.32.13 [Ulpian]: "It is not sexual intercourse but the intent to be married [*maritalis affectio*] which creates marriage"). Needless to say, both sexual intercourse and cohabitation were normal features of marriage.

21. On other ritual surrounding weddings cf. Gardner 1986, 44, citing Varro *LL* 6.29; Macrobius 1.15.21 on suitable times for weddings; *Dig.* 23.2.5 (Pomponius) on the procession to accompany the bride from her home to that of her husband (*deductio*). Williams (1958) and Manson (1978, 250ff.) examine aspects of the ceremony in detail. Cf. Cat. 61, but on the understanding that it includes elements from the Greek literary tradition (Fordyce 1968, 235–54). Balsdon (1962, 181–86) gives a lucid and interesting description of the full wedding ceremony. Cf. Marquardt 1886, 42–57.

22. Cf. Polyb. 31.27.5 on the payment of the dowry of the Corneliae in the second century B.C.; Cic. *Att.* 11.25.3, 11.23.3 on the repayment of Tullia's dowry by Dolabella after her divorce in the first century B.C.; and Ulpian *Tit.* 6.8 (second century A.D.) on the rules for repayment at the end of a marriage.

23. Cf. *P.Mich.Inv.* 4703–2217, discussed by Sanders (1938). Pomeroy 1985, 86–89, provides a sample of Hellenistic Egyptian contracts in Greek. Some of the first-century A.D. wax tablets from Herculaneum record the details of the dowry arrangements of Paullina, married to L. Cominius Primus and later divorced from him (see Arangio-Ruiz and Pugliese-Carratelli 1955 and Cosentini 1971 on this dowry. Corbett's discussion [1930, 146–204] of dowry is both comprehensive and impressive. See more recently Saller 1984b; and Gardner 1985 on the function of dowry.

24. Ulpian *Tit.* 6.3–5. Dowries could be made up by contributions from different parties. The mother would commonly be one of the contributors. Other relations and even family friends might offer parts of the dowry. Aemelia bestowed large dowry payments on her daughters in her will (Polyb. 31.26ff.); "Turia" contributed to the dowries of her female relatives (*CIL* 6.1527.42ff.); the empress Livia endeared herself to members of the senatorial order by contributing to their daughters' dowries

(Dio 58.2.3); Pliny contributed to the dowries of his friends' daughters (Plin. *Ep.* 2.4, 6.32).

25. Dixon 1984c, 99–100.

26. Ulpian *Tit.* 6.6–8 on rules for repayment, 9–13 on deductions for marital misconduct; *Dig.* 24.3.47 (Scaevola). Again, Corbett covers the whole subject (1930, 182–202).

27. On the obligation of a father to provide dowry cf. Corbett 1930, 152–54. The obligation was probably social until the Augustan laws on marriage. Cf. *Dig.* 23.3.28 and 30 (Paul); 23.2.19 (Modestinus).

28. The formula is referred to incidentally in a number of texts, e.g., Val.Max. 7.7.4; Aul.Gell. *NA* 4.3.2, 17.21.44; Liv. *Ep.* 59; Suet. *Caes.* 52.3. On medical aspects of this link between marriage and procreation see now Gourevitch 1990.

29. "quod tibi sempiternum / salutare sit: liberis procreandis– / ita di faxint–volo te uxorem / domum ducere" (*Aul.* 146–49).

30. "liberorum quaerundorum causa ei, credo, uxor data est" (Plaut. *Capt.* 889).

31. *P.Mich.Inv.* 508, for the contract which dates to the time of the emperor Augustus. See Schiaparelli 1920; Wolff 1937; and *Serm.* 51.22, 278.9, for the references by St. Augustine to such contracts in late antiquity.

32. Aul.Gell. *NA* 4.3.1–2, 17.21.44; cf. Val.Max. 2.1.4, who sets the story earlier.

33. Plut. *Rom.* 22 dates divorce (initiated only by the husband) to the regal period, from the eighth to the sixth century B.C. Cic. *Phil.* 2.28.69; and *Dig.* 48.5.44 (Ulpian) suggest that divorce was possible at the time of the Twelve Tables, in the fifth century B.C. Cf. Val.Max. 2.9.2; Liv. 9.43.25 on the divorce of L. Annius (307–6 B.C.).

34. Aul.Gell. *NA* 4.3.2; Val.Max. 2.1.4 ("ne cupiditatem quidem liberorum coniugali fidei praeponi debuisse arbitrantur").

35. The anecdotes told, for example, by Plutarch and Valerius Maximus about second-century B.C. characters tend not to have such an emotional content.

36. Plut. *Aem.P.* 5.1.

37. Cf. modern Israel, where Jewish marriages can be dissolved only by the husband, though in most cases this is a formality.

38. Dixon 1985c, 359–61.

39. Liv. 1.9.14

40. Dio 56.3.3.

41. Tac. *Ann.* 3.34, A.D. 21. The prince Drusus said that he would not be as happy in fulfilling his civic duty if he were deprived of his "most beloved wife, the mother of their many children."

42. Treggiari, in her forthcoming work on marriage (1991), cites a number of references in her chapter entitled *Coniugalis Amor,* which she has

kindly allowed me to view in typescript. I have also discussed this ideal in Dixon 1991. Cf. Tac. *Germ.* 18; *Ann.* 3.15.2, 12.5.5.

43. E.g., *CIL* 6.35536, 9810, 27853. See also the many examples given in Lattimore 1942, 279 nn. 107, 108.

44. Ov. *Met.* 8.708.

45. Plin. *Ep.* 3.16.10: "si tam diu tantaque concordia . . . quam ego cum Paeto"—in answer to her son-in-law's query whether she would expect her daughter to die if he were condemned. These people were all associated with Stoic philosophy and opposition to the Empire. Stories about the courage and exemplary wifely loyalty of the women of this group circulated throughout the early Empire (see Plin. *Ep.* 3.16, 7.19, 9.13.5; Dio 16.5–6; and *ILS* 6261).

46. *Dig.* 23.2.1.

47. Paulus *Sent.* 5.15. See n. 92 below.

48. Corbett 1930 remains an invaluable source. Corbett's main emphasis is on the evidence of Justinian's sixth-century compilation of law, the *Digest,* but he includes references to earlier literary sources, such as Livy and Cicero. The great authority for the republican period is Watson, who deals with marriage in several of his works, notably *The Law of Persons in the Later Roman Republic* (1967). Crook (1967a, 99–106; cf. 40–42), Humbert (1972), and Gardner (1986, chaps. 3–6) give more readable treatments of marriage from the social *and* legal points of view. The authors listed here all provide useful bibliographies on specific questions, and I shall refer throughout the chapter to many such works but consider it beyond the scope of this volume to give extensive consideration to detailed controversies. I am also conscious of the comprehensive character of Treggiari 1991, on Roman marriage, which would make any such attempt superfluous.

49. Unless his paternal grandfather was alive. This rider should always be understood, but it is more convenient and realistic to assume that the death of a father usually rendered a child *sui iuris* (which in the case of a male meant that he became a *paterfamilias*) than to repeat this possibility each time.

50. Gai. 1.189–95 on *tutela mulierum* in imperial times; Cic. *Flacc.* 84 on the need for the permission of *tutor(es)* to pass into the husband's *manus.* See esp. Watson 1967, 149–52. The *tutor* did not actually give permission for the *marriage* but for certain financial implications of the marriage. A woman *in tutela* had full power to dispose of money (a *res nec mancipi*) and certain property as she wished, but a transfer of slaves, land, and other items (some, but not all, livestock) classed at law as *res mancipi* required the presence and assent (*auctoritas*) of her *tutor* to validate the transactions. A marriage contracted without the consent of a living *paterfamilias* was void. This was not the case with a marriage contracted without the permission of the *tutor* or *tutores.* In practice, a *tutor* might be

closely involved in the proceedings in his function as friend of the family or close relation.

51. Cornell 1989.

52. Dion.Halic. 2.25.1.6. Juvenal (6.287–90) looks back to an unspecified period in the past when Roman peasant women were too exhausted by hard work to think of adultery, which these authors apparently saw as a "modern" invention, a common twentieth-century delusion.

53. Liv. 1.58.

54. Quoted by Aulus Gellius (*NA* 10.23.4) in the second century A.D., some three hundred years later.

55. Dion.Halic. 2.26.27.

56. Plut. *Rom.* 22.

57. The details of the ceremony are given in Gai. 1.112. It had almost disappeared by the early Empire, which was inconvenient because certain patrician priesthoods could be filled only by couples (or men) married by this method, and usually on the understanding that their parents had also been married by this method (Tac. *Ann.* 4.16. See also Boethius on Cic. *Top.* 14; Servius on Verg. *Aen.* 4.103; and Marquardt 1886, 34).

58. Gai. 1.113. A woman could also conduct a *coemptio* to change *tutores* or, until the time of the emperor Hadrian (A.D. 117–38), before making a valid will. This had no effect on her status unless she made the *coemptio* with her husband, in which case she entered his *manus* (whether that had been her intention or not) just as if it had been part of a marriage ceremony (Gai. 115a–b).

59. Gai. 1.111. Watson (1967, 19–23) thinks that by Cicero's time *usus* could be avoided if a woman's *paterfamilias* (and possibly the *tutor*) withheld consent to *usus* as such. For a bibliography on the controversial aspects see esp. Watson 1967, 23 n. 3, as well as Watson 1976 and 1979.

60. Polyb. 18.35.6, 41.26. See also Dixon 1985a, 64–67.

61. Val.Max. 4.4.9.

62. Cic. *Top.* 23.

63. I prefer this terminology to the expressions "marriage *cum manu*" and "marriage *sine manu*" coined by Watson. Convenient as they are, they give the appearance of being legal Latin terms, a false impression I wish to avoid.

64. On Gai. 1.108–15b. Cf. Koschaker 1937, which de Zulueta cites. Schulz (1951, 102–3) quotes Jhering (1880) on the change in marriage preference: "Better natures, however, far from seeing progress in this evolution rightly regarded it as a sign of ever-spreading demoralization." Schulz himself deplores this approach and praises what he perceives as a triumph of a humanistic view of Roman marriage. De Zulueta and Schulz seem to be transitional between the old style of social evolutionary thinking and the more recent trends.

65. Cf. Watson 1967, 20–21, on the significance of the decision for par-

ticular families and estates; and Crook 1967a, 104, and 1986, 61.

66. According to Saller (1986, 15), "By the time girls married in their late teens, more than half had probably lost their fathers."

67. This was certainly the original purpose of *tutela mulierum perpetua* and its link with agnatic family relationship (see Dixon 1984a, 345–49).

68. Rawson 1976, *pace* Treggiari 1979a.

69. The *Lex Voconia* of ca. 169 B.C. forbade members of the top property class to institute women as heirs. There were, however, many ways of benefiting women if testators wished it (Dixon 1985b). The *Lex Oppia*, passed in the second Punic War and restricting female display of wealth, was rescinded in 196 B.C. Liv. 34.1–8 gives a colorful reconstruction of the debate and the female demonstration that attended the rescission. See Haury 1976.

70. Lightman and Zeisel 1977.

71. Hallett 1984; Dixon 1985c, 369–71.

72. Val.Max. 2.9.21; Liv. 9.43.25.

73. Val.Max. 6.3.9.

74. "Adulterii graviorem poenam deprecatus, ut exemplo maiorum propinquis suis ultra ducentesimum lapidem removeretur suasit" (Tac. *Ann.* 2.50, A.D. 17).

75. "Mariti iudicio permissa; isque prisco instituto propinquis coram de capite famaque coniugis cognovit et insontem nuntiavit" (Tac. *Ann.* 13.32).

76. Richlin's (1981) thorough treatment of the sources on adultery and the punishments meted out informally represents a great advance. Other studies tend to concentrate on the legalities. There were complex rules in the Julian legislation about when or where a husband or father did have the right to kill an adulterer, but it is very difficult to relate these to practice. Cf. Rabello 1972; and Csillag 1976, 195–99.

77. "Nam culpam inter viros ac feminas vulgatam gravi nomine laesarum religionum ac violatae maiestatis appellando clementiam maiorum suasque ipse leges egrediebatur" (Tac. *Ann.* 3.24).

78. On the rules governing adultery trials see *Dig.* 48.5.

79. Cic. *Leg.* 3.7; Dion.Halic. 2.25.7; Aul.Gell. *NA* 4.3.2. See also the sources cited in n. 28, above.

80. Val.Max. 2.9.2.

81. Liv. 8.22.3, 10.31.9, 25.2.9. See also Bauman 1974 on the trials of certain matrons by the plebeian aediles in 213 B.C.

82. Doubt has been thrown on the confused account of Livy 4.1, in particular by Last (1945), but a law was passed in the mid-fifth century B.C. which validated marriage between the two primary divisions of Roman society at that time, namely, the patricians and plebeians. Corbett 1930, 30, discusses the background of the earlier prohibition and the evidence for it.

83. Ulpian 5.3–7 lists those categories with whom *conubium* existed in

his day, the second century A.D. Berger 1953, 415, gives a useful bibliography up to about 1952 on the subject. See also Leonhard 1900; and Kunkel 1930, 2262.

84. Corbett 1930, 31–34, has a good discussion of the evidence of such a law, although Corbett himself does not believe in its existence. See also Watson 1967, 33–38, for the opposing view. Both authors list the relevant texts. I incline to Corbett's view, that such unions were not illegal but were probably frowned upon in certain quarters. Epitaphs attest such unions but are chiefly from the imperial period. See now Humbert 1987.

85. The legislation of 18 B.C. was actually masterminded by Augustus but formally proposed by the consuls of that year (both bachelors) with the aim of encouraging Roman citizens, especially those of the upper classes, to marry and have legitimate children. Augustus himself openly put forward the second block of legislation, which was more severe, particularly in its penalties for adultery or childlessness. The suggestion that there was a third block of legislation has been quashed by Badian (1985). Cf. Dixon 1988, 84–86.

86. Levy 1925, 6–52; cf. Csillag 1976, 128–33.

87. On the legislation in general see Williams 1962; Astolfi 1970; Hallett 1973; Kaser 1975, 1.318–21; Csillag 1976; Frank 1976; Nörr 1977; Besnier 1979; Cairns 1979; Raditsa 1980; and Galinsky 1981. The remains of the laws are collected in Riccobono 1945, 168.

88. See esp. Suet. *Aug.* 34; and cf. Aug. *RG* 8.5: "legibus novis me auctore latis multa exempla maiorum exolescentia iam ex nostro saeculo reduxi et ipse multarum rerum exempla imitanda posteris tradidi." The depiction of his own family on the Ara Pacis Augustae (Altar of Augustine Peace) also promoted this example. See plate 16.

89. Dio 56.1–10. Cf. Suet. *Aug.* 34.

90. Interested parties (husbands and fathers of adulteresses) had first option in prosecutions, but if they had not taken it up after sixty days, anyone (even slaves and noncitizens) could bring the case (*Dig.* 48.5.2 [Ulpian]).

91. Plin. *Ep.* 6.31.5; see also Sherwin-White's (1966, 393–94) discussion of the case.

92. Schulz 1951, 135–36, citing *Dig.* 24.2 *pr.* 1, 24.2.9; Kaser 1975, 1.326–28. Of course, divorce could also be initiated by the *paterfamilias* of one or both parties, but the law gradually limited the paternal power to dissolve a happy marriage against the wishes of the married pair. See above, chap. 2, on the gradual checks on *patria potestas.*

93. Gardner (1986, 91–93) stresses that bigamy in imperial times would expose the bigamist to a charge of adultery or fornication and cites post-classical rulings to support this. In classical times, the effect of two unions would be to invalidate one. Cf. the case described in Cic. *de Or.* 1.183, which does not give the court's decision about a man who had a

wife in Spain and one in Rome. After his death, a question arose concerning the status of the child of the second marriage, and the court had to determine whether the first marriage had been dissolved by divorce as demonstrated by his acting as if he were not married. Cf. Corbett 1930, 143.

94. Corbett 1930, 243–45; Kaser 1975, 2.176–78.

95. Humbert 1972, 326–40; Kaser 1975, 2.168. Cf. Goody 1983, 134–46, on the reasons for these prohibitions.

96. Gai. 1.59ff.; but see Corbett 1930, 50–51. It looks as if father-daughter incest was punished as an abomination (Tac. *Ann.* 6.19; Dio 58.22), but this was not true of bigamy.

97. Liv. 20 (frag. pub. in Kruger 1870, 372); cf. Tac. *Ann.* 12.6, where Vitellius argues in the senate that marriage between cousins had once been unknown in Roman society but had since become commonplace. This was part of his speech urging the senate to accept the marriage of the emperor Claudius to his niece, the younger Agrippina, a union that until then would have been void.

98. Liv. 42.34.3, set in 171 B.C. Since Ligustinus refers to having two married daughters and four sons who have attained adult status (as well as two younger sons), the marriage must have been contracted more than twenty years earlier.

99. Cic. *Phil.* 2.99, where Cicero would certainly have lost no opportunity to stigmatize M. Antonius's marriage; Plut. *Ant.* 9.1–2; *Brut.* 13.2; Cic. *Clu.* 5.11. Vitellius's argument in his speech to the senate (Tac. *Ann.* 12.6) is based on the assumption that cousin marriage is commonplace in his day, A.D. 49. Saller and Shaw (1984a) have contested Goody's (1983) contention that cousin marriage was a preferred form of marriage in Roman society, but this selection (which is by no means exhaustive) shows that it was certainly popular.

100. August. *Civ.Dei.* 15–16.

101. Kaser 1975, 2.166–67. Goody (1983) argues that the Christian church set out to destroy traditional modes of property dispersal by setting up the Church in competition with family obligations and that the attack on cousin marriage was an important element of this strategy.

102. E.g., Corbett 1930, 30–47.

103. *C.Th.* 3.7.2; *CJ* 1.9.6 (Valentinian, Theodosius, and Arcadius, A.D. 388). Transgressors were subject to the penalties for adultery.

104. Where Greek inscriptions take up this practice, it is clearly in imitation of the Roman style (Lattimore 1942, 280, on a set of inscriptions from Neoclaudiopolis by Greek-speaking Roman citizens).

105. Cf. Segal 1968, 22–28.

106. Quoted by Aulus Gellius, *NA* 1.6.2, and used by Augustus in one of his speeches encouraging his contemporaries to marry. The statement was part of a speech by a second-century B.C. censor. Quotes from Sen-

eca's *de Matrimonio* were used by St. Jerome to argue against marriage (*adv. Iovinianum* = Sen. frag. 13 Haase 1872). Seneca's work, which was probably based on Theophrastus, included a section (48 ff.) on the irreconcilability of philosophy and marriage.

107. See esp. Veyne 1978; Hallett 1984; and Bradley 1987.

108. Cic. *fam*. 14.4.6 ("fidissima atque optima uxor"); 14.2.2 ("mea lux, meum desiderium"); 14.2.3 ("mea vita"). Cf. 14.3.5 ("mihi te carius nihil esse nec umquam fuisse").

109. *Tristia* 3.3.24 ("carissima"), 3.3.52 ("lux mea"), 3.3.55 ("optima coniunx").

110. *CIL* 6.1527.44–45, 51–66 (Durry).

111. *CIL* 6.1527.ii.2a–21 on "Turia"; Plin. *Ep*. 3.16 on Arria the elder, 6.24 on a woman who suicided with her terminally ill husband; Plut. *Brut*. 13 and Dio 44.13–14 on Porcia; Val.Max. 4.6 and 6.7 on heroic and strikingly faithful wives; Appian *BC* 4.39–40 and Tac. *Hist*. 1.3 on wives in civil wars.

112. Many have been collected by Lattimore (1942, 275–80, esp. 278–79). See also Harrod 1909, 66–72, esp. 71; and Dixon 1991. A few examples from *CIL* 6 (Rome and environs) include 33182, 25678, and 26776.

113. She was forty at the time of her death, seven when he "took her to his bosom" ("gremio ipse recepit"). Cf. the fourteen-year-old wife Aelia Tychene, commemorated by her husband (*CIL* 6.25301).

114. Bradley 1986, 92 n. 43, on the tombstone terminology. Cf. Bradley 1987, 36 and n. 11, on the ideal of marital harmony.

115. Williams 1962, 28; Lilja 1965, 176–77; Hallett 1973; Lyne 1980, 5–7; Rudd 1981, 15–154.

116. Plin. *Ep*. 7.5. Pliny's adoption of the motif of the excluded lover falls perfectly within the erotic elegiac tradition. See Guillemin 1929, 140–41. This is equally true of Sulpicia's poetry and Ovid's claim that the image of his absent wife hovers before him (Ov. *Tristia* 3.3.15–20) or Statius's possession by love (*Silvae* 3.5.22–36). See my discussion of these themes in Dixon 1991. It was traditionally supposed that the six poems by "Sulpicia" in the Tibullan *Corpus* (3.13–4.7) were penned by Tibullus himself rather than by the poet Sulpicia, who is known to have moved in the literary circle of Messalla Corvinus and *fl. ca*. 15 B.C. Her work has gained greater attention—and appreciation (e.g., Ellerman 1982; Lowe 1988, 205; Roessel 1990, 250)—in recent years, and most critics now accept her authorship of the surviving elegies (e.g., Alfonsi 1946, 96; Putnam 1973, 5; Ellerman 1982; Ball 1983, 166–67; Roessel 1990, 247–50). Not all assume that her poetry is directed to her husband, and recent attention has been focused on the role reversal of a respectable woman singing the praises of a lover (Hinds 1987, 33; Roessel 1990, 247–50). Hinds even contemplates the possibility that the poem involves a more complex reversal of roles and is

really written by a man masquerading as a woman (e.g., Hinds 1987, 46), but this is simply one of a range of possibilities which he suggests.

117. Plut. *Cat.mai.* 17; Luc. 4.1263–77; Plut. *Praec.Con.* (*Moralia*) 139.9; Sen. *de Matrimonio* (= frag. 13 Haase 1872) 84–85.

118. Plut. *Praec.Con.* (*Moralia*) 138.4. Cf. Luc. 4.1280–87 on true love, which grows with time and is founded in character and mutual knowledge; and Cat. 61.102–5, 109–12, and esp. 169–71 (Fordyce) on the ardor of the newlyweds.

119. Sen. *Ep.mor.* 104; Tac. *Ann.* 4.22 for the murder. The man's first wife had to answer charges of sorcery against him, which also implies passion between spouses. The account of the suicide of Seneca is in Tac. *Ann.* 15.63–64.

120. Burn 1953, 11–12; Hopkins 1966, 261; Huttunen 1974, 56–58.

121. Val.Max. 4.6.1–3.

122. See esp. Hallett 1984, 223–43, 343–46; and Dixon 1985c, 369–71, on the identification with brothers and children rather than husbands. Examples of wives showing outstanding loyalty in times of crisis include Sulpicia, who escaped her own mother's protective custody to go into dangerous flight with her husband (Val.Max. 6.7.3), and Cicero's wife Terentia, who supported him in every way throughout his exile (Cic. *fam.* 14.1–4; see Dixon 1984c, 80–87, reprinted in Rawson 1986a, 95–102). Consider again Velleius Paterculus's claim (2.67.2) that wives consistently showed the greatest loyalty throughout the civil war.

123. Cf. Lattimore 1942, 278 and n. 98. See *CIL* 2.78; 3.3572; 5.7763; 6.2318, 13299; 8.7384, 7337. Literary references include Sen. *de Matrimonio* 72–77; Liv. 10.23; Val.Max. 2.1.3; and Tac. *Ann.* 2.86. And see also the list in Csillag 1976, 232–33 n. 235. Other references include Prop. 4.11.68 and the odd attempt by Horace (3.14) to extend the language to Livia ("unico gaudens mulier marito"), whose divorce from her first husband in order to marry Augustus was particularly scandalous, since she was expecting a child. Humbert 1972, 327–40, and Lightman and Zeisel 1977 both follow the development of the ideal into Christian times, when it took on a new force. Cf. Williams 1958, 23–24, 25.

124. *CJ* 5.10.1 (A.D. 392). See Dixon 1988, 49–50.

125. Cf. Watson's (1989) study of the term *filiaster,* which Meyer interpreted as "illegitimate child" rather than "stepson."

126. See also Treggiari 1981b.

127. Cf. the examples of Jones (1985, 33–38) for American slavery and Bush (1990, 108–10) for Caribbean slavery.

128. Corbett 1930, 24–53.

129. Crook 1967a, 101. Augustan legislation made bigamists liable for adultery or fornication (Corbett 1930, 143; Gardner 1986, 91–93).

130. *Dig.* 23.2.44 (Paul). This question of relative social status is explored below, in the discussion of *concubinae.*

131. Gai. 1.56; *Inst.* 1.10 on *conubium;* Gai. 1.29 on Junian Latins. See Weaver 1991.

132. Gai. 1.78.

133. Garnsey (1970a, esp. 221–33) on these and other status terms.

134. See esp. Parker 1928, 237; Garnsey 1970b; and Campbell 1978. The gradual legal acknowledgment of such unions is also discussed in chap. 2, above, and the effect on the status of the children of the union is discussed in chap. 4.

135. Cf. Parker 1928, 237; MacMullen 1963, 126–27; Campbell 1978 and 1984, 302; and for Britain, Allason-Jones 1989, 60–61.

136. Herodian 3.8.4–5, *pace* Garnsey 1970b.

137. See, e.g., *FIRA* 1.231 (no. 27, A.D. 71) on auxiliaries, and the many examples of Roxan 1978, e.g., 2.137 (no. 79, A.D. 65), 2.168 (no. 102, A.D. 157), and 2.196 (no. 123, A.D. 179). Parker 1928, 238–42, and Campbell 1978, 159, have detailed discussion of such *diplomata.* Note that they are rarely for legionaries.

138. In Parker's words, "Not infrequently their tombstones were put up by loving wives and dutiful daughters and in the second century a large proportion of legionaries were drawn . . . from a class which gave their birthplace as *castris*" (1928, 237). Cf. Allason-Jones 1989, 59; and Birley 1981, 45–46.

139. *Dig.* 1.5.17 (Ulpian) on the Edict of Caracalla. But Campbell points out (1978, 164 n. 84) that *diplomata* were still issued after A.D. 212; see, e.g., Roxan 1978, 1.99 (no. 77, A.D. 236).

140. The early imperial jurist Masurius Sabinus noted that earlier authors had called such women *paelices* but that they had come to be known as *amicae* or *concubinae. Amica* (girlfriend) is seen as a frank term, *concubina* as a more honorable one (*Dig.* 50.16.144 [Paul]). On the distinction between *amica* and *concubina* in Plautus see Watson 1967, 1–2; and Treggiari 1981a, 60, which reviews these texts.

141. *Dig.* 23.2.44; 23.2.23 (Celsus) on senators and their children; 23.2.16 (Paul), specifically on daughters of senators.

142. *Dig.* 32.49.4, where Ulpian, in relation to the estate of the man, says that the difference between a wife and a concubine is essentially one of status ("sane enim nisi dignitate nihil interest").

143. *SHA Marcus* 29.10.

144. Although the male partner and the *concubina* sometimes had children from previous alliances (Rawson (1974, 291 and n. 49). Treggiari (1981a, 68–69) considers this point and quotes St. Augustine's comment that partners in concubinage tried to avoid children and were sorry if they had any (*Conf.* 4.2, 6.12–15).

145. Suet. *Dom.* 12.3. Cf. *Dig.* 25.4.1 *pr.* (Ulpian), stating that it is more honorable for an owner to keep a freedwoman as his concubine than it is to keep her as a *materfamilias* (technically, a wife *in manu mariti,* but

eventually used as a general term for a respectable matron).

146. *Dig.* 20.1.8 (Ulpian) and 42.5.38 (Paul), cited in Treggiari 1981a, 72.

147. *Dig.* 25.7.3 (Modestinus), 25.7.1.1 (Ulpian).

148. Tac. *Ann.* 12.53; Gai. 1.91, 1.160. See also Berger 1953, 697.

149. Weaver 1986, 166. Cf. also Weaver 1972, 168–69.

150. *Dig.* 23.2.13, but see *CJ* 5.4.3 (Septimius Severus).

151. Weaver 1986, 147, arguing that such terminology is therefore of little use in determining the legal status of partners. His inclusion of kin terms such as *pater, mater, frater, soror,* and *filii* is misplaced. Unlike *liberi, pater-familias,* etc., these terms are not confined to specific legal relationships.

*Chapter 4. Children in the Roman Family*

1. Shaw 1992, esp. tables 1 and 2.

2. Plut. *Numa* 12.2; *FV* 321 (Ulpian). On the cross-cultural parallels see, e.g., Shorter 1977, 174 (seventeenth-century France); Gibbs 1960, 73–74 (eighteenth-century England). See also Dixon 1988, 136 n. 3.

3. Sen. *Ep.mor.* 99.14 upbraids a friend for his unphilosophic mourning for a child as yet better known to his nurse than to his father. Pliny even cautions Aefulanus Marcellinus against reproaching their mutual friend Minicius Fundanus for his great grief at the loss of a thirteen-year-old daughter (*Ep.* 5.16, esp. 8–10; she was actually twelve [*ILS* 1030]).

4. Cic. *Disp.Tusc.* 1.93.4 on general practice. Cf. *Att.* 10.18, where he refers to his daughter's premature child as "a thing" ("quod est natum"). His comments on Lentulus are not as harsh, but he seems to have no interest in the baby beyond performing his duty in the disposition of property (*Att.* 12.18a).

5. Note the contrast between Pliny's description of his friend's desolation at the death of his daughter and the stark commemorative inscription, *ILS* 1030. In *Ep.* 5.16.8, Pliny apologizes sympathetically for the father, who is unable in spite of his training to gain solace from philosophy and rise above his grief. Golden's (1988) discussion of the issues involved is sensitive. He concentrates on Greek examples, but his points are applicable to the Roman world as well. See also Hopkins 1983, 217–26; and Dixon 1988, 104, 113–14.

6. Compare Burn 1953, 4; Hopkins 1983, 225; and Bradley 1986, 217. Griessmair (1966, e.g., 15–16) looks at the age aspect of "untimely death" in Greek sources in his thorough study of the phenomenon, and Nock (1972) looks at the survival into Christian writings of a certain fear of those who die before their time.

7. Cic. *Disp.Tusc.* 1.93–94.

8. Hor. *Serm.* 1.6, esp. 81–92; Tac. *Agr.* 4; Marcus *Med.* 1.1–17.

9. E.g., Cic. *Disp.Tusc.* 3.1.2. Bradley (1987, 49 n. 37) has a collection of attractive images from childhood, but these are usually invoked to il-

lustrate general points. Cf. Wiedemann 1989, 22–24 and esp. 45 n. 44, quoting Fannius's statement (Cic. *de Re Pub.* frag. incert. 3 Ziegler 1964, 137.3) that childhood cannot be praised for its own sake, only for its potential ("non enim res laudanda sed spes est").

10. Illustrations of this process usually show the midwife lifting the child immediately after birth (see plate 24). Legal and literary sources concentrate on the act of the *paterfamilias,* often referred to as *tollere liberos,* literally "to raise children," an expression that comes to have our extended meaning of raising children. On the ritual and problems connected with its interpretation, especially its legal implications, see Volterra 1951, 952; Belmont 1973; and Rousselle 1988, 51. Other aspects, including the religious, are discussed by Néraudau (1984, 70–74) and Eyben (1986, 324–27); French (1987) concentrates on the medical aspects.

11. Marquardt 1886, 83–84; Dixon 1988, 240; and the references in the preceding note. On the present, cf. *Dig.* 50.16.194 on the *natalicium.* See plate 19 for a child wearing the *bulla.* I am not sure whether the *bulla* was (as is often asserted) confined to boys.

12. Perhaps we should not too hastily assume the absence of special ritual for girls. Many Australian aboriginal groups have proved to be rich in all-female rites which never appeared in early ethnographic accounts because male anthropologists relied on male informants. Cf. Bell 1983, 84, on the significance of the *jilimi* (women's house) and elsewhere the imperfect male knowledge and appreciation of female ceremonial associated with it (11).

13. Marquardt 1886, 42–57; Fordyce 1968, esp. 236, on Cat. 61 and 62; Harmon 1978, 1598–1600; Courtney 1980, 285–86, on Juv. 6.200–205 and other parts of the same satire. Weddings are also represented in art, e.g., in the Aldobrandini frieze and sarcophagus reliefs (see plates 1–3).

14. But the age varied (see Marquardt 1886, 128–30). I do not accept Rousselle's contention (1988, 59–61) that a boy's puberty was determined by close physical analysis, e.g., by his family watching for his first ejaculation. Some physical inspection was traditional, but this gradually gave way to a notional age of male puberty at 14 (Gai. 1.196; *Inst.* 1.22 *pr.*). Cf. n. 36 below.

15. Plin. *Ep.* 1.9 and Sherwin-White 1966, 106; Cic. *Att.* 5.20.9; *Mur.* 69; Marquardt 1886, 124–30.

16. Cic. *Cael.* 11–12.

17. The full charm of the brief description of the baby in Cat. 61.212–13 is difficult to convey in English. While the expression *semihiante labello* ("with half-smiling little mouth/lip") can be translated, its graphic quality is elusive. See Martial 5.34; *CIL* 6.18086, which records the neighbors' exclamation, "O dulce Titu!"; and cf. *CIL* 14.1731 from Ostia, on the child Acerva. See plates 16–24 for portrayals of childhood and youth in the art of the Roman world.

18. Manson 1978, 258–59, and 1983, 154; and for the association on coins of *pietas* with love of children see Manson 1975. See also Dixon 1988, 104–14. Neither Néraudau nor Wiedemann looks specifically at the appreciation of young children per se, but Néraudau (1984, 60–61) does examine the Roman evidence for what Ariès termed *mignotage* and has an excellent discussion (335–71) of Roman attitudes towards children (i.e., progeny) in general. Wiedemann (1989, 90–91) looks at parental affection for children from about age ten to early adult life, somewhat modifying his material (39–43) on the view of children as security for parents.

19. E.g., Cic. *Att.* 1.10.6, 7.2.4; Fronto *ad Amicos* 1.12. Consider the proverbial blindness of parents to their children's faults (Hor. *Serm.* 1.3.43–58).

20. This is even evident in private and official imperial statuary (Kleiner 1977, 178–79, and 1978; Pollini 1985; and see plates 14 and 16–24 in this volume). Cf. Ariès's comments (1962, 33–34 and nn. 1–7) on the representation of children in mediaeval art as miniature adults. This phenomenon also occurs in Roman depictions of children, e.g., plate 15.

21. "ita sum ab omnibus destitutus ut tantum requietis habeam quantum cum uxore et filiola et mellito Cicerone consumitur." It is important to add that he was regretting the absence from Rome of his friend Atticus and brother Quintus, who provided him with trustworthy masculine friendship and political advice. On the concept of the family as haven see above, chap. 1, and Lasch 1977.

22. Luc. 3.894–96: "Iam iam non domus accipiet te laeta, neque uxor / optima nec dulces occurrent oscula nati / praeripere et tacita pectus dulcedine tangent."

23. Bradley 1987, 49 n. 37. Manson (1978, 258–59; 1983, 153–54) contrasts the terminology of Plautus's second-century plays with the language used of young children in first-century B.C. literature. As I have argued elsewhere (1991), anecdotes about happy marriages are grounded overwhelmingly in examples from this period, and the interest in the subject as a literary and epigraphic commonplace is later than the second century B.C. On this debate see above, chap. 3.

24. Consider the information collected by Rawson (1986b) on *alumni,* who were nearly all very young; by Bradley (1986) on nurselings and (1987) on *collactanei* (foster brothers and sisters); and by Dixon (1984b) on the relationships signified by the childish terms *mamma* and *tata.* See also Heraeus 1937, 158–80, and Vogt 1974, 107–14, on relations with pedagogues and other caregivers.

25. On *liberi* as a term denoting freeborn children see Benveniste 1936, esp. 57 n. 1; and Manson 1978, 251. Wiedemann (1989, 32–34) argues that *pueri* and *puellae* referred to the child as part of the household, while *liberi* signified their place in the wider community. Cf. *Dig.* 50.16.204 for

a summary of the uses of *pueri*. On the terminology in general see also Slusanski 1974; Néraudau 1984, 44–58; and Gray-Fow 1985.

26. Bradley (1986, 218) feels that Plutarch's description of his dead two-year-old daughter (*Mor.* 608A–612B, *Consolatio ad uxorem*) does not fit her age.

27. Quint. *Inst.Or.* 6 pr. 10–12; Plin. *Ep.* 5.16.2.

28. Cf. the young Cicero boys in their mid-teens (*Att.* 6.1.12).

29. Plin. *Ep.* 5.16.7.

30. *CIL* 6.18086.15–17.

31. For example, according to their biographers, Cato the younger was always chosen to lead childish games (Plut. *Cat.min.* 3.1), and the infant Nero was unsuccessfully attacked by snakes (Suet. *Nero* 6.4; cf. *Aug.* 94). See Wiedemann 1989, 49–64, on children in imperial biographies generally; and Lyman 1974, 79–80, for examples of saints' childhoods.

32. E.g., *TLL* 1349.

33. See Kaser 1975, 1.352–54 on *tutela* and 1.369–72 on *cura*. Cf. *Dig.* 6.1.60 (Pomponius) on the limited criminal culpability of the *furiosus* and *infans*; and Gai. 3.109 on the similarity of intellect between an *infans* or *qui infanti proximus est* and the *furiosus*. *Inst.* 1.23 makes explicit the analogy between the *curator furiosi*, etc., and the *curator minoris*. On the similarities and differences between *tutela mulierum* and *tutela impuberum* see Watson 1967, 146; and Dixon 1984a, 346 and n. 12.

34. Table 5.3 (e.g., *FIRA* 1.37–39).

35. *CJ* 6.30.18 (A.D. 426) on *infantes* as being under seven years. Cf. Thomas 1976, 459.

36. Puberty could be determined by inspection rather than a fixed age, although this was not usual in the case of girls, and the presumptive age of fourteen for boys gradually superseded inspection (Gai. 1.196; Ulpian 11.28; *Inst.* 1.22 pr.). Cf. n. 14 above.

37. Gai. 1.191.

38. See the references in Watson 1967, 102–5; and Dixon 1984a, 350–51.

39. Gai. 1.183–85 on the appointment of such a *tutor dativus*, made possible by the *Lex Atilia* of 186 B.C. and extended to the provinces by the *Lex* (or *Leges*) *Iulia et Titia*; *Dig.* 38.17.2 (Ulpian) and *Inst.* 3.3 on the mother's obligation to make application where no agnatic or testamentary *tutor* was available.

40. Solazzi 1928–29, 1; Watson 1967, 131. Cf. Thomas 1976, 458 (*pace* Arangio-Ruiz 1954, 494): "Consistently with the original function of *tutela*, the functions and duties of the *tutor*, though he was appointed to the child, were concerned with the estate not with his personal welfare."

41. Kaser 1975, 1.276–77; Plaut. *Ps.* 303–4 (192 B.C., which Watson 1967, 157, takes to refer to the statute soon after its enactment. See also

Rotondi 1966, 271–72; and Watson 1971, 42. Cf. *Dig.* 4.4.16.1 (Ulpian) on the republican edict concerning *minores*.

42. Kaser 1975, 1.369–71; Thomas 1976, 466–68.

43. *SHA Marcus* 10.12. Cf. *Dig.* 4.4.11.2. Kaser (1975, 1.369) notes that young women were brought under *cura* as *tutela mulierum* declined. This is plausible but difficult to substantiate because of the tendency of ancient (and modern) legal authors to overlook the female sex. Female "minority" might have ended two years earlier (cf. *C.Th.* 2.17.3).

44. *Dig.* 27 seems to merge *tutela* and *cura* throughout (cf. *Inst.* 1.23 and Thomas's commentary on it [1975, 56–58]).

45. *Dig.* 14.6.1 (Ulpian); see also Daube 1969, 89–90.

46. See the examples collected by Wiedemann (1989, 39–42) to illustrate his argument that "classical Romans saw their children primarily as an investment in future security" (39).

47. Consider Pliny's picture of the old age of the childless Domitius Tullus, who had adopted his niece as a device for keeping her fortune within the control of himself and her father and had married a respectable widow when his age and condition made him an object of disgust (Plin. *Ep.* 8.18, esp. 9); or the much more respectable Fannia, who had contracted her own fatal illness while tending her aged relative by marriage, the Vestal Iunia (*Ep.* 7.19.1–3).

48. Ov. *Met.* 8.630–88. See the discussion in Bradley 1985b, 328.

49. The association of the two led to the proverbial expression *hereditas sine sacris* (inheritance without funeral rites) for a gift without strings (Plaut. *Capt.* 775; *Trin.* 484; Festus 370 [Lindsay 290 M]).

50. Musonius frag. 15 Lutz; Plut. *de Amore Prolis* 497E; Polyb. 36.17.7.

51. Bradley's analysis (1985b) of apprenticeship contracts in Roman Egypt is invaluable evidence for this process, and his observations are important for the assessment of ancient childhood. Cf. Westermann 1914.

52. See, e.g., Forbes 1955 on aspects of child labor in the ancient world; Booth 1979; and Wiedemann 1989, 155–56. Slave parents commemorated children, and slaves are known to have bought freedom for family members (cf. Rawson 1966, esp. 75–82), but note Bradley 1984, 53–80, on the disruption of slave families by sale.

53. On this, see esp. Dixon 1983, 1985c; and Hallett 1984.

54. Cic. *Att.* 15.15.

55. The Hortensii Hortali were bailed out by Augustus in acknowledgment of M. Hortensius Hortalus's decision to have four children (Suet. *Tib.* 47; Tac. *Ann.* 2.37).

56. Hor. *Serm.* 1.6, esp. 5–22, 71–80.

57. See esp. Cic. *Mur.* 17; *de Leg. Ag.* 2.3. Cf. Wiseman 1977.

58. The tomb of Eurysaces the baker is depicted in Lyttelton and Forman 1984, 100–101; the inscription is *CIL* 6.28567. The memorial of

Naevoleia Tyche is illustrated in Will 1979, 39; inscription *CIL* 10.1030. Some would argue that the ship represents the voyage of the soul.

59. Macmullen 1963, 102–3, 115; Garnsey 1970a, 247–50; *Dig.* 49.18.1–5.

60. Parker 1928, 237; Campbell 1984, 439–45. Campbell disputes the standard view that children of legionaries born during their term of service were not legitimate but gives a good summary of the evidence for it. Cf. Campbell 1978, 155.

61. Always provided that the manumission met the requirements of the *Lex Aelia Sentia* (Gai. 1.31, 40).

62. Hopkins 1978, 187; and see Crook 1967a, 41–43, for a neat summary of ways in which Roman citizenship might be acquired. Cf. the apostle Paul (who was a Roman citizen at birth) and the envious commander who had had to purchase his own citizenship (*Acts* 22:27–28).

63. Plut. *Cic.* 26.6; Hor. *Serm.* 1.6.29.

64. Suet. *Gramm.* 21.

65. Cf. Plin. *Ep.* 9.19 on the maintenance of historical writings but also of the family tradition of Stoicism and a vague republicanism (Plin. *Ep.* 7.19; Macmullen 1966, 5–10. Other stories, e.g., of mourning parents and heroic husbands and wives, were also maintained in families (e.g., Plin. *Ep.* 3.16, 6.24; Cic. *Att.* 12.20.2, 12.22.2; Sen. *ad Helviam* 16.7). On the *imagines,* consider Juv. 8.19; Vitruv. 6.3–6; and references in Marquardt 1886, 241nn. 1—2; Zadoks-Josephus Jitta 1932; and Hopkins 1983, 255–56. On magistrates' keeping official records within their homes see Culham 1989.

66. Dio 56.3.4, a modified version of the Loeb translation by E. Cary; cf. Plaut. *Mil.gl.* 703–4.

67. Eur. *Med.* 1032–35. Cf. *CIL* 6.19914, 22066, 28644, 27866 and see Lattimore 1942, 187–91, esp. 190, and nn. 138 and 139, for Roman examples, including the abbreviation of this sentiment. The whole phenomenon is discussed exhaustively by Griessmair (1966) with reference to Greek literature and epitaphs, many of them in the Roman world.

68. E.g., the adoption of the younger Pliny by his maternal uncle (Plin. *Ep.* 8.18.4; Sherwin-White 1966, 70); and the adoption of Atticus by Q. Caecilius (Val.Max. 7.9.1; Cic. *Att.* 3.20.1; Corn.Nep. *Att.* 5.2). Cf. the Greek practice (Gernet 1920, 129–31; Cox 1988, 389).

69. On the adoption of young children see, e.g., *P.Oxy.* 16.1895 (Winter 1933, 59) on the adoption of a nine-year-old girl in A.D. 554. Cf. *FIRA* 3.37–39 (no. 16), with Arangio-Ruiz's commentary. On the adoption of females, consider the niece of Domitius Tullus, mentioned above n. 47 (Plin. *Ep.* 8.18.4).

70. One Livia attempted to impose this condition on Dolabella as her heir, but the legality of the procedure was questioned (Cic. *Att.* 7.8.3).

71. E.g., the sons of Aemilius Paulus still arranged his burial, and one of them, Scipio Aemilianus, honored their biological mother, although both had been adopted into other families by the time of their father's death (Polyb. 18.35–36, 31.26). And consider the case of Tullius, whose will was overturned because he passed over his son, who had been adopted by an uncle (Val.Max. 7.7.2), or the son who had been adopted and whose will was overturned because he had made no mention in it of his biological father or his brothers (Val.Max. 7.7.2).

72. Gai. 1.97; *Inst.* 1.11, esp. *pr.*

73. Goody's 1973 article (1973b) sets out the problem admirably. See also Bourdieu 1972, 1977; Howell 1976; and the opening remarks of Saller 1991.

74. Plut. *Aem.P.* 35; Liv. 45.40.7–8. For a close analysis of the reasons for the failure of the Roman elite to reproduce see above all Hopkins 1983 and Corbier 1990; and see Corbier 1991 for a study of adoption as a partial remedy.

75. See esp. Bradley 1984, 56–68; and Rawson 1986c, 78–80.

76. Sen. *de Sen.* (*Ep.mor.* 12).3 on the slave recalling in old age his favored status as a child; Slater 1974 on the sexual element in some relationships. See most recently Nielsen 1990.

77. See below, n. 161 and the associated text, for definitions of *vernae* and *alumni.* Cf. Rawson 1986c, 196–77; Nielsen 1987; and Bellemore and Rawson 1990. And cf. *CIL* 6.27827, in which a *mamma* (probably foster mother) laments that a (clearly beloved) young girl has died before being able to perform the expected benefits for her.

78. The records are very fragmentary, so the sequence and details are not entirely clear, but it looks as if the mother did regain the girl, then died soon afterwards. There was a subsequent wrangle which revived the question of the girl's status. See Arangio-Ruiz 1948, 1959; Deiss 1966, 71–79; and Weaver 1991.

79. The statement that a memorial was for the deceased and the members of the *familia,* e.g., LIBERTIS LIBERTABUSQVE POSTERISQVE EORUM ("to the freed male and female slaves and to their descendants"), sometimes with a reference to the survival of the family name, was common. Examples include memorials to Flavius Syntrophe (*FIRA* 3.298–301 [no. 96]) and to Iunia Libertas of Ostia (Calza 1939; *AE* 94 [1940]; de Visscher 1963). Such foundations included property that would yield an income to pay for offerings on the Day of Violets and the Day of Roses, when graves and memorials were tended.

80. References to *captatio* (inheritance-hunting) abound in the literature of the Empire, particularly in works of the satirists, e.g., Hor. *Serm.* 2.5.23ff. and Juv. 4.155–57, but Plaut. *Mil.gl.* 705—16, written in the second century B.C., has a character claim that he does not need to marry and have children because his more distant relatives cultivate him in the

hope of inheriting. Tac. *Ann.* 3.25 claims that Augustus's "family" legislation failed because the benefits of childlessness were so great. See below, on deliberate childlessness.

81. Plin. *Ep.* 2.20 has an amusing attack on the blatant techniques of Pliny's enemy Regulus, but compare Pliny's gratified reference to the fact that he and Tacitus are frequently linked in the wills of friends (*Ep.* 7.20.6), supported by their joint naming in *CIL* 6.10229, the so-called *testamentum Dasumii,* now thought to be by Domitius Tullus (Eck 1978; Syme 1985a, 1985b; Champlin 1986). Cf. Plin. *Ep.* 5.1, in which Pliny, as one of several joint heirs, finally came to a compromise solution with the excluded son of the testatrix.

82. Flory 1978 gives many examples of slaves and former slaves of a particular *familia* forming small kinlike groupings to commemorate each other at death; Hopkins 1983, 211–17, has a fascinating discussion of burial clubs. Cf. Le Bras 1936, 35–36, on legal aspects.

83. See plates 22 and 23, and cf. the figures cited by Hopkins (1983, 225) for Roman Italy. Cf. Cic. *Disp.Tusc.* 1.93, cited above, on the attitude towards "untimely" death.

84. Dio 56.3. This precedes the quote given above, also from Augustus's speech to the bachelor knights to persuade them to marry and have children. See below, on deliberate childlessness.

85. McDaniel 1948 has some fascinating examples of the folklore.

86. Étienne 1973.

87. E.g., the philosopher Favorinus (Aul.Gell. *NA* 12.1.17, 22–23) and the orator Vipstanus Messalla (*Dial.* 28–29).

88. Plut. *Cat.mai.* 20 on Cato the elder; Cic. *Brutus* 210 and Tac. *Dial.* 28–29 on Cornelia; Suet. *Aug.* 64 on Augustus; Nicolaus 4 on Atia.

89. Cf. Hieron. *ad Laetam* (*ep.* 7 = 107 Vallers) 10. Augustus's daughter Julia and Julia's daughters maintained this tradition, but Julia presumably learned from her stepmother Livia, who also produced Augustus's clothes (Suet. *Aug.* 64).

90. See the examples given in Marquardt 1886, 93 n. 1; Plut. *T.Gr.* 1; *Gr.* 8 on Cornelia, who saw to it that her children were trained in the (then controversial) Hellenic culture. Lower down the social scale, Horace's father showed a similar dedication to his son's education (Hor. *Serm.* 1.6.71–92).

91. Cf. Cic. *Cael.* 9 on Caelius's attachment to Cicero himself and *de Amicitia* 1 on Cicero's own attachment in his youth to Q. Mucius Scaevola or *Att.* 5.20.9 and 6.1 on young Quintus and Marcus accompanying him on his provincial command. On the custom in general see Plin. *Ep.* 8.14.4ff.; Tac. *Dial.* 34.1; and Quint. *Inst.Or.* 12.11.5, all referring to an unspecified past. Cf. Bonner 1977, 84–85.

92. Cf. Cic. *Cael.* 9; and Wiedemann 1989, 158.

93. Wiedemann 1989, 162. Bradley 1985b provides an excellent study

of apprenticeship in the Roman world, with extensive references to earlier work. See also Treggiari 1979b; and Wiedemann 1989, 154–56.

94. *CIL* 6.9213.

95. Varro (Nonius 156). It is sometimes difficult to tell from Roman art whether children performing this function are slaves or children of the family; cf. the Pompeian wall painting of a banqueting scene (e.g., Feder 1978, 25) with plate 15 in this volume. Demause (1974, 20 and n. 83) rightly points out that this service is a traditional part of childhood. In many parts of the modern world, parents, especially mothers, wait on the children even when they have reached adult status. A sociologist's public statement about this phenomenon in modern Australia provoked an angry reaction from teenagers, who insisted that they did do unpaid work about their home ("We are not useless—teenagers answer critic," *Brisbane Courier Mail,* 8 January 1990).

96. Val.Max. 5.8.3 (Manlius Torquatus), 5.8.2 (Brutus); Plut. *Cor.* 36 (Volumnia); Appian *BC* 4.37; Dio 47.8.5 (Iulia, mother of M. Antonius).

97. E.g., Plaut. *Most.* 118–21; the whole of Juv. 14; Tac. *Dial.* 28; Hor. *Serm.* 1.6.71–92.

98. Hor. *Carm.* 3.6.37–41 and Tac. *Dial.* 28–29 both look back to an earlier, better age; Nicolaus 15 commends Atia's attentiveness to her young son's morals.

99. Cic. *Att.* 10.4.6 (rather a different view from *Disp.Tusc.* 3.1.2). On biographers see esp. Wiedemann 1989, chap. 2; and Bradley 1978, 14–15, 23.

100. Cic. *Disp.Tusc.* 3.64. On the motif of the punishment of Eros (Cupid), consider the Pompeian painting depicted in Néraudau 1984, following p. 30, as well as pp. 244–45.

101. Demause 1974; Saller 1991. This contrasts with the grim picture of family life in the age of Augustine conjured up by Shaw (1987b) and Wiedemann (1989, 105–6). On assaults on children in other periods, i.e., "beatings" or "discipline," as they are commonly termed, cf. Wiedemann 1989, 28–30.

102. Plut. *Cat.mai.* 20.4. Elsewhere, Cato is quoted as criticizing men who beat their wives and children (*Cat.mai.* 20.2), but this sounds like a comment on a standard practice. The references of Wiedemann 1989, 105–6, are more to teachers than to parents; cf. the famous Pompeian picture of boys holding a schoolmate for the master to beat (e.g., Wiedemann 1989, pl. 4).

103. Aul.Gell. *NA* 12.1.22–23.

104. See the examples assembled in Dixon 1988, 120–26 and chap. 6. Cf. Dixon 1984b, Bradley 1986, Joshel 1986, and Nielsen 1989; and see n. 157 below.

105. Bradley 1984, 53–58, on forcible separations, especially of mothers and young children.

106. This subject is discussed in chap. 3, above, and in more detail in Dixon 1988 chap. 4, esp. pp. 84–97.

107. And possibly a third, if the *Lex sublata* of Prop. 2.7 concerns an attempted bill of 28 B.C. (see Hallett 1973; and Besnier 1979). Badian (1985) persuasively argues against this. On the timing of the *Lex Iulia* and the *Lex Papia Poppaea* see Corbett 1930, 120–21; and Csillag 1976, 29–35.

108. E.g. Musonius frag. 15 Lutz; Juv. 6.594–96 (abortifacients), 602–3 (exposure).

109. This was probably because the insistence on repeated marriage and production of children ran counter to the Christian ideology, which put a different value on celibacy and officially disapproved of remarriage, especially for women. The Julian strictures on adultery, however, were better regarded and have been better preserved (see Riccobono 1945, 166–98; and Csillag 1976, 77–80, for attempted reconstructions). Provincial legislation such as the *Lex Malecitana* and the *Lex Iulia municipalis* provide some information by analogy.

110. Ancient references include Dio 54.16, 56.1–10; Aug. *RG* 6, 8.5; Suet. *Aug.* 34; Ulpian 11.20. See also Corbett 1930, 120–21; and Dixon 1988, 98 n. 2, 100 n. 18, 102–3 n. 39.

111. Three children secured full privileges for freeborn Italians (*ingenui*); four, for freed slaves (counting only those produced after manumission); possibly five for provincials (Gai. 1.145, 194; Dio 56.10. See also Sherwin-White 1966, 558, on Plin. *Ep.* 10.2.1, and the references he lists there).

112. Cf. Cic. *pro Marcello* 23, urging Caesar to restore traditional morality; Hor. *Carm.* 3.6 on the need for a moral revival after the civil wars; Aug. *RG* 6, 8.5 on the marriage laws and 7.3, 10, 19.2 on the religious revival.

113. Cf. Jörs 1882; Field 1945; Brunt 1971, 154, 565–66; Csillag 1976, 45; Nörr 1977 and 1981.

114. Dio 56.7.5, set in A.D. 9.

115. *Gnomon Id.* 24–32, which seems to exempt people below a certain standard of wealth. See also Tac. *Ann.* 2.51 and Aul.Gell. *NA* 2.153–55. Cf. Brunt 1971, 561—62; and Wallace-Hadrill 1981, 58–59.

116. Suet. *Aug.* 34; Dio 56.1.2. The accounts differ somewhat, and the precise timing is awkward, but there clearly was at least one major demonstration at the games, probably (as Dio indicates) before the legislation of A.D. 9.

117. Dio 56.8.2–3. Cf. Aul.Gell. *NA* 1.6.2 on Augustus's use of a second-century B.C. censor's speech which began, "Since nature has decreed that we cannot live at all comfortably with our wives, or live at all without them, we should consider the long-term benefits rather than immediate happiness."

118. Tac. *Ann.* 3.25; *Germ.* 19.5; Plin. *Ep.* 4.15.3.

119. On the alimentary schemes see Veyne 1957—58; Duncan-Jones

1974, 317–18; and Dixon 1988, 86–88. Plate 14 depicts the emperor Trajan making payments to the free poor, who bring their children forward to him.

120. Gilfillan 1965.

121. In Plin. *Ep.* 10.2.2–3, where he gives the reasons for his (successful) application for the right of three children, he points out that he has married three times and his latest wife has recently suffered a miscarriage. For more on this see *Ep.* 8.10, 11.

122. Musonius 15 Lutz. Cf. the situation of Hortensius Hortalus under Tiberius (Suet. *Tib.* 47; Tac. *Ann.* 2.37). Corbier (1985, 518–20) looks at the decline of noble families, but "dying out" seems often to mean simply that the families slipped out of their senatorial status (Brunt 1971, 141–42; Hopkins 1983, 60—76).

123. Musonius 15 Lutz; Plin. *Pan.* 26, 27; Plut. *de Amore Prolis* 497E. Abortion was known at least from the time of Plautus (*Truc.* 200–201; see also Nardi 1971; and Eyben 1980, 11).

124. On the exposure of handicapped children see Sen. *de Ira* 1.15; Cic. *de Leg.* 3.19; Liv. 27.37; Soranus *Gyn.* 2.9–10. On exposure as a more general means of family limitation see Tac. *Germania* 19; *Dig.* 40.4.29 (Scaevola); Juv. 6.603, and Courtney 1980, 342, on it; Aul.Gell. *NA* 12.1.23.

125. Hopkins 1965b; Eyben 1980. A kind of rhythm method was known, but it advocated intercourse during what we now consider to be the most fertile time of the menstrual cycle.

126. E.g., Suet. *Aug.* 65.4; *Claud.* 27.1.

127. The slaveowner's right to expose slave children was checked by the third century (*CJ* 8.51.1). On fathers see *Dig.* 25.3.4 (Paul) and *CJ* 9.16.7; *CJ* 8.51.3 for later confirmation.

128. Cf. Stone's comment (1977, 41) that the European elite, which first practiced "modern" contraception, was the group which manifested growing parental interest, especially in the new formal education. The 1949 British *Report of the Royal Commission on Population* contains some interesting observations about the declining British birthrate from the mid-nineteenth century, especially marked from the 1920s, e.g. par. 411, linking family limitation to the "education" (probably class) of the parents, and par. 100, on the argument that the fewer the children, the more chance each has for "a better start . . . in life."

129. "is demum infortunatus est homo / pauper qui educit in egestatem liberos," quoted by Aulus Gellius (*NA* 2.23.21), who compares it unfavorably with its Greek source.

130. 58, Sen. *de Matrimonio* frag. 13 Haase = Hieron. *adv. Iovinianum* 1, p. 191.

131. Tac. *Ann.* 15.19 (A.D. 62): "quando quis sine sollicitudine parens,

sine luctu orbus longa patrum vota repente adaequaret." For other references to parental anxiety see Ov. *Rem.* 547–48; Hor. *Carm.* 4.5.9–14; Sen. *ad Marciam* 24.2; Juv. 10.289–91 (mothers). Cf. Ov. *Met.* 2.91–94, where Apollo belatedly shows a paternal concern for Phaethon.

132. See above all Garnsey 1970a; and Garnsey and Saller 1987, 123–5.

133. Some scholars, following Mommsen (1887, 429–31), believe that marriage between freeborn and freed Roman citizens was illegal (i.e., void) in the early and even mid-Republic and that Augustus's legislation on marriage actually widened the categories by applying this restriction only to senators (Corbett 1930, 31–34; Watson 1967, 32–37, concludes that Augustus was actually introducing a restriction). On soldier marriage see esp. Parker 1928, 237–47; Corbett 1930, 39–42; Garnsey 1970b; and Campbell 1978, as well as chap. 3, above.

134. Rawson 1966, 77 and n. 9. They were later admitted to the schemes but gained a smaller subsidy (Duncan-Jones 1974, 288, based on *CIL* 11.1147). Illegitimate children could not be entered on the formal register of births initiated under Augustus (*FIRA* 1943: 3.5–7 [no. 5]; Bruns 1909, 1.72; Crook 1967a, 47).

135. Gai. 1.82 and *Inst.* 1.4 *pr.* on the child of a slave mother. The rules concerning the offspring of unions between Romans and free Latins or foreigners (Gai. 1.79–81; Ulpian 5.4) became largely irrelevant after the Edict of Caracalla in A.D. 212, which conferred Roman citizenship on most free subjects of the empire (*Dig.* 1.5.17 [Ulpian]), but until then, freeborn non-Romans tended to be a mildly underprivileged group, although they had local citizenship (as Alexandrians, Syrians, etc.) if they met local requirements. The officeholding aristocracy of each city-state generally had Roman citizenship (Garnsey 1970a, 242–45; Garnsey and Saller 1987, 121).

136. Gai. 1.76–96 deals with this topic, but unfortunately the text is quite defective at this point. The discussion is concerned primarily with the question of which children come under the *potestas* of the father rather than the (related) questions of citizenship and legitimacy as such (see de Zulueta 1953, 2.32–33. On the *Lex Minicia* see Berger 1953, 557; and Rotondi 1966, 338).

137. Weaver 1972, 170–96, 307–12.

138. Suet. *Aug.* 46; Plin. *NH* 7.60.

139. Cf. Suet. *Aug.* 42.

140. Junian Latin parents could gain citizenship for themselves and their offspring by applying for it when the first child reached one year of age (Gai. 1.80, 94–95; Crook 1967a, 53). Junian Latins in the imperial period were former slaves whose manumission did not meet the requirements of the *Lex Aelia Sentia* (Gai. 1.17). See Weaver 1990, 1991.

141. Gai. 1.194. Cf. *CIL* 6.1877.

142. Gai. 1.65–87. See also Plin. *Ep.* 10.11, where Pliny has to argue separately for his friend's citizenship, then for his right to exert *patria potestas* over his children.

143. The effect of such an institution would probably be to make the whole will void, so that the rules of succession on intestacy would apply (Gai. 2.110; Voci 1960, 1.384–85; Jolowicz 1965, 256 n. 4, 260–62; Watson 1971, 61–70; Kaser 1975, 1.682–83, 690; Thomas 1976, 487).

144. *FIRA* 3.428–20 (= *BGU* 1.140; Hadrian A.D. 119), but Campbell (1978, 158) believes the privilege might actually date to Trajan. On soldiers' wills in general see Campbell 1984, 210–29; Gai. 2.109–10, 114; and *Inst.* 2.11.

145. See esp. Campbell 1978; 1984, 301–3 and app. 3. Garnsey (1970b) denies that Septimius Severus lifted the ban.

146. For examples see Parker 1928, 237; and Macmullen 1963, 126–28. See Campbell 1984, 439–45, on the archaeological evidence.

147. Cic. *Mur.* 16–17; *de Leg. Ag.* 2.3; Plut. *Cic.* 1.

148. Cic. *Att.* 12.7, 15.15.

149. Through the marriage of his granddaughter Vipsania to Tiberius. Cf. Tac. *Ann.* 2.43.

150. Crook 1967a, 64–67. Apart from moral and occupational bars, freeborn male Roman citizens of the right age were eligible if they had the requisite wealth and political success.

151. *CIL* 6.10634, cited in Rawson 1966, 75.

152. All the authors mentioned here note the particular difficulties. See esp. Kajanto 1972, 1977; and Weaver 1972, chap. 3.

153. Rawson 1966, 1974, 1986c, 1991; Weaver 1972, 1986. Others include Treggiari, e.g., 1969, 1975, 1981a, 1981b; Huttunen 1974; Flory 1978; and Bradley 1986, 1987.

154. See, e.g., Weaver 1972, 137–47. Weaver (1986, 1991) has made a particular study of the implementation of the *SC Claudianum* (A.D. 52), which originally condemned to slavery any woman who knowingly cohabited with a slave without the permission of the slave's owner (e.g., Chantraine 1967; Weaver 1986, 1991). Rawson 1986c is also an example of numerical analysis of status indicators.

155. Rawson 1966, 76; Treggiari 1969, 212–13.

156. Rawson 1966, 78–79; Treggiari 1969, 15 n. 11. See *Dig.* 40.2.11–13 on the possibility of freeing parents or "natural children."

157. Bradley 1984, 59–69. For other works on various aspects of the lives of slave or freed children see the papers by Rawson and Weaver in Rawson's (1991) edited collection; Treggiari 1969, 208–15, on freed slaves in the Republic, and 1975 on the family life of slaves; Weaver 1972, 93–196, specifically on the slaves of the imperial family and their connections; Flory 1975, 1978; Bradley 1984, chap. 4, and on the work of slave

(and free) children, 1985b; and Wiedemann 1989, 154–56.

158. Plaut. *Mil.gl.* 696.

159. "nutriendus" (*Dig.* 32.99.3 [Paul]). Bradley 1986, 207–11, collects and discusses the evidence for the wet-nursing of slave children. See Treggiari 1979c, 189–90, and Rawson 1986c, 191, for speculation about the reasons for sending young slave children off to the country. Note the reference in Plin. *Ep.* 2.17.22 to the need to separate the slave quarters from the luxury villa so that guests would not be disturbed by the shouts of the young slaves ("voces servulorum").

160. *CIL* 6.21279a. Two slaves from Domitian's *familia* commemorated the freed Ti. Claudius Epaphus as *nutricius suus bene merens,* as if he had reared them both (*CIL* 6.5405).

161. On *vernae* see esp. Chantraine 1967, 170–71; Weaver 1972; and Rawson 1986c, 186–95, esp. 186–87 on the meaning of the term; on *alumni,* Rawson 1986c, 173–86; Nielsen 1987. Cf. n. 77.

162. Rawson 1986c, 187–88.

163. Martial 5.34. Sen. *de Sen.* 2. On *delicia* see Nielsen 1990.

164. *collacteus/a* or *collactaneus/a.* See Rawson 1986c, 147, for an example of such a relationship in the imperial household. Cf. *CIL* 6.6324, to a four-year-old girl, apparently dedicated by the son of the girl's nurse. See also Bradley 1987, 57–62.

165. *CIL* 6.27827. She is not characterized as a *verna* or *alumna* but has clearly been freed at a very early age by the dedicator. On the applications of *mamma* and the masculine equivalent *tata* see Heraeus 1937; Dixon 1984b, 1988, 146–49; and Nielsen 1989. Bradley 1985a has a very good discussion of many of the terms applied to childcare at Rome in different social contexts, with the emphasis on men involved in childcare.

166. Rawson 1986c, 188–90.

167. *CIL* 6.15983; Suet. *Gramm.* 7. On *alumni* see also Rawson 1986c, 173–86, and Nielsen 1987. Plates 20 and 21 show grave reliefs in memory of foundlings (*alumnae* or Greek *threptoi* or *threptai*).

168. Weaver 1986, e.g., 148–49. On illegitimates generally in Roman society see Rawson 1966, 82 n. 9, and 1991b.

169. *Dig.* 40.2.16.11 (Ulpian) on close kinship (i.e., slave, child, or sibling) and elsewhere (40.2.16.20.3) cites Marcellus's view that a woman is also permitted to free her son. *Dig.* 40.2.16.13 (Ulpian) includes the *collactaneus* and *alumnus* in a list of relationships. In *Dig.* 40.2.16.14, Marcianus concedes that *alumni* and any children in whose rearing the owner has taken a special interest should be included. And see *Dig.* 40.2.16.16 (Ulpian) for the general rule.

170. Bradley 1984, 59–69, for the sale of slave children; Sen. *de Ira* 1.15 on the tradition of exposing or killing deformed children.

171. Sen. *de Sen.* 2.

172. Rawson 1986c, where it is argued that *verna* has a similar application. Cf. Dixon 1984b, 1988, 146–47, and Nielsen 1989 on the correlative fostering terms *mamma, tata, nutritores,* etc.

*Chapter 5. The Roman Family through the Life Cycle*

1. Cf. Luc. 5.222–27.
2. See esp. Wiedemann 1989, 32, 39–43, and the texts cited therein, esp. the epitaphs.
3. Cf. Segalen 1986, 92, on kinship in modern urban France: "The widest range of relatives is invited to those great rituals that mark the ending of one stage of life; in a French context these are baptism, first communion, marriage and—in particular—funerals. These family reunions are only points in a general process of identification with the family that has its own range of functions."
4. Cicero (*Leg.* 2.29) refers to the statutory requirement that *feriae* (festivals) in general entail a cessation of labor (which he characteristically associates with the servile population) and litigation, and he points out that the calendar is designed so that festivals fall after the periods of greatest agricultural activity. Cf. Cato *de Ag.* 138; and Col. 2.21 on farm holidays during family festivals.
5. Plin. *Ep.* 1.9. And see the commentary on this by Sherwin-White (1966, 106–7).
6. A proceeding rather extravagantly detailed by Statius (*Silvae* 4.8.37–41), who pictures himself as performing these actions on the birth of a friend's child. See plate 23 for a depiction of a newborn baby being raised up.
7. Cf. Suet. *Nero* 6.2; Festus *Epit.* p. 120 s.v. "*lustrici*"; Daremberg and Saglio 1877, 2a:1420; Marquardt 1886, 83–86; Harmon 1978, 1596–97; Dixon 1988, 237–40.
8. Sherwin-White's statement (1966, 106) that the ceremony normally took place in the boy's home on the occasion of the Liberalia, on 17 March, is, as he points out, clearly contradicted by Plin. *Ep.* 1.9 (quoted above) and by other accounts, which also make it plain that there was no fixed age for the procedure. Cf. Cic. *Att.* 5.20.9 on young Quintus and see the list of examples, with ages and text references, supplied by Marquardt (1886, 128–30, and for the public ritual at Rome, 124–26). The subject is discussed in greater detail in chap. 4, above.
9. Cic. *Mur.* 69 and Heitland 1874, 94, on this passage; Cic. *Cael.* 11–12 on typical activities during the *tirocinium,* the period of apprenticeship served by elite youth in the forum and in military life.
10. Gai. 1.112 and Dion.Halic. 2.25 (*confarreatio*); Gai. 1.113 (*coemptio*).
11. *Pace* Harmon 1978, 1598–99: "The notion of *usus* (Serv. *auct. ad Georg.* 1.31) implies no ceremony." Wedding ritual as described in

Catullus's *Epithalamia,* 61 and 62, contains some Greek elements, in deference to the literary tradition (Fordyce 1968, 236). Other sources for the wedding ceremony include Juv. 6, esp. 25 and 200–205, and Courtney 1980, 285–86, on this. On the origins of these ceremonies and the archaeological evidence for them see Marquardt 1886, 42–57; Harmon 1978, 1598–1600; and Torelli 1984, 23–51, 117–56. See plates 1 and 2 for depictions of Roman wedding ceremonies.

12. Toynbee 1971, 43–61, lists many of these elements, some of which are illustrated by plates showing funeral practices. See also plate 11 in this volume. Marquardt 1886, 346–60, and Harmon 1978, 1600–1603, contain further references from the ancient sources. As in the case of ceremonies generally, especially domestic ones, the best sources for detail of standard practices tend to be satirists (Lucian *de Luctu* 10–13, on Greek practice; Juv. 1.72, 7.207–9, etc.) or philosophers (Luc. 3.830–1010; Sen. *ad Marciam, ad Helviam;* Cic. *Disp.Tusc.* 1.93) critical of convention; censorious Christian authors (Tert. *de Corona* 10); grammarians explaining odd usages (e.g., Varro *de vita p.R.* 3.110; Festus 282 Lindsay) or poets making a point, as where Propertius (2.13a) tells Cynthia all the things she need not do for him when he dies. Cicero *de Leg.* 2.55–62 gives us the more formal and public rules governing mourning obligations.

13. Cf. Festus 61 Lindsay (Paulus)—"denicales feriae colebantur cum hominis mortui causa familia purgabatur"—in spite of his suggestion that all mourners were subject to some form of ritual purification (Festus 3 Lindsay). This passage also refers to the ritual cleansing of the house of the dead person *aqua et igni* (literally, "by fire and water").

14. In much of the West, Christmas has for many irreligious people become more of a celebration of the family than one of the birth of Christ.

15. On the Fornacalia see Ov. *Fasti* 2.527 and Scullard 1981, 73. On the Terminalia, Ov. *Fasti* 2.635–84; Varro *LL* 6.13; and Scullard 1981, 17, 79–80.

16. Ov. *Fasti* 5.419–44; Fowler 1933, 306–7; Scullard 1981, 118–19 on the dead in general Ov. *Fasti* 5.426 ("compositique nepos busta piabat avi") and 5.479–80 show that feasts of the dead were associated particularly with deceased kin.

17. Wills and memorial foundations sometimes specified these occasions, together with the birthday or death day of the deceased, as occasions for commemoration and supplied the means of providing the appropriate offerings; e.g., *AE* 94 (1940): 15–18 requires offerings on the Parentalia, the Day of Violets, and the Day of Roses ("INPENDI VOLO IN ORNATIONEM SEPVLCHRI / ET SACRIFICIS DIE PARENTALIORVM / H-S. C. VIOLAE. HS. C. ROSAE. HS. C."). Cf. *CIL* 6.10234.15 on the Day of Violets, and Toynbee 1971, 63, on roses in offerings to the dead.

18. Cf. Plaut. *Aul.* 23–25 on daily attention to the Lar; and Orr 1978, 1567, for full references regarding holidays and 1571 on the Genius. Plate

9 shows a shrine in a wealthy Pompeian house with a painting of the Genius flanked by two Lares.

19. See Fowler 1933, 307.

20. Ov. *Fasti* 2.617–20 on the Caristia or Cara Cognatio. "The *Parentalia* was practically a yearly renewal of the rite of burial" (Fowler 1933, 308; cf. Harmon 1978, 1603 and n. 38).

21. Val.Max. 2.1.8. This is still mentioned in the fifth-century A.D. calendar of Polemius Silvius (Fowler 1933, 308 n. 6, 309 n. 1).

22. Ov. *Fasti* 2.631–38.

23. "Proxima cognati dixere Caristia cari, / et venit ad socios turba propinqua deos. / scilicet a tumulis et, qui periere, propinquis / protinus ad vivos ora referre iuvat, / postque tot amissos, quicquid de sanguine restat, / aspicere et generis dinumerare gradus" (Ov. *Fasti* 2.617–22).

24. Cic. *Mur.* 27 implies that women could inherit family *sacra,* but perhaps not if they had brothers. It is not clear whether wives who were not in the *manus* of their husbands took on their family rites. They might well in any case have wished to join in rites commemorating a dead parent, and it would seem natural to follow these with a gathering on the Caristia with their "own" family.

25. The term *sui heredes* (their own heirs) is explained by the jurists by the fact that the family property is, in effect, held in trust by the *paterfamilias* for the next generation (*Dig.* 28.2.11 [Paul]). The concept of the *bonus paterfamilias* is sometimes invoked at law to mean the good householder, who maintains property and where possible improves on it, to be passed on to his heirs. Cf. Plut. *Cat.mai.* 21.8 for Cato's advice to his son that it was the act of a widow, not of a man, to allow an inherited estate to run down.

26. See Thomas 1976, 415 and n. 27.

27. L. Annius had allegedly incurred general disapprobation resulting eventually in a loss of status imposed by the censor in the third century B.C. because he had divorced his respectable young wife without calling a *consilium* to justify the step (Val.Max. 2.9.2. Cf. Cic. *Fin.* 2.54–55 and Plin. *Ep.* 1.9.2 on other *consilia*).

28. Liv. 1.58. See above, chap. 3, for the decline of the husband's power and its impact on the *consilium* as a domestic court.

29. See Bauman 1984–85; and Thomas 1990.

30. Tac. *Ann.* 2.50, on the trial in A.D. 17 (under Tiberius) of Appuleia Varilla *exemplo maiorum;* 13.32, on that of Pomponia Graecina in A.D. 57 (under Nero) for foreign superstition, a charge of which she was acquitted by her husband "prisco instituto propinquis coram."

31. Cic. *Att.* 15.11.

32. Aul.Gell. *NA* 12.1.5 shows us a mother present for her daughter's lying-in and supervising subsequent arrangements for the care of the new child. Plin. *Ep.* 3.16 tells us of the anxious care provided for Arria by her

daughter and son-in-law when Arria's husband had been condemned to death. The education of the orphaned Ummidius Quadratus and his sister had been supervised by their grandmother. Once he had his own residence, Ummidius Quadratus continued to pay respectful attendance on her, with both sides skirting around their differences (Plin. *Ep.* 7.24).

33. Note Cic. *Sest.* 6: "ademit Albino soceri nomen mors filiae, sed caritatem illius necessitudinis et benevolentiam non ademit"; and Cicero's relations with his own sons-in-law, e.g., *Att.* 9.11.3 (Furius Crassipes after his divorce from Tullia); *fam.* 9.11–12; *Att.* 14.14.1, 14.16.2, 14.17, 14.17a (Dolabella after divorce and Tullia's death).

34. The child's death is assumed by Shackleton-Bailey (1966, 5.314) and Wiedemann (1989, 85) but is not mentioned anywhere in the ancient texts.

35. Plut. *Pomp.* 53; Suet. *Caes.* 26–27.

36. This naturally favored those whose fathers or other male relations had achieved high office in their day. Women also seem to have been important in the political process—consider the role of Brutus's mother Servilia in 44 B.C. (Cic. *Att.* 15.11) or that of Seneca's aunt and mother when he sought the consulship (Sen. *ad Helviam* 14.3).

37. See Plin. *Ep.* 1.10 on the usual obligation. Cf. Cicero's letters to Atticus vainly urging him to support Quintus as a brother-in-law ought to do (*Att.* 1.15, 1.16.14), as well as the help Cicero himself received during his exile from his son-in-law L. Calpurnius Piso Frugi (*post Red.* 7–8). Cf. Cicero's own statement that he needed to make a new marriage alliance to counteract the betrayal of his former wife with the support of new connections ("novarum necessitudinum fidelitas") (*fam.* 4.14.3).

38. See Shaw 1987a on the age of women at marriage; and Saller 1987a on men.

39. The rift between Messalina and her mother is one of the rare examples of mother-daughter conflict in the sources (Tac. *Ann.* 11.37–38). Cf. Dixon 1988, 223.

40. *Att.* 5.1.3–4. It is a pity that we do not have Atticus's replies. Cicero's accounts and subsequent developments make it clear that Atticus continued to side with his sister, and Cicero with his brother, which is hardly surprising.

41. Goody (1973a, 37–38, 54 nn. 39 and 41) relates the tendencies (both actual and perceived) to different systems of property use and transmission as well as residence. Gluckman (1965, 225), in considering the perception of women as evil witches in some African societies, relates this to the Zulu belief that wives make trouble between brothers and the matrilineal Yao view that they compete with a man's sisters. (I would say that it is the obligation to the children of the marriage vs. the nephews and nieces that is at issue in the latter case.) He considers other systems, such as the Hindu and the Chinese, in which wives are particularly seen as causing conflict between the demands of the conjugal and wider kin units

(1965, 248). Segalen (1986, 18) refers also to the role of women in the inevitable restructuring of the Yugoslav basic household (*zadruga*).

42. Cf. Crook 1967b; and Saller 1986, 16. There are examples of such joint households, e.g., that of the Aelii Tuberones in the second century B.C. (Val.Max. 4.4.8; Plut. *Aem.P.* 5) and that of the Crassus brothers in the first century B.C. (Plut. *Crass.* 1), but the sources suggest that these were remarkable in their own day, at least within the elite (cf. Rawson 1986b, 7). Barker (1985) has found many examples of joint households in Roman Egypt.

43. Tac. *Ann.* 2.43; cf. 1.4, 1.69.

44. Sen. *ad Marciam* 2.3–4.

45. Cf. Dixon 1985c, 370 and n. 38, and the examples cited there. On the tendency of elite women to align with brothers rather than husbands, consider the argument of Hallett 1984.

46. Plut. *Caes.* 9–10.

47. Plut. *Cat.mai.* 24. This was also the case with the wives of the Aelii Tuberones and the Licinii Crassi, cited above. In their cases, the point of particular interest was that the brothers continued joint residence after the death of their fathers.

48. Ov. *Fasti* 2.626: "quae premit invisam socrus iniqua nurum"; Juv. 14.220–21: "elatam iam crede nurum, si limina vestra / mortifera cum dote subit."

49. Plut. *Ant.* 87.1 (Octavia); Sen. *ad Helviam* 2.4 (his mother's un-named stepmother); Plin. *Ep.* 9.13 (Fannia); Suet. *Galba* 4.1 (Livia).

50. Tac. *Ann.* 1.6. This in spite of the fact that Livia seems to have main-tained Julia in her exile. Once Livia died, Tiberius allowed his former wife to starve to death (Tac. *Ann.* 4.71; cf. Phillips 1978, 76). Germanicus was her grandson.

51. E.g., Juv. 6.626–33 (the poisonous stepmother); Cic. *Clu.* 26–27 (the allegedly bloodthirsty stepmother Sassia). See Plin. *Ep.* 6.33 for his triumphant court case concerning the will of the octogenarian who had changed his will after his marriage to a much younger woman; Pliny rep-resented the daughter of the old man in the court case.

52. Hallett 1984, 257–58. For the hostile stereotype see Dixon 1988, 155–59; Gray-Fow 1988; and Noy 1991.

53. E.g., Vespasian (Suet. *Vesp.* 3.21; *Dom.* 12.3) and the emperor Mar-cus, who "took to himself as concubine the daughter of his wife's pro-curator, rather than put a stepmother over his numerous children" (*SHA Marcus* 29.10).

54. Marcus Antonius promoted the interests of Clodius, a son from Fulvia's former marriage (Plut. *M.Ant.* 28; cf. Cic. *Att.* 14.13A), which suggests not only that the boy lived with Antonius but that their interests were closely identified. Augustus's stepfather was also paternally protec-tive (Nicolaus 3.5).

55. *C.Th.* 2.21, 3.8; *CJ* 5.9. Cf. Humbert 1972, 387–446. The burden of all of these rulings was that children had a right to their patrimony and to their mother's dowry, even if she became its owner at law on the death of her first husband.

56. Apul. *Apol.* 71.

57. Liv. 39.9.2–4. See Pailler 1990 for a good discussion of the implications of this story for family relationships.

58. Dixon 1988, 179–87, has some examples. The most detailed ones are from the ruling imperial family, where mothers had often been instrumental in getting sons to power and the sons eventually came to resent the continuing maternal claims based on this. I argue that this scenario might have been acted out in other elite political families for lesser stakes.

59. Thomas 1982 and Daube 1969, 88, exaggerate this tendency, which I see as expressing fantasy rather than any recorded reality. Cf. the views of Saller (1986, 17–19).

60. E.g., Liv. 8.7.1ff. for the story of T. Manlius Torquatus, whose father allowed him to be killed for going against military orders, even though he had behaved heroically. Cf. the examples of Val.Max. 5.8 and those cited by Liebenam (1900, 916).

61. The ruling, passed in the reign of the emperor Vespasian (A.D. 69–79), meant that a *filiusfamilias* who had incurred such a debt could escape from its consequences by claiming an *exceptio* against his creditor (see Berger 1953, 698; and Daube 1969, 89–90. The ruling and its rationale are cited in *Dig.* 14.6.1 [Ulpian]).

62. See esp. Veyne 1978, 37. Cf. Daube 1969, 81–82, 91; and Rawson 1986b, 14. Saller 1987a, 33 (table 2), supplies the statistical probabilities on paternal death.

63. *Dig.* 14.6.99.2 Ulpian).

64. De Beauvoir's argument (1970, 126 n. 1)–"Du jour où elle reçut une dot de son père, elle eût une parfaite indépendance économique"—is based on the erroneous assumption that the daughter was the owner of her dowry. In fact, it was owned and administered by the husband (albeit for her benefit and that of the joint household) for the duration of the marriage. See the many entries of *Dig.* 23.3; Watson 1967, chap. 7; and Thomas 1976, 429 and n. 93.

65. Eyben (N.d., chap. 1) has a mass of entries portraying the elite male youth as frivolous. The image of the foolish old man in Plautus has been much discussed. Eyben (1989) provides a number of references in his helpful bibliography. Cf. the characterization of Hor. *Ars Poetica* 169–74.

66. In Peter Weir's film *The Dead Poets' Society,* one schoolboy, a potential doctor, reminds his friend, a potential lawyer, that they are both unable to defy their fathers.

67. E.g., Cic. *Att.* 13.41, 42; 14.10, 19; 15.26. See also Saller 1986.

68. Lacey 1968, 117–18; Golden 1981, 322 n. 21. Chevallier (1954, 50)

sets an average of thirty years to the period during which one male generation can impose its will before being supplanted. Cf. *Ath.Pol.* 4.3.4.

69. Mitford 1956, 53: "Death duties can be avoided altogether if the
owner of an estate gives it to his heir and then lives another five years. . . .
Their heirs, so far from longing to step into their shoes, will do anything
to keep them alive."

70. Mitford 1963, 5, on Uncle Matthew and son Tom. Cf. Chevallier
1954, 49, for the young vintners' chafing to oust their fathers and their
old-fashioned methods. In a sample dialogue, the typical son reminds his
father of his own conflicts with *his* father and the grandparent's eventual
retirement. Again, the argument is between sons in their thirties and fathers in their sixties.

71. Cic. *de Sen.* 37 (Appius Claudius); Plut. *Cat.mai.* 24 (Cato); Suet.
*Aug.* 64–65 (Augustus). *Dig.* 25.3.5 does set out guidelines for judges on
the duty of maintenance, which extends beyond the parent-child relationship (cf. *Dig.* 37.15), but this duty is not equivalent to the Greek requirements (see Harrison 1968, 1.77–78; and Schaps 1979, 83–84).

72. This was the *querela inofficiosi testamenti* (*Dig.* 5.2). See Dixon 1988,
59, on its application to mothers' wills. Note the procedure followed by
Pliny when he was a joint heir of the estate of a woman who passed over
her own son (*Ep.* 5.1). Attested cases of genuine exheredation (as distinct
from legal devices and special arrangements balancing dowry against
inheritance [cf. Gardner 1985, 451–52]) by fathers are in fact surpris-
ingly rare.

73. Cic. *de Sen.* 22. Cf. Watson 1967, 156–57, and see Ulpian *Tit.* 12.3;
*Dig.* 27.10.13, 15; Val.Max. 3.5.2.

74. Cic. *de Sen.* 7: "deplorare solebant . . . quod spernerentur ab eis, a
quibus essent coli soliti."

75. Eyben (N.d., chap. 3) on "the conflict of generations" in the army
and politics.

76. A tradition inherited from the Greek comedies, which Plautus and
Terence imitate. The father is treated more sympathetically in Terence's
comedies (Eyben 1989, 237).

77. Hor. *Ars Poetica* 173–74.

78. Cf. Cic. *fam.* 2.16.6 on the old men of his own youth and Tac. *Agr.*
4.4–5 on Agricola's diversion by his mother from excessive philosophical
enthusiasm. On the efforts of Cicero, Quintus, and Atticus to dominate
the behavior of young Quintus see Cic. *Att.* 13.42, 14.10, 14.19. Cf.
Vel.Pat. 2.67.2 on the period of the proscriptions and the hierarchy of
loyalties, in which sons (or children, *filii*) rank lowest, an observation not
supported by the actual examples given by authors of this and similar
periods—Appian *BC* 4.20; Tac. *Hist.* 1.3.1; Plut. *Cic.* 47. See Hinard
1990. On father-son hostility in general see Hopkins 1983, 244–45. On

parricide see, e.g., Veyne 1978, 36; and Thomas 1981, 659, 679. See also Saller's excellent (1986) discussion, esp. pp. 9, 18–19.

79. E.g., Goode 1963; Lake 1985, 173, 217 n. 2, citing Hartmann 1981; Hareven 1987, xvii.

80. The stress varies in its cultural emphasis; e.g., depending on the economic and structural requirements of a particular system, it might be on conjugal loyalty, parent-child solidarity, cooperation between cousins or brothers-in-law. Cf. Gluckman 1965, 225; and Cox 1988, 380 and n. 2, citing Plakans 1984, 159, on the usefulness of dyads in examining family relationships.

81. E.g., Finley 1981, 160, but consider the question of retirement from the Roman senate (McAlindon 1957) and the recycling of elderly slaves for childcare (Vogt 1974, 108–9). Obligations to the state were legally remitted or reduced for age (Cic. *de Sen.* 34). On Greek practice cf. Lacey 1968, 117–18, 130–31; Golden 1981, 322 n. 21; and, in literature, Philetas's retirement from herding (Longus, *Daphnis and Chloe* 2.3.3).

82. See Burn 1953, 16; Hopkins 1966, 263, for a median life expectancy below thirty; Frier 1982, 1983, for a life expectancy of twenty-five years (based on skeletal remains); Saller 1987, 33 (table 2), for the likelihood, for example, that 41 percent of ordinary Romans (43 percent of senatorial Romans) were likely to have a living father at the age of twenty and note that "at birth only one in ten Romans had a living paternal grandfather; by the time they reached their teens the proportion diminished to one in fifty" (33). These figures are based on computer simulations of the Roman population. The difference between senatorial and other experience reflects the lower age of senatorial men at first marriage, a phenomenon readily explained by the need for in-law support to gain political office, discussed above.

83. Eyben 1989, 231, where he rejects the views of Van Hooff (1983) and Philibert (1984). Consider Hor. *Ars Poetica* 155–78; Varro cited by Censorinus 14.2; Sen. *Ep.* 12.6 for the divisions of life (in reality, the masculine citizen's life stages), usually into *pueritia, adulescentia, iuventus,* and *senectus* or *senecta.* On the terminology of old age, its etymology, and its usage see Slusanski 1974, 563–69.

84. Cic. *de Sen.* 2.

85. Slusanski 1974, 105, shows that authors often dated old age from the mid-forties. Varro allegedly dated it from sixty years (Censorinus 14.2), distinguishing it from the military classification of the *seniores* (45–60 years). Cf. Eyben 1989, 236, and his reference to Berelson 1934, 4–7.

86. Cic. *de Sen.* 19, 64.

87. Consider Augustus's use of ancient precedents and speeches to justify his legislative reforms (*RG* 8.5 [*exempla maiorum*]; Suet. *Aug.* 34; Liv. *Per.* 59. Cf. Aul.Gell. *NA* 1.6.2).

88. Cic. *de Sen.* 37. Cato the elder himself tyrannized over his adult, married son (Plut. *Cat.mai.* 24).

89. See Dixon 1988, 47–51, 188–94.

90. " . . . QVI MALVIT LVC / TVM LINQVERE QVAM GRATIAS / REDDERE SVIS DERISOR AVIAE / S QVIA SE DICEBAT NVTRIRE / BACHILLVM SVMMAE SENEC / TAE . . . " ("who preferred to abandon the light [of day] rather than to pay his due to his relations. Mocker of his grandmother, for he used to say he would look after her and be her support in her extreme old age") (*CIL* 6.18086.3–8).

91. Sen. *ad Marciam:* "iuvenis, iam matri iam patri praesidium ac decus: (17.1); "non erit qui me defendat, qui a contemptu vindicet" (19.2).

92. Saller and Shaw 1984b, 136–37, on the low incidence of dedications to grandparents. Even allowing for the Roman custom of erecting one's own memorial in one's lifetime, it is striking that the inscriptions by parents to children so outweigh those by children to parents (Dixon 1988, 138 n. 40, 214. Cf. Hopkins 1965a, 324 n. 54; and Huttunen 1974, 60–61). Hopkins (1983, 205–6 and n. 5) reviews the archaeological evidence for the proposition that it was rare for tombs around Rome to cater for more than one or two generations. Lattimore (1942, 190) comments on the fact that children do not conventionally express grief at the loss of parents in epitaphs.

93. Examples are legion. Consider the famous *pietas* of Vergil's Aeneas towards his aged father; Tac. *Hist.* 1.3.1 on the good and bad examples of family behavior; Cic. *Rosc.* 53 on disinheritance of a son. Cf. Val.Max. 7.8.2.

94. Saller 1988, esp. 395, 399.

95. Hor. *Ars Poetica* 169–74.

96. Juv. 10.188–245.

97. E.g., Domitius Tullus, who could not move or brush his own teeth without the assistance of slaves (Plin. *Ep.* 8.18.8–9). His loathsome character and history might have colored Pliny's view, for he describes him as disgusting, particularly as a marriage partner: "senis ita perditi morbo, ut esse taedio posset uxori." Cf. Juv. 10.201–2: "usque adeo gravis uxori natisque sibique ut captatori moveat fastidia Cosso." Courtney (1980, 473) discusses other examples of this stock theme.

98. Cic. *de Sen.* 7 summarizes the standard complaints, which are then addressed (through the *persona* of Cato the elder) in order, in rhetorical fashion: exclusion from the active life (15–20), physical infirmity (21–38), reduction of enjoyments (39–66), the approach of death (66–84). Complaints about the old are treated in 35–36 (silliness and forgetfulness), 55 (garrulity), and 65 (crankiness). Cato admits only to garrulity.

99. Cf. Hor. *Ars Poetica* 144–78, in which the *puer* quickly gives way to the more interesting *iuvenis* (who passes from youthful fecklessness to manly gravity), then the rather unpleasant *senex*.

100. I have not yet been able to procure Esler 1989. Bremmer 1987 is concerned primarily with the representation of elderly Greek women but touches on the Roman stereotypes. Her general point holds, namely, that the male literary focus is primarily on women as sex objects and that older women are perceived as being asexual and therefore of little interest to the poet. Richlin (1983, 109–16) and Sullivan (1991, 200) make an excellent case for a more violent reaction to older women. They look particularly at hostile sexual imagery of older women and at the depiction of old women as witches. See Dixon 1988 on the evidence from prose authors and epitaphs.

101. Cic. *de Sen.* 2: "hoc enim onere, quod mihi commune tecum est, aut iam urgentis aut certe adventantis senectutis et me ipsum levari volo."

102. Sen. *Ep.mor.* 12 (*de Sen.*).1: "quid mihi futurum est, si tam putria sunt aetatis meae saxa?"

103. Sen. *Ep.mor.* 12.3.

104. Sen. *ad Helviam* 19.2; see above, n. 91.

105. *CIL* 6.18086.3–8, quoted above, in n. 90. Cf. Wiedemann 1989, 40–42.

106. Bradley (1985b, 328), who also cites Musonius Rufus 15 on the idealized image of children caring for parents and Plut. *de Lib. Educ.* 11 on the need for the poor to educate their children in order to gain support from them in old age.

107. Harrison 1968, 1.77–78; Schaps 1979, 83–84. Sons could plead in their defense that the parents had failed to provide them with a trade or skill (Plut. *Sol.* 22).

108. Cato *RR* 2.7.

109. Plut. *Cat.mai.* 5 for his disgust at Cato's views; Suet. *Claud.* 25 and Dio *Ep.* 61(60).29.7. (Xiph.) on the Claudian legislation.

110. See esp. Vogt 1974, 105–14; cf. *CIL* 6.21279 by his *patrona* Licinia Venera to Licinius Meropymus: "To the departed shades. Licinius Meropymus, who lived more or less 50 years, 3 months, 20 days. Licinia erected this for her well-deserving freed slave, sweetest nurturer [*nutritor*] of my children and of my *alumni*." See also Bradley 1986, esp. 221–22, cautioning against oversentimentalizing the relationship between nurse and nurseling; Dixon 1988, 127–28, 151–53. Cf. Shorter 1977, 185–86, on French nurses.

111. Plin. *Ep.* 6.3.2, 5.16.

112. Cic. *de Amicitia* 74, esp.: "nec, si qui ineunte aetate venandi aut pilae studiosi fuerunt, eos habere necessarios, quos tum eodem studio praeditos dilexerunt. isto enim modo nutrices et paedagogi iure vetustatis plurimum benevolentiae postulabunt. qui neglegendi quidem non sunt, sed alio quodam modo aestimandi." This would presumably apply also to slave children who had grown up with a young master or mistress, such

as Seneca's Felicio, above, or the *pueri* assigned to the newborn Lentulus (Cic. *Att.* 12.30.1).

113. Fronto *Ep. ad Ant.* 1.5 (102).

114. Martial 11.39. Cf. Plaut. *Bacch.* 162.

115. Consider the inclusion of the nurse in the family tomb of the Cornelii Scipiones (*CIL* 6.16128). Individual commemorations of dependents include *ILS* 8351–53; *CIL* 6.4352 and 6.10229.35 and 47ff. Cf. the reference to Licinius Meropymus, *CIL* 6.21279, quoted in n. 110 above; and the nurses commemorated in the examples of Treggiari 1976, 88.

116. Gai 1.19; *Dig.* 40.2.9–16 lists the various special relationships. Ulpian summarizes the principle in 40.2.16; the exemption is for proper relationships, not sexual whims: "neque enim deliciis, sed iustis affectionibus dedisse iustam libertatem legem Aeliam Sentiam credendum." Cf. Suetonius's unfavorable comments on Nero's treatment of his former nurse's son (not a slave) (*Nero* 35.5); and *CIL* 6.16057, to a slave child of the Rubellii Blandi, also a foster brother (*collactaneus*).

117. Tac. *Dial.* 29.

118. Disability was also held to make slaves fit for childcare. Cf. the apocryphal story of the slave who fell out of a tree, at which Pericles exclaimed, "That slave has just become a pedagogue!" (Stobaeus *Eclogia* 2,233 ed. Wachsmuth, cited in Vogt 1974, 110 n. 20). Wiedemann (1989, 144–45) provides other examples and apparently endorses the ancient view that physical fitness is not requisite for care of young children!

119. Heraeus 1937, 158–80; Vogt 1974, 112; Dixon 1984b; Nielsen 1990b.

120. Cf. the *avia educans* of Quint. *Inst.Or.* 6 pr. 8; and for other examples of grandparental relationships, Dixon 1988, 154.

121. Tac. *Ann.* 4.22 (Urgulania and her grandson Plautius Silvanus); Plin. *Ep.* 7.24.5 on Ummidia Quadratilla, who lived for pleasure and died just short of the age of eighty. Pliny approves of this respect for youthful innocence.

122. Plin. *Ep.* 7.19 on Fannia's illness; 7.24.5 on Ummidia's idle existence, spent gambling and watching her pantomime artistes; Ov. *Fasti* 541–42 on the lower-class old couple celebrating the feast of Anna Perenna, along with other age groups.

123. According to tradition, old men were pushed into the Tiber—this was the explanation of the expression *senes depontani* (Festus [Pauli *Exc.* p. 66L = 75M]). Eyben (1989, 240) cites modern authors on such traditions. Hopkins (1983, 244–45) treats father-son tension in general in Roman society.

124. See the examples scattered throughout Cic. *de Sen.*, e.g., 10 and 13. Cf. Plin. *NH* 7.153–59 and *Ep.* 9.19 on his patron Verginius Rufus or, less flatteringly, Tac. *Ann.* 4.52 on Cn. Domitius Afer, whose forensic eloquence weakened with old age but who disregarded this and continued his prosecutions.

125. This emerges by implication from the portrait of the elder Cato, who knew the fathers and grandfathers of young contemporaries (Cic. *de Sen.* 29, 49). I have noticed that my own culture places stress on the family as the major safeguard against the perceived trials of old age but that in practice the elderly, though deriving comfort from the idea and attention of children and grandparents, gain their major social satisfaction from mixing with their peers.

126. Lambert 1982, 53–54. Cf. Reinhold's startling statement (1976, 49): "Reverence and obedience to fathers were second nature to Roman youths"; and see the quotes and discussion in Bradley 1985b, 327–28.

127. Cic. *fam.* 2.16.6, not about his own son, but about the younger generation as a whole: "recordor enim desperationes eorum qui senes erant adulescente me. eos ego fortasse nunc imitor et utor aetatis vitio." (See pp. 148–49 for a translation.) Cf. Tac. *Dial.* 28–29 for another generalization about "the youth of today." Bertman 1976 stresses the essential harmony between the generations of elite males in imperial Rome.

# Chronological Guide
# to Roman History

For the reader unfamiliar with Roman history, it might be useful
to summarize some of the landmarks. A detailed knowledge of
events and emperors' reigns should not be necessary, but this will
at least give the reader some idea of what is meant by "regal period" or "mid-Republic," as well as which emperor reigned during
which century.

Regal period, 753–509 B.C. (traditional dates)
Republic, ca. 509–27 B.C.
    Early Republic, 509–262 B.C.
        Publication of the Twelve Tables, mid-fifth century B.C.
        Roman expansion throughout continental Italy.
    Mid-Republic, ca. 262–133 B.C.
        Second Punic War with Hannibal ends 201 B.C.
        Roman expansion throughout Mediterranean.
        Increased wealth.
    Late Republic, 133–27 B.C.
        Dated from plebeian tribunate of Tiberius Sempronius
            Gracchus.
        Further expansion outside Italy.

Rise of the expert (but amateur) jurists, the most influential being Q. Mucius Scaevola (consul 95 B.C.) and Servius Sulpicius Rufus (consul 51 B.C.)

Cicero's letters date to this period.

Empire, dated from Augustus's establishment of the new principate, 27 B.C.

Julio-Claudians, 27 B.C.–A.D. 68: Augustus, Tiberius, Gaius (Caligula), Claudius, Nero

Augustan legislation on marriage and the family passed amid great protest.

Flavians, 69—79 A.D.: Vespasian, Titus, Domitian

"Year of the Four Emperors" (Galba, Otho, Vitellius, Vespasian), 69 A.D.

Adoptive emperors, 96–138 A.D.: Nerva, Trajan, Hadrian

Pliny's letters date to this period.

Antonines, 138–92 A.D.: Pius, Marcus (Antoninus, or Aurelius), Commodus

Severans, 193–211 A.D.: Septimius Severus, Caracalla and Geta, then Caracalla alone, Elagabalus, Alexander Severus

Septimius Severus revoked the ban on soldier marriage, 197 A.D.

Edict of Caracalla, 212 A.D., widely extended Roman citizenship within the Empire.

Period of the great classical jurists: Gaius had taught and written in the mid-second century, under the Antonines; Ulpian and Paul flourished in the early third century.

# Bibliography

Alfonsi, L. 1946. *Albio Tibullo e gli autori del "Corpus Tibullianum."* Milan: Società editrice "Vita e Pensiero."

Allason-Jones, L. 1989. *Women in Roman Britain.* London: British Museum.

Amundsen, D. W., and C. J. Diers. 1969. "The Age of Menarche in Classical Greece and Rome." *Human Biology* 41:125–32.

—————. 1970. "The Age of Menopause in Classical Greece and Rome." *Human Biology* 42:79–86.

Anderson, M., ed. 1971. *Sociology of the Family.* Harmondsworth: Penguin.

—————. 1980. *Approaches to the History of the Western Family, 1500–1914.* London: Macmillan.

Andreau, J., and H. Bruhns, eds. 1990. *Parenté et stratégies familiales dans l'antiquité romaine.* Rome: École française de Rome.

Arangio-Ruiz, V. 1948. "Il processo di Giusta." *Parola del passato* 3:129–50.

—————. 1954. "Le Persone *sui iuris* e la capacità di agire: *tutela e cura.*" In *Istituzioni di diritto romano,* 492–507. Naples: Giuffrè.

—————. 1959. "Testi e documenti IV. Tavolette ercolanesi (il processo di Giusta)." *Bollettino dell'istituto di diritto romano* 62 (3d ser. 1): 223–45.

Arangio-Ruiz, V., and G. Pugliese-Carratelli. 1955. "Herculaneum Tablets—Tabulae Ceratae Herculanenses." *Parola del passato* 10:448–77.

Ariès, P. 1962. *Centuries of Childhood: A Social History of Family Life.* Translated by R. Baldiek. New York: Vintage Books. Originally published as *L'enfant et la vie familiale sous l'ancien régime* (Paris: Plon, 1960).

Astolfi, R. 1970. *La Lex Iulia et Papia*. Padua: Facoltà di giurisprudenza dell'Università di Padova.

Badian, E. 1985. "A Phantom Marriage Law." *Philologus* 29:82–98.

Baldwin, B. 1976. "Young and Old in Imperial Rome." In *Conflict of Generations in Ancient Greece and Rome*, 221–33. *See* Bertman 1976.

Ball, R. J. 1983. *Tibullus the Elegist: A Critical Survey*. Gottingen: Vanderhoeck & Ruprecht.

Balsdon, J. P. V. D. 1962. *Roman Women: Their History and Habits*. London: Bodley Head.

Barker, D. 1985. "Some Findings from the Census Returns of Roman Egypt." *Ancient Society: Resources for Teachers* (Sydney) 15:138–47.

Bauman, R. A. 1974. "Criminal Prosecutions by the Aediles." *Latomus* 33:245–64.

————. 1983. *Lawyers in Roman Republican Politics: A Study of the Roman Jurists in Their Political Setting, 316–82 BC*. Münchener Beiträge zur Papyrusforschung zur antiken Rechtsgeschichte, 75. Rome: Bretschneider.

————. 1984–85. "Family Law and Roman Politics." *Scritti in onore di Antonio Guarino* 3:1283–1330.

Beauvoir, S. de. 1970. *La Vieillesse*. Paris: Gallimard.

Bell, D. 1983. *Daughters of the Dreaming*. Sydney: McPhee Gribble.

Bellemore, J., and B. Rawson. 1990. "*Alumni*: The Italian Evidence." *Zeitschrift für Papyrologie und Epigraphik* 83:1–19.

Belmont, N. 1973. "Levana ou comment '*élever*' les enfants." *Annales: économies, sociétés, civilisations* 28:77–89.

Beloch, J. 1886. *Die Bevölkerung der griechisch-römischen Welt*. Leipzig: Duncker & Humbolt.

Bender, D. 1967. "A Refinement of the Concept of the Household: Families, Co-residence, and Domestic Functions." *American Anthropologist* 69:493–504.

Benveniste, E. 1936. "*Liber* et *Liberi*." *Revue des études latines: mélanges Marcel Durry* 14:53–58.

Berelson, L. 1934. "Old Age in Ancient Rome." Ph.D. diss., University of Virginia.

Berger, A. 1953. *Encyclopedic Dictionary of Roman Law. Transactions and Proceedings of the American Philological Association*, n.s. 43, pt. 2. Philadelphia: American Philosophical Society.

Berkner, L. K. 1975. "The Use and Misuse of Census Data for the Historical Analysis of Family Structure." *Journal of Interdisciplinary History* 4:721–38.

Bertman, S., ed. 1976. *The Conflict of Generations in Ancient Greece and Rome*. Amsterdam: Gruner.

Besnier, R. 1979. "Properce (élégies II, VII et VIIa) et le premier échec de la législation démographique d'Auguste." *Revue historique de droit français et étranger* 57:191–203.

Birks, P., and G. McLeod. 1987. *Justinian's Institutes.* London: Duckworth.

Birley, A. [1964] 1981. *Life in Roman Britain.* Reprint. London: Batsford.

Blok, J., and P. Mason, eds. 1987. *Sexual Asymmetry: Studies in Ancient Society.* Amsterdam: Gieben.

Bonner, S. F. 1977. *Education in Ancient Rome.* London: Methuen.

Booth, A. D. 1979. "The Schooling of Slaves in First-Century Rome." *Transactions and Proceedings of the American Philological Association* 109:11–19.

Bouchard, G. 1972. *Le Village immobile: Sennely-en-Sologne au XVIIIe siècle.* Paris: Plon.

Bouloiseau, M., et al., eds. 1962. *Contributions à l'histoire démographique de la révolution française.* Paris: Bibliothèque nationale.

Bourdieu, P. 1972. "Marriage Strategies as Strategies of Social Reproduction." In *Family and Society: Selections from the Annales: économies, sociétés, civilisations,* edited by R. Forster and O. Ranum, 117–44. Baltimore: Johns Hopkins Press.

———. 1977. *Outline of a Theory of Practice.* Cambridge: Cambridge University Press.

Bradley, K. R. 1978. *Suetonius' Life of Nero: An Historical Commentary.* Collection Latomus, 157. Brussels.

———. 1984. *Slaves and Masters in the Roman Empire: A Study in Social Control.* Collection Latomus, 164. Brussels.

———. 1985a. "Child Care at Rome: The Role of Men." *Historical Reflections/Réflexions historiques* 12:485–523.

———. 1985b. "Child Labour in the Roman World." *Historical Reflections/Réflexions historiques* 12:311–30.

———. 1986. "Wet-nursing at Rome–A Study in Social Relations." In *The Family in Ancient Rome,* 201–29. See Rawson 1986a.

———. 1987. "Dislocation in the Roman Family." *Historical Reflections/Réflexions historiques* 14:33–62.

———. 1989. "History Old and New: A Perspective." *Échos du monde classique/Classical Views* 33:333–40.

Bremmer, J. N. 1987. "The Old Women of Ancient Greece." In *Sexual Asymmetry,* 191–206. See Blok and Mason 1987.

Brennan, T., ed. 1989. *Feminism and Psychoanalysis.* Cambridge: Cambridge University Press.

Bridenthal, R., and C. Koonz, eds. 1977. *Becoming Visible: Women in European History.* Boston: Houghton & Mifflin.

Brown, P. 1989. *The Body and Society: Men, Women, and Sexual Renunciation in Early Christianity.* New York: Columbia University Press.

Bruns, C. G. 1909. *Fontes iuris romani antiqui.* Tübingen: Mohr (Paul

Siebeck). Reprint. Darmstadt: Scientia Verlag, 1969. 2 vols. in 1.

Brunt, P. A. 1971. *Italian Manpower, 225 BC–AD 14.* Oxford: Clarendon Press.

Buck, C. D. 1949. *A Dictionary of Selected Synonyms in the Principal Indo-European Languages: A Contribution to the History of Ideas.* Chicago: University of Chicago Press.

Buckland, W. W. 1932. *Elementary Principles of the Roman Private Law.* Cambridge: Cambridge University Press.

Burn, A. R. 1953. "*Hic breve vivitur:* A Study of the Expectation of Life in the Roman Empire." *Past and Present* 4:2–31.

Bush, B. 1990. *Slave Women in Caribbean Society, 1650–1838.* Bloomington: Indiana University Press.

Cairns, F. 1979. "Propertius on Augustus' Marriage Law (II.7)." *Grazer Beiträge* 8:185–205.

Calza, G. 1939. "Epigrafe sepolcrale contenente disposizioni testamentarie." *Epigraphica* 1:160–62.

Campbell, J. B. 1978. "The Marriage of Soldiers under the Empire." *Journal of Roman Studies* 68:153–66.

———. 1984. *The Emperor and the Roman Army, 31 BC–AD 235.* Oxford: Clarendon Press.

Carandini, A., and S. Settis. 1980. *Schiavi e Padroni nell' Etruria Romana: la Villa di Sette Finestre dallo scavo alla mostra.* Rome: De Donato.

Carney, T. F. 1961. *A Biography of C. Marius.* Proceedings of the African Classical Association, suppl. 1. Assen: Van Gorcum.

Carp, T. 1980. "*Puer senex* in Roman and Medieval Thought." *Latomus* 39:736–39.

Champlin, E. 1986. "*Miscellanea Testamentaria.*" *Zeitschrift für Papyrologie und Epigraphik* 62:247–55.

———. 1987. "The Testament of the Piglet." *Phoenix* 41:174–83.

Chantraine, H. 1967. *Freigelassene und Sklaven im Dienst der römischen Kaiser.* Wiesbaden: Steiner.

Chevallier, G. [1954] 1972. *Clochemerle Babylon.* Translated by E. Hyams. Reprint. Harmondsworth: Penguin.

Cixous, H. 1970. *Le Troisième Corps.* Paris: Grasset.

Cixous, H., and C. Clément. 1986. *The Newly Born Woman.* Minneapolis: University of Minnesota Press.

Collins, J. H. 1951–52. "Tullia's Engagement and Marriage to Dolabella." *Classical Journal* 47:162–68.

Corbett, P. E. 1930. *The Roman Law of Marriage.* London: Clarendon Press.

Corbier, M. 1985. "Idéologie et pratique de l'héritage (Ier siècle av. J-C.– IIe siècle ap. J-C)." Actes du colloque de Lecce, 19–24 September 1983. *Index* 13:501–28, 648–50.

———. 1990. "Les Comportements de l'aristocratie romaine (IIe siècle av. J-C.–IIIe siècle ap. J-C.)." In *Parenté et stratégies familiales. See* Andreau and Bruhns 1990.

―――――. 1991. "Divorce and Adoption as Roman Familial Strategies." In *Marriage, Divorce, and Children in Ancient Rome,* 47–78. *See* Rawson 1991a.

Cornell, T. 1989. "Rome: The History of an Anachronism." Paper delivered at a symposium of the Association of Ancient Historians, "City-States in Classical Antiquity and Medieval Italy," at Brown University, Providence, R.I., 7–9 May.

Cosentini, C. 1971. "La dote di Paolina (TH 87, I e II)." *Studi in onore di Edoardo Volterra.* Publication of the Faculty of Jurisprudence, University of Rome. Milan: Giuffrè.

Courtney, E. 1980. *A Commentary on the Satires of Juvenal.* London: Athlone Press.

Cox, C. A. 1988. "Sibling Relationships in Classical Athens: Brother-Sister Ties." *Journal of Family History* 13:377–95.

Crook, J. A. 1967a. *Law and Life of Rome.* London: Thames & Hudson.

―――――. 1967b. *"Patria Potestas." Classical Quarterly* 17:113–22.

―――――. 1986. "Women in Roman Succession." In *The Family in Ancient Rome. See* Rawson 1986a, 58–82.

Csillag, P. 1976. *The Augustan Laws on Family Relations.* Budapest: Akademiai Kiado.

Culham, P. 1989. "Archives and Alternatives in Imperial Rome." *Classical Philology* 84:100–115.

Curchin, L. 1982. "Familial Epithets in the Epigraphy of Roman Spain." In *Mélanges Étienne Gareau,* 179–82. Ottawa: Éditions de l'Université.

―――――. 1983. "Familial Epithets in the Epigraphy of Roman Britain." *Britannia* 14:255–56.

Daly, M. 1979. *Gyn-ecology: The Metaethics of Radical Feminism.* London: Women's Press.

Daremberg, C., and E. Saglio. 1877. *Dictionnaire des antiquités grecques et romaines d'après les textes et les monuments.* Paris: Hachette.

Daube, D. 1969. *Roman Law: Linguistic, Social, and Philosophical Aspects.* Edinburgh: Edinburgh University Press.

Davis, J. C. 1962. *Decline of the Venetian Nobility as a Ruling Class.* Baltimore: Johns Hopkins Press.

Degler, C. N. 1980. "Women and the Family." In *The Past before Us,* 308–26. *See* Kammen 1980.

Deiss, J. J. 1966. *Herculaneum: Italy's Buried Treasure.* New York: Thomas Y. Crowell.

Demause, L., ed. 1974. *The History of Childhood.* New York: Harper & Row.

de Visscher, F. 1963. *Le Droit des tombeaux romains.* Milan: Giuffrè.

Dickison, S. 1973. "Abortion in Antiquity." *Arethusa* 6:159–66.

Dixon, S. 1983. "A Family Business: Women's Role in Patronage and Politics at Rome ca. 80–44 BC." *Classica et Mediaevalia* 34:50–59.

————. 1984a. "*Infirmitas Sexus*: Womanly Weakness in Roman Law." *Tijdschrift voor Rechtsgeschiedenis* 52:343–71.

————. 1984b. "Roman Nurses and Foster-Mothers: Some Problems of Terminology." *AULLA, Papers and Synopses from the 22nd Congress of the Australian Universities Language and Literature Association* 22:9–24.

————. 1984c. "Family Finances: Tullia and Terentia." *Antichthon* 18:78–101. (Reprinted in Rawson 1986a, 111–15.)

————. 1985a. "Polybius on Roman Women and Property." *American Journal of Philology* 106:147–70.

————. 1985b. "Breaking the Law to Do the Right Thing: The Gradual Erosion of the Voconian Law in Ancient Rome." *Adelaide Law Review* 9:519–34.

————. 1985c. "The Marriage Alliance in the Roman Elite." *Journal of Family History* 10:353–78.

————. 1988. *The Roman Mother*. London: Croom Helm; Norman: Oklahoma University Press.

————. 1991. "The Sentimental Ideal of the Roman Family." In *Marriage, Divorce, and Children in Ancient Rome*, 99–113. See Rawson 1991a.

Donahue, C. 1978. "The Case of the Man Who Fell into the Tiber." *American Journal of Legal History* 22:1–54.

Donzelot, J. 1979. *The Policing of Families*. New York: Pantheon.

Duby, G. 1967. "Structures et parenté de la noblesse dans la France du nord au 11e et 12e siècles." In *Miscellanea Mediaevalia in Memoriam Jan Frederik Niermeyer*. Groningen: Wolters.

Duff, P. W. 1928. *Freedmen in the Early Roman Empire*. Rev. ed. Cambridge: Heffer, 1958.

Duncan-Jones, R. 1964. "The Purpose and Organisation of the *Alimenta*." *Papers of the British School at Rome* 32:123–46.

————. 1974. *The Economy of the Roman Empire: Quantitative Studies*. Cambridge: Cambridge University Press.

Durry, M. 1950. *Éloge funèbre d'une matrone romaine*. Paris: Budé.

————. 1955. "Le Mariage des filles impubères dans la Rome antique." *Revue internationale des droits de l'antiquité*, 3d ser., 2:263–73.

————. 1969. "Le Mariage des filles impubères à Rome." *Revue des études latines: mélanges Marcel Durry*, 47:17–25, and "Autocritique et mise en point," 27–41.

Earl, D. 1967. *The Moral and Political Tradition of Rome*. London: Thames & Hudson.

Eck, W. 1978. "Zum neuen Fragment des sogenannten Testamentum Dasumii." *Zeitschrift für Papyrologie und Epigraphik* 30:277–95.

Elder, G. H. 1978. "Family History and the Life Course." In *Transitions*, 17–64. See Hareven 1978.

Ellerman, K. 1982. "Sulpicia og hendes digte." *Museum Tusculanum* 48:61–90.

Engels, F. 1884. *The Origins of the Family, Private Property, and the State.* Chicago: Kerr.

Erikson, E. 1963. *Childhood and Society.* New York: Norton.

Esler, A. 1989. "Horace's Old Girls: Evolution of a *Topos.*" In *Old Age in Greek and Latin Literature,* chap. 7. *See* Falkner and de Luce 1989.

Étienne, R. 1973. "La Conscience médicale antique et la vie des enfants." *Annales de Démographie Historique* 21, *Enfant et Sociétés,* 15–61.

Eyben, E. 1977. *De jonge Romein volgens de literaire Bronnen der periode ca. 200 v. Chr. tot ca. 500 n. Chr.* (with English summary). Brussels: Paleis der Akademie.

————. 1980–81. "Family Planning in Graeco-Roman Antiquity." *Ancient Society* 11–12: 5–82.

————. 1986. "Sozialgeschichte des Kindes im römischen Altertum." In *Zur Sozialgeschichte der Kindheit,* 317–56. *See* Martin and Nitschke 1986.

————. 1989. "Old Age in Greco-Roman Antiquity and Early Christianity: An Annotated Select Bibliography." In *Old Age in Greek and Latin Literature. See* Falkner and de Luce 1989.

————. N.d. *The Young Ones in Ancient Rome* (provisional title). London: Routledge. Forthcoming.

Falkner, T. M., and J. de Luce, eds. 1989. *Old Age in Greek and Latin Literature.* New York: State University of New York Press.

Feder, T. H. 1978. *Great Treasures of Pompeii and Herculaneum.* New York: Abbeville.

Field, J. A. 1945. "The Purpose of the *Lex Iulia* et *Papia-Poppaea.*" *Classical Journal* 40:398–416.

Finley, M. I. 1963. "Generalisation in Ancient History." In *Generalisation in the Writing of History,* 19–35. *See* Gottschalk 1963.

————. 1981. "The Elderly in Classical Antiquity." *Greece and Rome* 28:156–71.

————. [1975] 1986. *The Use and Abuse of History.* Reprint. London: Hogarth.

Flandrin, J. L. 1979. *Families in Former Times.* Cambridge: Cambridge University Press. Originally published as *Familles: parenté, maison, sexualité dans l'ancienne société* (Paris: Hachette, 1976).

Flory, M. B. 1975. "Family and *Familia:* A Study of Social Relations in Slavery." Ph.D. diss., Yale University.

————. 1978. "Family and *Familia:* Kinship and Community in Slavery." *American Journal of Ancient History* 3:78–95.

Forbes, C. A. 1955. "The Education and Training of Slaves in Antiquity." *Transactions and Proceedings of the American Philological Association* 86:321–60.

Fordyce, C. J. [1961] 1968. *Catullus: A Commentary*. Reprint. Oxford: Oxford University Press.

Fowler, W. W. [1899] 1933. *The Roman Festivals of the Period of the Republic*. Reprint. London: Macmillan.

Frank, R. I. 1976. "Augustus' Legislation on Marriage and Children." *California Studies in Classical Antiquity* 8:41–52.

Frayn, J. M. 1984. *Sheep-Rearing and the Wool Trade in Italy during the Roman Period*. Liverpool: Francis Cairns.

Frazer, J. G. 1890. *The Golden Bough: A Study in Magic and Religion*. Reprint. London: Macmillan, 1922.

French, V. 1987. "Midwives and Maternity Care in the Greco-Roman World." In *Rescuing Creusa: New Methodological Approaches to Women in Antiquity*, edited by M. B. Skinner, special issue of *Helios*, n.s., 13, no. 2:69–84. Lubbock, Tex.: Texas Tech. University Press.

Friedl, E. 1962. *Vasilika: A Village in Modern Greece*. New York: Holt, Rinehart, & Winston.

———. 1977. "Some Aspects of Dowry and Inheritance in Boeotia." In *Mediterranean Countrymen*, edited by J. Pitt-Rivers, 113–35. Westport, Conn.: Greenwood.

Frier, B. W. 1982. "Roman Life Expectancy: Ulpian's Evidence." *Harvard Studies in Classical Philology* 86:213–51.

———. 1983. "Roman Life Expectancy: The Pannonian Evidence." *Phoenix* 37:328–44.

———. 1985. *The Rise of the Roman Jurists: Studies in Cicero's pro Caecina*. Princeton: Princeton University Press.

Galinsky, G. K. 1981. "Augustus' Legislation on Morals and Marriage." *Philologus* 125:126–44.

Gardner, J. 1984. "A Family and an Inheritance: The Problems of the Widow Petronilla." *Liverpool Classical Monthly* 9, no. 9:132–33.

———. 1985. "The Recovery of Dowry in Roman Law." *Classical Quarterly* 35:449–53.

———. 1986. *Women in Roman Law and Society*. London: Croom Helm, 1986.

Garnsey, P. 1970a. *Social Status and Legal Privilege in the Roman Empire*. Oxford: Clarendon Press.

———. 1970b. "Septimius Severus and the Marriage of Soldiers." *California Studies in Classical Antiquity* 3:45–53.

———. 1979. "Where Did Italian Peasants Live?" *Proceedings of the Cambridge Philological Society*, n.s. 25:1–15.

Garnsey, P., and R. Saller. 1987. *The Roman Empire: Economy, Society, and Culture*. Berkeley and Los Angeles: University of California Press.

Gaudemet, J. 1962. "Les Transformations de la vie familiale au Bas-empire et l'influence du christianisme." *Romanitas* 4:58–85.

———. 1978. "Tendances nouvelles de la législation familiale au IVe siècle." In *Transformation et conflits au IVe siècle après J-C.*, edited by A. Alföldi and J. Straub, 187–207. *Antiquitas,* Reihe 1, Abhandlungen zur alten Geschichte, 29. Bonn: Rudolf Habelt.

Gelzer, M. 1912. *Die Nobilität der römischen Republik.* Stuttgart: Teubner. Translated as *The Roman Nobility* by R. Seager. Oxford: Blackwell, 1969.

Gernet, J. 1920. *Droit et société dans la Grèce ancienne.* Reprint. New York: Arno Press, 1979.

Gibbs, M. A. 1960. *The Years of the Nannies.* London: Hutchinson.

Gilfillan, S. C. 1965. "Lead Poisoning and the Fall of Rome." *Journal of Occupational Medicine* 17, no. 2:53–60.

Gluckman, M. 1956. *Custom and Conflict in Africa.* Oxford: Blackwell.

————. 1965. *Politics, Law, and Ritual in Tribal Society.* Oxford: Blackwell.

Golden, M. 1981. "Demography and the Exposure of Girls at Athens." *Phoenix* 35:316–31.

————. 1988. "Did the Ancients Care When Their Children Died?" *Greece and Rome* 35:152–63.

Goode, W. J. 1963. *World Revolution and Family Patterns.* Glencoe, Ill.: Free Press.

————. 1964. *The Family.* Englewood Cliffs, N.J.: Prentice-Hall.

Goody, J., ed. 1958. *The Developmental Cycle in Domestic Groups.* Cambridge: Cambridge University Press.

————. 1972. "The Evolution of the Family." In *Household and Family in Past Time,* 103–24. *See* Laslett and Wall 1972.

————. 1973a. "Bridewealth and Dowry in Africa and Eurasia." In *Bridewealth and Dowry,* edited by J. Goody and S. J. Tambiah, 1–58. Cambridge: Cambridge University Press.

————. 1973b. "Strategies of Heirship." *Comparative Studies in Society and History* 15:3–20.

————. 1983. *The Development of the Family and Marriage in Europe.* Cambridge: Cambridge University Press.

Goody, J., J. Thirsk, and E. Thompson, eds. 1976. *Family and Inheritance: Rural Society in Western Europe, 1200–1800.* Cambridge: Cambridge University Press.

Gottschalk, L. 1963. *Generalisation in the Writing of History.* Chicago: University of Chicago Press.

Gourevitch, D. 1990. "Se marier pour avoir des enfants: le point de vue du médecin." In *Parenté et stratégies familiales,* 139–51. *See* Andreau and Bruhns 1990.

Gray-Fow, M. J. G. 1985. "The Nomenclature and Stages of Roman Childhood." Ph.D. diss., University of Wisconsin.

————. 1988. "The Wicked Stepmother in Roman Literature and History: An Evaluation." *Latomus* 47:741–57.

Griessmair, E. 1966. *Das Motiv der Mors Immatura in den griechischen metrischen Grabinschriften*. Innsbruck: Universitätsverlag Wagner.

Grimshaw, P., C. McConville, and E. McEwen, eds. 1985. *Families in Colonial Australia*. Sydney: George Allen & Unwin.

Guillemin, A. M. 1929. *Pline et la vie littéraire de son temps*. Paris: Société d'Édition Les Belles Lettres.

Haase, F., ed. 1872–74. *Luci Annaei Senecae Opera Quae Supersunt*. 3 vols. Leipzig: Teubner.

Hallett, J. P. 1973. "The Role of Women in Roman Elegy: Counter-cultural Feminism." *Arethusa* 6:103–24.

—————. 1984. *Fathers and Daughters in Roman Society: Women and the Elite Family*. Princeton: Princeton University Press.

Hareven, T. K. 1978. *Transitions: The Family and the Life Course in Historical Perspective*. New York: Academic Press.

—————. 1987. "Family History at the Crossroads." *Journal of Family History* 12:ix–xxiii.

Harmon, D. P. 1978. "The Family Festivals of Rome." *Aufstieg und Niedergang der römischen Welt* 2.16.2:1592–1603.

Harris, B. J. 1976. "Recent Work on the History of the Family: A Review Article." *Feminist Studies* 3:159–72.

Harris, W. V. 1986. "The Roman Father's Power of Life and Death." In *Studies in Roman Law in Memory of A. Arthur Schiller*, edited by R. S. Bagnall and W. V. Harris, 81–95. Leiden: Brill.

Harrison, A. R. W. 1968. *The Law of Athens: 1. The Family and Property*. Oxford: Clarendon Press.

Harrod, S. G. 1909. *Latin Terms of Endearment and Family Relationship: A Lexicographical Study Based on Vol. VI of the CIL*. Ph.D. diss., Princeton University.

Hartmann, H. 1981. "The Family as the Locus of Gender, Class, and Political Struggle: The Example of Housework." *Signs* 6:367–68.

Haury, A. 1976. "Une 'année de la femme' à Rome, 195 avant J-C?" In *L'Italie préromaine et la Rome républicaine: mélanges offerts à Jean Macqueron I*, 427–36. Rome: de Boccard.

Heitland, W. E. 1874. *Oratio pro L. Murena*. Cambridge: Cambridge University Press.

Henrion, R. 1940. "Des origines du mot *familia*." *L'Antiquité classique* 9:37–39.

Heraeus, W. 1937. "Die Sprache der römischen Kinderstube." *Archiv für Lateinische Lexikographie und Grammatik* 13:149–72.

Herlihy, D. 1983. "The Making of the Medieval Family: Symmetry, Structure, and Sentiment." *Journal of Family History* 8:116–30.

Hillard, T. 1983. "*Materna auctoritas*: The Political Influence of Roman *matronae*." *Classicum* 22:10–13.

Hinard, F. 1990. "Solidarités familiales et ruptures a l'époque des guerres civiles et de la proscription." in *Parenté et stratégies familiales,* 555–70. *See* Andreau and Bruhns 1990

Hinds, S. 1987. "The Poetess and the Reader: Further Steps toward Sulpicia." *Hermathena* 143 : 29–46.

Hobson, D. W. 1985. "House and Household in Roman Egypt." *Yale Classical Studies* 28 : 211–29.

Hopkins, K. 1965a. "The Age of Roman Girls at Marriage." *Population Studies* 18 : 309–27.

——. 1965b. "Contraception in the Roman Empire." *Comparative Studies in Society and History* 8 : 124–51.

——. 1966. "On the Probable Age Structure of the Roman Population." *Population Studies* 20 : 245–64.

——. 1978. *Conquerors and Slaves.* Cambridge: Cambridge University Press.

——. 1980. "Brother-Sister Marriage in Roman Egypt." *Comparative Studies in Society and History* 22 : 303–54.

——. 1983. *Death and Renewal: Sociological Studies in Roman History.* Cambridge: Cambridge University Press.

Howell, C. 1976. "Peasant Inheritance Customs in the Midlands, 1280–1700." In *Family and Inheritance,* 112–55. *See* Goody, Thirsk, and Thompson 1976.

Humbert, M. 1972. *Le Remariage à Rome: étude d'histoire juridique et sociale.* Milan: Giuffrè.

——. 1987. "Hispala Faecenia et l'endogamie des affranchis sous la Republique." *Index* 15 : 131–48.

Humphreys, S. C. 1978. *Anthropology and the Greeks.* London: Routledge & Kegan Paul.

Hunt, D. 1970. *Parents and Children in History: The Psychology of Family Life in Early Modern France.* New York: Harper & Row.

Huttunen, P. 1974. *The Social Strata in the Imperial City of Rome: A Quantitative Study of the Social Representation in the Epitaphs Published in CIL VI.* Oulu, Finland: University of Oulu.

Jolowicz, H. F. 1932. *Historical Introduction to the Study of Roman Law.* Cambridge: Cambridge University Press.

Jones, J. 1985. *Labor of Love, Labor of Sorrow: Black Women, Work, and the Family from Slavery to the Present.* New York: Vintage.

Jörs, P. 1882. *Ueber das Verhaltnis der Lex Iulia de Maritandis Ordinibus zur Lex Papia Poppaea.* Diss., Bonn.

Joshel, S. R. 1986. "Nurturing the Master's Child: Slavery and the Roman Child-Nurse." *Signs* 12 : 3–22.

Kajanto, I. 1968. *On the Problem of the Average Duration of Life in the Roman Empire.* Helsinki: Finnish Academy of Sciences.

——. 1970. "On Divorce among the Common People of Rome." *Re-*

vue des études latines: mélanges Marcel Durry 47:99–113.

————. 1972. "On the First Appearance of Women's *Cognomina.*" In *Acts of the Sixth International Congress on Greek and Latin Epigraphy,* 402–4. Munich: Beck.

————. 1977. "On the Peculiarities of Women's Nomenclature." In *L'onomastique latine,* 147–58. Paris: Éditions du Centre National de la Recherche Scientifique.

Kammen, M. 1980. *The Past before Us: Contemporary Historical Writing in the U.S.* Ithaca: Cornell University Press.

Kampen, N. 1981. *Image and Status: Roman Working Women in Ostia.* Berlin: Mann.

————. 1982. "Social Status and Gender in Roman Art: The Case of the Saleswoman." In *Feminism and Art History,* edited by M. D. Garrard and N. Broude, chap. 4. London: Harper & Row.

Karras, M., and J. Wiesehöfer. 1981. *Kindheit und Jugend in der Antike: eine Bibliographie.* Bonn: Rudolf Habelt.

Kaser, M. 1938. "Der Inhalt der Patria Potestas." *Zeitschrift der Savigny-Stiftung für Rechtsgeschichte, Romanistische Abteilung* 58:62–87.

————. [1955] 1975. *Das römische Privatrecht.* 2 vols. Munich: Beck.

Kelly, J. M. 1976. *Studies in the Civil Judicature of the Roman Republic.* Oxford: Clarendon Press.

Kelly-Gadol, J. 1977. "Did Women Have a Renaissance?" In *Becoming Visible,* 137–64. *See* Bridenthal and Koonz 1977.

Kertzer, D. I., and R. P. Saller, eds. 1992. *The Family in Italy from Antiquity to the Present.* New Haven: Yale University Press.

Klapisch-Zuber, C. 1983. "La 'mère cruelle.' Maternité, veuvage, et dot dans la Florence des XIVe–XVe siècles." *Annales: économie, sociétés, civilisations* 38:1097–1109.

Kleiner, D. E. 1977. *Roman Group Portraiture: The Funerary Reliefs of the Late Republic and Early Empire.* New York: Garland.

————. 1978. "The Great Friezes of the Ara Pacis Augustae: Greek Sources, Roman Derivatives, and Augustan Social Policy." *Mélanges de l'école française de Rome: antiquité* 90:753–85.

Koschaker, P. 1937. "Eheformen bei den Indogermanen." *Zeitschrift für Ausländisches und Internationales Privatrecht,* special issue, 11:77–140b.

Krause, J. T. 1958. "Changes in English Fertility and Mortality." *Economic History Review,* 2d ser., 11:52–70.

Kruger, P. 1870. "Anecdotum Livianum." *Hermes* 4:371–72.

Kunkel, W. 1930. "*Matrimonium.*" *Realencyclopädie der Klassischen Altertumswissenschaft* 14:2259–86.

Lacan, J. 1977. *Écrits: A Selection.* Edited and translated by A. Sheridan. London: Tavistock Press. Originally published as *Écrits* (Paris: Éditions du Seuil, 1966).

Lacey, W. K. 1968. *The Family in Classical Greece*. London: Thames & Hudson.

Lake, M. 1985. "Helpmeet, Slave, Housewife: Women in Rural Families, 1870–1930." In *Families in Colonial Australia*, 173–85. *See* Grimshaw, McConville, and McEwen 1985.

Lambert, G. R. 1982. *Rhetoric Rampant: The Family under Siege in the Early Western Tradition*. London, Ontario: Faculty of Education, University of Western Ontario.

Lanfranchi, F. 1936. "Le definizioni e il concetto del matrimonio nei retori romani." *Studia et documenta historiae et iuris* 2:148–57.

Langer, W. L. 1974. "Infanticide: An Historical Review." *History of Childhood Quarterly* 1:353–65.

Lasch, D. 1977. *Haven in a Heartless World: The Family Besieged*. New York: Basic Books.

Laslett, P. 1987. "The Character of Familial History, Its Limitations, and the Conditions for Its Proper Pursuit." *Journal of Family History* 12:263–84.

Laslett, P., and R. Wall, eds. 1972. *Household and Family in Past Time*. Cambridge: Cambridge University Press.

Last, H. 1945. "The Servian Reforms." *Journal of Roman Studies* 35:30–48.

Lattimore, R. B. 1942. *Themes in Greek and Latin Epitaphs*. Urbana: University of Illinois Press.

Leach, E. 1961. *Rethinking Anthropology*. London: Athlone Press.

Le Bras, G. 1936. "Les Fondations privées du haut empire." In *Studi in onore di S. Riccobono*, 3:21–67. Palermo.

LeBrun, F. 1971. *Les Hommes et la mort en Anjou aux 17e et 18e siècles: essai de démographie et de psychologie historique*. Paris: Mouton.

Lenel, O. 1927. *Das Edictum Perpetuum: ein Versuch zu seiner Wiederherstellung*. Leipzig: Tauchnitz.

Leonhard, R. 1900. "*Concubinatus*." *Realencyclopädie der Klassischen Altertumswissenschaft* 4, no. 1:835–38.

LePlay, P. G. F. 1871. *L'Organisation de la famille*. Paris.

Lesquier, J. 1918. *L'armée romaine d'Egypte d'Auguste á Dioclétien*. Cairo: Institut français d'archéologie orientale du Caire.

Lévi-Strauss, C. 1949. *Les Structures élementaires de la parenté*. Paris: La Haye, Mouton.

———. 1967. *Structural Anthropology*. New York: Doubleday.

Levy, E. 1925. *Der Hergang der römischen Ehescheidung*. Weimar: Böhlau.

Lewis, N., and M. Reinhold, eds. 1990. *Roman Civilization. Selected Readings I: The Republic and the Augustan Age*. New York: Columbia University Press.

Liebenam, W. 1900. "*Consilium*." *Paulys Real-Encyclopädie der klassischen Altertumswissenschaft* 4, pt. 1:915–22. Stuttgart: Druckenmüller.

Lightman, M., and Zeisel, W. 1977. "*Univira*: An Example of Continuity and Change in Roman Society." *Church History* 46:19–32.

Lilja, S. 1965. *The Roman Love Elegists' Attitude to Women*. Annales academiae scientiae fennicae, ser. 13:135, 1. Helsinki: Suomalainen Tiedeakatemia. Reprint. New York: Garland, 1978.

Lions, P., and M. Lachiver. 1967. "Denombrement de la population de Brueil-en-Vevin en 1625." *Annales de démographie historique* 16:521–37.

Lowe, N. J. 1988. "Sulpicia's Syntax." *Classical Quarterly* 38:193–205.

Lyman, R. 1974. "Barbarism and Religion: Late Roman and Early Medieval Childhood." In *The History of Childhood*, 75–100. *See* Demause 1974.

Lyne, R. O. A. M. 1980. *The Latin Love Poets*. Oxford: Oxford University Press.

Lyttelton, M., and W. Forman. 1984. *The Romans: Their Gods and Their Beliefs*. London: Orbis.

McAlindon, D. 1957. "The Senator's Retiring Age: 65 or 60?" *Classical Review* 7:108.

McDaniel, W. B. 1948. *Conception, Birth, and Infancy in Ancient Rome and Modern Italy*. Coconut Grove, Fla.: Privately printed.

MacDonnell, W. R. 1913. "The Expectation of Life in Ancient Rome." *Biometrika* 9:366–80.

MacDowell, D. M. 1978. *The Law in Classical Athens*. London: Thames & Hudson.

Macfarlane, A. 1979. Review of *The Family, Sex, and Marriage in England, 1500–1800*, by L. Stone. *History and Theory* 18:103–26.

————. 1986. *Marriage and Love in England, 1300–1840: Modes of Reproduction*. Oxford: Blackwell.

Macmullen, R. 1963. *Soldier and Civilian in the Later Roman Empire*. Cambridge: Harvard University Press.

————. 1966. *Enemies of the Roman Order: Treason, Unrest, and Alienation in the Empire*. Cambridge: Harvard University Press.

————. 1986. "Women's Power in the Principate." *Klio* 68:434–43.

Maiuri, A. 1960. *Roman Painting*. Geneva: Skira.

Mann, J. C. 1983. *Legionary Recruitment and Veteran Settlement during the Principate*. Edited by M. M. Roxan. 2 vols. British Institute of Archaeology Occasional Publication, 7. London.

Manson, M. 1975. "La *pietas* et le sentiment de l'enfance à Rome d'après les monnaies." *Revue Belge de numismatique et de sigillographie* 121:21–80.

————. 1978. "*Puer Bimulus* (Catulle, 17, 12–13) et l'image du petit enfant chez Catulle et ses prédécesseurs." *Mélanges de l'école française de Rome* 90:247–91.

—————. 1983. "The Emergence of the Small Child at Rome." *History of Education* 12:149–59.

Marquardt, J. 1886. *Das Privatleben der Römer*. Vol. 1. Leipzig: Hirzel.

Martin, J., and A. Nitschke, eds. 1986. *Zur Sozialgeschichte der Kindheit*. Munich: Verlag Karl Alber.

Medick, H. 1976. "The Proto-industrial Family Economy: The Structural Function of Household and Family during the Transition from Peasant Society to Industrial Capitalism." *Social History* 3:291–315.

Meyer, P. 1895. *Das römische Konkubinat nach den Rechtsquellen und den Inschriften*. Leipzig: Teubner. Reprint. Aalen: Scientia, 1966.

Michel, J. H. 1979. "Mariage romain et ethnologie française." in *Maior viginti quinque annis*, 104–10. See Watson 1979.

Millar, F. 1977. *The Emperor in the Roman World*. London: Duckworth.

Mitford, N. 1956. "The English Aristocracy." *Encounter*. Reprinted in *Noblesse Oblige: An Enquiry into the Identifiable Characteristics of the English Aristocrat*. London: Futura, 1980.

—————. 1963. *Don't Tell Alfred*. Harmondsworth: Penguin.

Mitteis, L. 1912. *Grundzüge und Chrestomathie der Papyruskunde*. Vol. 2, pt. 2. Leipzig: Teubner.

Mommsen, Th. 1887. *Römisches Staatsrecht*. Vol. 1. Leipzig: Hirzel.

Moreau, P. 1983. "Structures de parenté et d'alliance à Larinum d'après le *Pro Cluentio*." In *Les 'bourgeoisies' municipales italiennes aux IIe et Ier siècles av. J-C.*, edited by M. Cébeillac-Gervasoni, 99–123. Paris: Centre national de recherches scientifiques and L'Institut français de Naples.

Morgan, L. H. 1871. *Systems of Consanguinity and Affinity of the Human Family*. Washington, D.C.: Smithsonian. Reprint. Netherlands: Oosterhout, 1970.

—————. 1877. *Ancient Society, or Researches in the Lines of Human Progress from Savagery through Barbarism to Civilization*. London: Macmillan.

Mount, F. 1982. *The Subversive Family: An Alternative History of Love and Marriage*. London: Jonathan Cape.

Münzer, F. 1920. *Römische Adelsparteien und Adelsfamilien*. Stuttgart: Metzler.

Murdock, G. P. 1949. *Social Structure*. New York: Macmillan.

Nardi, E. 1971. *Procurato aborto nel mondo greco-romano*. Milan: Giuffrè.

Needham, R., ed. 1971. *Rethinking Kinship and Marriage*. London: Tavistock Press.

Néraudau, J-P. 1979. *La Jeunesse dans la littérature et les institutions de la Rome républicaine*. Paris: Budé.

—————. 1984. *Être enfant à Rome*. Paris: Collection Realia, Les Belles Lettres.

Newman, L. 1972. *Birth Control: An Anthropological View*. Addison-Wesley

Modules in Anthropology, 27. Reading, Mass.

Nicholas, B. 1962. *An Introduction to Roman Law.* Oxford: Clarendon Press.

Nielsen, H. S. 1987. "*Alumnus:* A Term of Relation Denoting Quasi-Adoption." *Classica et Mediaevalia* 38:141–88.

——. 1989. "On the Use of the Terms of Relation '*mamma*' and '*tata*' in the Epitaphs of *CIL* VI." *Classica et Mediaevalia* 40:191–223.

——. 1990. "*Delicia* in Roman Literature and in the Urban Inscriptions." *Analecta Romana Instituti Danici* 19:79–88.

Nock, A. D. 1972. "Tertullian and the '*Ahori*.'" In *A. D. Nock: Essays on Religion and the Ancient World,* edited by Z. Stewart, 712–19. Oxford: Clarendon.

Nörr, D. 1977. "Planung in der Antike: über die Ehegesetze des Augustus." In *Freiheit und Sachzwang. Beiträge zu Ehren H. Schelskys,* 309–34. Opladen: Westdeutscher Verlag.

——. 1981. "The Matrimonial Legislation of Augustus: An Early Instance of Social Engineering." *Irish Jurist* 16:350–64.

Noy, D. 1991. "Wicked Stepmothers in Roman Society and Imagination." *Journal of Family History* 16.

Orr, D. G. 1978. "Roman Domestic Religion: The Evidence of the Household Shrines." *Aufstieg und Niedergang der römischen Welt* 2.16.2:1557–91.

Packer, J. E. 1975. "Middle and Lower Class Housing in Pompeii and Herculaneum." In *Neue Forschungen in Pompeji,* edited by B. Andreae and H. Kyrieleis, 133–46. Recklinghausen: Deutsches archäologisches Institut.

Pailler, J-M. 1990. "Les Bacchanales: une affaire de famille." In *Parenté et stratégies familiales,* 77–83. *See* Andreau and Bruhns 1990.

Paribeni, R. 1929. *La famiglia romana.* Rome: Optima. 2d ed. Bologna: Cappelli.

Parker, H. D. M. 1928. *The Roman Legions.* Oxford: Clarendon Press.

Paterson, J. 1982. "'Salvation from the Sea': Amphorae and Trade in the Roman West." *Journal of Roman Studies* 72:146–57.

Peppe, L. 1984. *Posizione giuridica e ruolo sociale della donna romana in età repubblicana.* Milan: Giuffrè.

Philibert, M. 1984. "Le Statut de la personne âgée dans les sociétés antiques et préindustrielles." *Sociologie et sociétés* 16:15–27.

Phillips, J. E. 1978. "Roman Mothers and the Lives of Their Adult Daughters." *Helios,* n.s., 6:69–80.

Plakans, A. 1984. *Kinship in the Past: An Anthropology of European Family Life, 1500–1900.* Oxford: Blackwell.

Plassard, J. 1921. *Le Concubinat romain sous le haut empire.* Paris: Sirey.

Pollini, J. 1985. *Portraiture of Gaius and Lucius Caesar.* Rome: Bretschneider.

Pollock, L. A. 1983. *Forgotten Children: Parent-Child Relations from 1500–1900.* Cambridge: Cambridge University Press.

Pomeroy, S. 1976. "The Relationship of the Married Woman to Her Blood Relatives in Rome." *Ancient Society* 7:215–27.

————. 1985. *Women in Hellenistic Egypt. From Alexander to Cleopatra.* New York: Schocken.

Popenoe, D. 1988. *Disturbing the Nest: Family Change and Decline in Modern Societies.* New York: de Gruyter.

Purcell, N. 1985. "Wine and Wealth in Ancient Italy." *Journal of Roman Studies* 75:1–19.

Putnam, M. 1973. *Tibullus: A Commentary.* Norman: University of Oklahoma Press.

Rabello, A. M. 1972. "Il *ius occidendi iure patris* della *lex Iulia de adulteriis coercendis* e la *vitae necisque potestas* del *paterfamilias.*" In *Atti del seminario romanistico internazionale,* 228–42. Perugia: Libreria Editrice Universitaria.

————. 1979. *Effetti personali della* "patria potestas." Università degli Studi di Milano, Istituto di Diritto Romano. Milan: Giuffrè.

Raditsa, L. F. 1980. "Augustan Legislation Concerning Marriage, Procreation, Love Affairs, and Adultery." *Aufstieg und Niedergang der römischen Welt* 2.13:278–339.

Rapp, R., E. Ross, and R. Bridenthal. 1979. "Examining Family History." *Feminist Studies* 5:174–200.

Rawson, B. 1966. "Family Life among the Lower Classes at Rome in the First Two Centuries of the Empire." *Classical Philology* 61:71–83.

————. 1974. "Roman Concubinage and Other *de facto* Marriages." *Transactions of the American Philological Association* 104:279–305.

————, ed. 1986a. *The Family in Ancient Rome: New Perspectives.* London: Croom Helm.

————. 1986b. "The Roman Family." In *The Family in Ancient Rome,* 1–37. *See* Rawson 1986a.

————. 1986c. "Children in the Roman *Familia.*" In *The Family in Ancient Rome,* 170–200. *See* Rawson 1986a.

————, ed. 1991a. *Marriage, Divorce, and Children in Ancient Rome.* Oxford: Oxford University Press, 1991a.

————. 1991b. "Adult-Child Relationships in Roman Society." In *Marriage, Divorce, and Children in Ancient Rome,* 7–30. *See* Rawson 1991a.

Rawson, E. 1976. "The Ciceronian Aristocracy and Its Properties." In *Studies in Roman Property,* edited by M. I. Finley, 85–102. Cambridge: Cambridge University Press.

Reed, E. 1969. *Problems of Women's Liberation.* New York: Pathfinder Press.

————. 1975. *Woman's Evolution from Matriarchal Clan to Patriarchal Family.* New York: Pathfinder Press.

Reinhold, M. 1976. "The Generation Gap in Antiquity." In *Conflict of Generations in Ancient Greece and Rome,* 15–54. *See* Bertman 1976.

Riccobono, S., ed. 1945. *Acta Divi Augusti*. Vol. 1. Rome: Accademia d'Italia.

Rich, A. 1976. "Women's Studies—Renaissance or Revolution?" *Women's Studies* 3:121–26.

Richlin, A. 1981. "Approaches to the Sources on Adultery at Rome." In *Reflections of Women in Antiquity*, edited by H. P. Foley, 379–404. New York: Gordon & Breach.

—————. 1983. *The Garden of Priapus: Sexuality and Aggression in Roman Humour*. New Haven: Yale University Press.

Rivière, P. G. 1971. "Marriage: A Reassessment." In *Rethinking Kinship and Marriage*, 57–74. *See* Needham 1971.

Roessel, D. 1990. "The Significance of the Name *Cerinthus* in the Poems of Sulpicia." *Transactions of the American Philological Association* 120: 243–50.

Rotondi, G. [1922] 1966. *Leges publicae populi Romani*. Reprint. Milan: Società Editrice Libreria.

Rousselle, A. 1988. Porneia: *On Desire and the Body in Antiquity*. Oxford: Blackwell.

Roxan, M. M., ed. 1978. *Roman Military Diplomas, 1954–1977*. British Institute of Archaeology Occasional Publication, 2. London.

—————. 1985. *Roman Military Diplomas, 1978–1984*. British Institute of Archaeology Occasional Publication, 9. London.

Rudd, N. 1981. "Romantic Love in Classical Times?" *Ramus* 10:140–58.

Saller, R. P. 1984a. "*Familia, Domus*, and the Roman Conception of the Family." *Phoenix* 38:336–55.

—————. 1984b. "Roman Dowry and the Devolution of Property in the Principate." *Classical Quarterly* 34:195–205.

—————. 1986. "*Patria potestas* and the Stereotype of the Roman Family." *Continuity and Change* 1:7–22.

—————. 1987a. "Men's Age at Marriage and Its Consequences in the Roman Family." *Classical Philology* 82:21–34.

—————. 1987b. "Slavery and the Roman Family." *Slavery and Abolition* 8:65–87.

—————. 1988. "*Pietas*, Obligation, and Authority in the Roman Family." In *Alte Geschichte und Wissenschaftsgeschichte: Festschrift für Karl Christ zum 65. Geburtstag*, edited by P. von Kneissl and V. Losemann, 392–410. Darmstadt: Wissenschaftlige Buchgesellschaft.

—————. 1991. "Corporal Punishment, Authority, and Obedience in the Roman Household." In *Marriage, Divorce, and Children in Ancient Rome*, 144–65. *See* Rawson 1991a.

—————. 1992. "Roman Heirship Strategies: In Principle and in Practice." In *The Family in Italy from Antiquity to the Present*. *See* Kertzer and Saller 1992.

Saller, R. P., and B. D. Shaw. 1984a. "Close-Kin Marriage in Roman Society?" *Man* 19:432–44.

————. 1984b. "Tombstones and Roman Family Relations in the Principate: Civilians, Soldiers, and Slaves." *Journal of Roman Studies* 74: 124–56.

Sanders, H. A. 1938. "A Latin Marriage Contract." *Transactions of the American Philological Association* 69:104–16.

Sawer, M. 1982. Review of *The Subversive Family*, by Ferdinand Mount. *Sydney Morning Herald*, 13 November.

Schaps, D. M. 1979. *Economic Rights of Women in Ancient Greece*. Edinburgh: Edinburgh University Press.

Schiaparelli, L. 1920. "Contratto di matrimonio." *Papiri Greci e Latini* 6:176–77.

Schulz, F. 1946. *History of Roman Legal Science*. Oxford: Oxford University Press.

————. 1951. *Classical Roman Law*. Oxford: Oxford University Press.

Scullard, H. H. 1981. *Festivals and Ceremonies of the Roman Republic*. London: Thames & Hudson.

Segal, E. 1968. *Roman Laughter*. Cambridge: Harvard University Press.

Segalen, M. 1972. *Nuptialité et alliance, le choix du conjoint dans une commune de l'Eure*. Paris: Maisonneuve et Larose.

————. 1986. *Historical Anthropology of the Family*. Translated by J. C. Whitehouse and S. Matthews. Cambridge: Cambridge University Press. Originally published as *Sociologie de la famille* (1981).

Shackleton-Bailey, D. 1965–70. *Cicero's Letters to Atticus*. 7 vols. Cambridge: Cambridge University Press.

Shaw, B. D. 1982. "Social Science and Ancient History: Keith Hopkins *in Partibus Infidelium*." *Helios*, n.s., 9:17–57.

————. 1984. "Latin Funerary Epigraphy and Family Relations in the Later Empire." *Historia* 33:457–97.

————. 1987a. "The Age of Roman Girls at Marriage: Some Reconsiderations." *Journal of Roman Studies* 77:30–46.

————. 1987b. "The Family in Late Antiquity: The Experience of Augustine." *Past and Present* 15:3–51.

————. 1992. "The Cultural Meaning of Death: Age and Gender in the Roman Empire." In *The Family in Italy from Antiquity to the Present. See* Kertzer and Saller 1992.

Sherudi, E. 1979. *Grandma Strikes Back*. New York: Nordon.

Sherwin-White, A. N. 1966. *The Letters of Pliny: A Historical and Social Commentary*. Oxford: Oxford University Press.

Shorter, E. [1975] 1977. *The Making of the Modern Family*. Reprint. Glasgow and London: Fontana/Collins.

Skydsgaard, J.-E. 1979. *Pompeii: en romersk Provinsby* (Pompeii: A Roman town). Copenhagen: Museum Tusculanums Forlag.

Slater, W. J. 1974. *"Pueri, turba minuta." Bulletin of the Institute of Classical Studies of the University of London* 21:133–40.

Slusanski, D. 1974. "Le Vocabulaire latin des *gradus aetatum.*" *Revue roumaine de linguistique* 19:103–21, 267–96, 345–69, 437–51, 563–78.

Smith, R. M., ed. 1984. *Land, Kinship, and Life Cycle.* New York: Cambridge University Press.

Solazzi, S. 1928–29. *Studi tutelari.* Naples: Jovene.

Solidoro, L. 1981. "La *familia* nell'editto di Lucullo." *Atti dell' Accademia di Scienze Morali e Politiche della Società Nazionale di Scienze, Lettere ed Arti di Napoli* 92:197–229.

Spurr, M. S. 1986. *Arable Cultivation in Roman Italy, 200 BC–200 AD.* Rome: British School at Rome.

Stone, L. 1965. *Crisis of the Aristocracy.* Oxford: Oxford University Press.

——————. 1977. *The Family, Sex, and Marriage in England, 1500–1800.* London: Weidenfeld & Nicholson.

——————. 1981. "Family History in the 1980's: Past Achievements and Future Trends." *Journal of Interdisciplinary History* 12:51–87.

Sullivan, J. P. 1991. *Martial. The Unexpected Classic.* Cambridge: Cambridge University Press.

Syme, Sir R. 1968. "The Ummidii." *Historia* 17:72–105.

——————. 1979. *Roman Papers.* Edited by E. Badian. 4 vols. Oxford: Clarendon Press.

——————. 1985a. "The Dating of Pliny's Latest Letters." *Classical Quarterly* 35:176–85.

——————. 1985b. "The '*Testamentum Dasumii*': Some Novelties." *Chiron* 15:41–63.

Thomas, J. A. C. 1975. *The Institutes of Justinian.* Amsterdam: North Holland Publishing.

——————. 1976. *Textbook of Roman Law.* Oxford: Oxford University Press.

Thomas, Y. 1981. "*Parricidium* I: le père, la famille, et la cité." *Mélanges d'archéologie et d'histoire de l'école française de Rome: antiquité* 93:643–715.

——————. 1982. "Droit domestique et droit politique à Rome: remarques sur le pécule et les honores des fils de famille." *Mélanges d'archéologie et d'histoire de l'école française de Rome: antiqué* 94:528–80.

——————. 1986. "A Rome, pères citoyens et cité des pères (IIe siècle av. J.-C.–IIe siècle après J.-C." In *Histoire de la famille,* edited by A. Burguière, C. Klapisch-Zuber, M. Segalen, and F. Zonabend, 194–229. 2 vols. Paris: A. Colin.

——————. 1990. "Remarques sur la jurisdiction domestique a Rome." In *Parenté et stratégies familiales,* 449–74. *See* Andreau and Bruhns 1990.

Torelli, M. 1984. *Lavinio e Roma*. Rome: Edizioni Quasar di Severino Tognon.

Toynbee, J. M. C. 1971. *Death and Burial in the Roman World*. London: Thames & Hudson.

Treggiari, S. 1969. *Roman Freedmen during the Late Republic*. Oxford: Clarendon Press.

―――. 1975. "Family Life among the Staff of the Volusii." *Transactions of the American Philological Association* 105:393–401.

―――. 1976. "Jobs for Women." *American Journal of Ancient History* 1:76–104.

―――. 1979a. "Sentiment and Property: Some Roman Attitudes." In *Theories of Property: Aristotle to the Present,* edited by A. Parel and T. Flanagan, 53–85. Waterloo, Ontario: Wilfrid Laurier Press.

―――. 1979b. "Lower Class Women in the Roman Economy." *Florilegium* 1:65–86.

―――. 1979c. "Questions on Women Domestics in the Roman West." In *Schiavitù, manomissione e classi dipendenti nel mondo antico,* 185–201. Rome: "l'Erma" di Bretschneider.

―――. 1981a. *"Concubinae."* *Papers of the British School at Rome* 49:59–81.

―――. 1981b. *"Contubernales* in *CIL* 6." *Phoenix* 35:42–69.

―――. 1982. "Consent to Roman Marriage: Some Aspects of Law and Reality." *Échos du monde classique/Classical Views* 26:34–44.

―――. 1991. *Roman Marriage*. Oxford: Oxford University Press.

Veyne, P. 1957–58. "La Table des *Ligures Baebiani* et l'institution alimentaire de Trajan." *Mélanges de l'école française de Rome: antiquité* 69:81–135; 70:205–22.

―――. 1978. "La Famille et l'amour sous le haut-empire romain." *Annales: économie, sociétés, civilisations* 33:35–63.

Voci, P. 1982. "Linee storiche del diritto ereditario romano I. Dalle origini ai Severi." *Aufstieg und Niedergang der römischen Welt* 2.14:392–448.

Vogt, J. 1974. *Ancient Slavery and the Ideal of Man*. Oxford: Blackwell.

Volterra, E. 1951. "Un osservazione in tema di *tollere liberos*." In *Festschrift Fritz Schulz,* 1:388–98. Weimar: Böhlau.

―――. 1952. "Ancora in tema di *tollere liberos*." *Iura* 3:216–17.

Waldstein, W. 1972. "Zum fall der 'Dos Licinniae.'" *Index. Quaderni camerti di studi romanistici, III. Ommagio à Max Kaser* 343–61.

Walker, A. J., and L. Thompson. 1983. "Intimacy and Intergenerational Aid and Contact among Mothers and Daughters." *Journal of Marriage and the Family* 44:841–49.

Wallace-Hadrill, A. 1981. "Family and Inheritance in the Augustan Marriage Laws." *Proceedings of the Cambridge Philological Society,* n.s. 27:58–80.

————. 1991. "Houses and Households: Sampling Pompeii and Herculaneum." In *Marriage, Divorce and Children in Ancient Rome*, 191–228. *See* Rawson 1991a.

Warmington, E. H., ed. [1935] 1961. *Remains of Old Latin*. Rev. ed. 4 vols. Reprint. Cambridge: Harvard University Press.

Watson, A. 1965. "The Divorce of Carvilius Ruga." *Tijdschrift voor Rechtsgeschiedenis* 33:38–50.

————. 1967. *The Law of Persons in the Later Roman Republic*. Oxford: Oxford University Press.

————. 1971. *The Law of Succession in the Later Roman Republic*. Oxford: Clarendon Press.

————. 1974. *Law-making in the Later Roman Republic*. Oxford: Clarendon Press.

————. 1975. *Rome of the XII Tables–Persons and Property*. Princeton: Princeton University Press.

————. 1976. "The Origins of *usus*." *Revue internationale des droits de l'antiquité*, 3d ser., 23:265–70.

————. 1979. "Two Notes on Manus." In *Maior viginti quinque annis: Essays in Commemoration of the Sixth Lustrum of the Institute for Legal History of the University of Utrecht*, edited by J. E. Spruit, 95–201. Assen: Van Gorcum.

————. 1981. *The Making of the Civil Law*. Rome: Bretschneider.

————, ed. and trans. 1985. *The Digest of Justinian*. 4 vols. Philadelphia: University of Pennsylvania Press.

Watson, G. R. 1969. *The Roman Soldier*. London: Thames and Hudson.

Watson, P. 1989. "*Filiaster: Privignus* or 'Illegitimate Child'?" *Classical Quarterly* 39:536–48.

Weaver, P. R. C. 1972. *"Familia Caesaris": A Social Study of the Emperor's Freedmen and Slaves*. Cambridge: Cambridge University Press.

————. 1986. "Status of Children in Mixed Marriages." In *The Family in Ancient Rome*, chap. 6. *See* Rawson 1986a.

————. 1990. "Where Have all the Junian Latins Gone? Nomenclature and Status in the Early Empire." *Chiron* 20:275–305.

————. 1991. "Children of Freedmen (and Freedwomen)." In *Marriage, Divorce, and Children in Ancient Rome*, 166–90. *See* Rawson 1991a.

Westermann, W. L. 1914. "Apprentice Contracts and the Apprentice System in Roman Egypt." *Classical Philology* 9:295–315.

Westrup, C. W. 1943. *Recherches sur les formes antiques de mariage dans l'ancien droit romain*. Copenhagen: Munksgaard.

Wheaton, R. 1987. "Observations on the Development of Kinship History, 1942–1985." *Journal of Family History* 12:285–301.

Wieacker, F. 1960. *Textstufen Klassischer Juristen*. Göttingen: Vandenhoeck & Ruprecht.

Wiedemann, T. 1989. *Adults and Children in the Roman Empire.* London: Routledge.

Will, E. L. 1979. "Women in Pompeii." *Archaeology* 32, no. 5: 34–43.

Williams, G. 1958. "Some Aspects of Roman Marriage Ceremonies and Ideals." *Journal of Roman Studies* 48: 16–29.

———. 1962. "Poetry in the Moral Climate of Augustan Rome." *Journal of Roman Studies* 52: 28–46.

Winter, J. G. 1933. *Life and Letters in the Papyri.* Ann Arbor: University of Michigan Press.

Wiseman, T. P. 1971. "Celer and Nepos." *Classical Quarterly* 21: 180–82.

———. 1977. *New Men in the Roman Senate, 139 B.C.–A.D. 14.* London: Oxford University Press.

Wolff, H. J. .1937. "Zwei juristische Papyri." *Aegyptus* 17: 470–78.

Wright, E. 1988. *A Question of Murder.* London: Fontana Paperback.

Yanagisako, S. J. 1979. "Family and Household: The Analysis of Domestic Groups." *Annual Review of Anthropology* 8: 161–205.

Young, M., and P. Willmott. 1957. *Family and Kinship in East London.* London: Routledge & Kegan Paul.

Zadoks-Josephus Jitta, A. N. 1932. *Ancestral Portraiture in Rome and the Art of the Last Century of the Republic.* Amsterdam: Noord-Hollandsche Uitgevers-mij.

Zanker, P. 1988. *The Power of Images in the Age of Augustus.* Ann Arbor: University of Michigan Press.

Ziegler, K. 1964. *M. Tullius Cicero Fasc. 39 de Re Publica.* Leipzig: Teubner.

Zulueta, F. de. 1946–53. *The Institutes of Gaius.* 2 vols. Oxford: Clarendon Press.

# Index

Most Latin terms (e.g. *Patria potestas*) and some relationships (e.g. Arria the Younger, daughter of Arria the Elder and Caecina Paetus) are explained briefly, but full details will be found by looking up the page references.

The name of a Roman male citizen had three elements, e.g. Caius/Gaius (C.) Cassius Longinus. Such names are usually listed by their central, gentile name. Cicero is, therefore, found under *T* for Tullius. Members of the imperial family, however, are listed under the names by which they are usually known, e.g. Tiberius, Germanicus, Livia. Names usually spelled with a *J* in English (e.g. Julia, daughter of Augustus) have been listed in the index under *J. U* and *V* are listed separately.

Abortion, 45, 122, 132, 195 n.17, 223 n.108, 224 n.123
Acerva, 215 n.17
*Actio rei uxoriae,* 50–51, 65, 76
*Adoptio. See* Adoption
Adoption, 5, 32, 41, 59, 112, 113, 123, 161, 219 n.68, 220 n.71, 220 n.74; definition, 112; testamentary, 112; by women, 112, 219 n.70; of women, 112, 218 n.47, 219 n.69; young children, 112, 219 n.69
*Adrogatio,* definition, 112. *See also* Adoption

Adultery, 44, 45, 69, 72, 73, 78, 80, 81, 83, 88, 96, 120, 121, 132, 139, 202 n.110, 207 n.52, 208 nn.74, 76, 78, 209 nn.85, 90, 93, 210 n.103. *See also Stuprum*
Aebutius, P., 144
Aefulanus Marcellinus, 214 n.3
Aelia Tychene, 211 n.113
Aelii Tuberones, 7, 22, 45, 186 n.25, 196 n.30, 232 nn.42, 47
Aelius Aelianus, 126
Aelius Tubero, Q., 51, 74
Aemilia (adoptive grandmother of

ANCIENT SOCIETY AND HISTORY

The series Ancient Society and History offers books, relatively brief in compass, on selected topics in the history of ancient Greece and Rome, broadly conceived, with a special emphasis on comparative and other nontraditional approaches and methods. The series, which includes both works of synthesis and works of original scholarship, is aimed at the widest possible range of specialist and nonspecialist readers.